My Left

Mag'

Is Out

by

E. R. Wilson

National Library of Canada Cataloguing in Publication Data

Wilson, E. R. (Earle R.)
  My left mag' is out

    Includes bibliographical references.
    ISBN 1-55212-776-1

    1. Wilson, E. R. (Earle R.) 2. Aviation mechanics (Persons)--
United States--Biography. 3. Airplanes--Maintenance and repairs--
Anecdotes. I. Title.
TL540.W562A3 2001   629.134'6'092   C2001-910752-8

TRAFFORD

This book was published *on-demand* in cooperation with Trafford Publishing. On-demand publishing is a unique process and service of making a book available for retail sale to the public taking advantage of on-demand manufacturing and Internet marketing. **On-demand publishing** includes promotions, retail sales, manufacturing, order fulfilment, accounting and collecting royalties on behalf of the author.

Suite 6E, 2333 Government St., Victoria, B.C. V8T 4P4, CANADA
Phone   250-383-6864   Toll-free   1-888-232-4444 (Canada & US)
Fax   250-383-6804   E-mail   sales@trafford.com
Web site   www.trafford.com   TRAFFORD PUBLISHING IS A DIVISION OF TRAFFORD HOLDINGS LTD.
Trafford Catalogue #01-0176   www.trafford.com/robots/01-0176.html

10   9   8   7   6   5   4   3

My Left Mag' is Out

by

E. R. Wilson

For My Children

Earl Jr., Karen, Stuart and Steve,
Not Necessarily in That Order.

All Unwittingly Made Sacrifices
While I Pursued a Career I Could Not Ignore.
They Were Sorely Missed During That Quest
When We Were Not Always Together.

and...

Grateful For an Unseen Hand
That Helped Me Through The Highs and Lows.

Acknowledgment

Twenty-miles south of the Wyoming-Colorado border there is a diminutive ranch of twenty-five acres, more or less, tucked into the landscape east of the Colorado Rockies. Twelve-miles to the west, the first ramparts of those mountains grace the sky. Farther beyond, the lofty splendors of Long's Peak, the Mummy Range and Crown Point are etched grandly against the bold sky.

Eleven head of beef cattle are on the little ranch. Also fourteen banty chickens, numerous cottontail rabbits underfoot and Western Kingbirds that nest in the cottonwoods. Mule deer occasionally cross the pastures, and now and then, ringneck pheasants forage for seeds amongst the shrubs in the back pasture. Hawks often overfly the pastures hunting for mice, and intimidate the bantys. Great horned owls prowl the night skies and solemnly announce their presence with eerie, haunting certitude. At times, coyotes answer the owls with concerts of howls and yips.

There are airliners high overhead flying their assigned routes to and from Denver and Seattle and Salt Lake City. They rumble on their east-west routes from Chicago and beyond to the West Coast. Lower, occasional light twins and single engine aircraft announce their passing with piston engines emitting throaty resonance. And there are turbo-props sounding their peculiar humming beat. My sub-conscience tunes into the sounds, attentive to any variations from the norm. There is also a busy gliderport three-miles north of the ranch.

Oletha Cole is here, too — she owns the ranch. I am indebted to her for a place to work on this manuscript, her calm, easy-going disposition, companionship and constant encouragement. She has been thoroughly understanding when, in fits of frustration, I have voiced doubts and anxieties; nevertheless, she has prevailed in her persuasion.

Since the inception of our time together she took a consummate interest in matters aviation, asking innumerable questions like a child who's discovered a new world. In turn, those sometimes lengthy question and answer sessions awakened long-dormant memories in my mind. These were added to my collection of notes, proving to be invaluable to the total effort.

She and her ranch provided surcease from the keyboard. I could walk away and find relief amongst the ranch's busy outdoor environment. It's also convenient to the mountains where further refreshment of mind and body is assured in the serenity of field, forest and stream. I will be forever grateful for her presence, generosity and enduring encouragement.

I am thankful for the many men and women in all walks of aviation who, over the years, provided the experiences, relationships and memories — wherever those characters in the play may be.

Time and distance are often barriers to renewing acquaintances, but they remain in my memory's storehouse. Inexorably Time has, bit-by-bit, claimed the lesser ones and will continue to do so. But not until Time claims me will the complete inventory of images vanish entirely from my mind.

The engineers who designed the airplanes and engines are acknowledged too, although they are personally unknown, faceless and remote from the world of maintenance. Their fertile brains provided many outstanding examples of airplanes that are long remembered. In doing so, they could not foresee also providing interesting, rewarding careers as a spinoff of their efforts, for many mechanics.

It would be remiss not to acknowledge the airplanes and engines in their own right. Collections of parts, components, structures, various designs, disparate operating characteristics and metals. There were some of both that seemed to have near-human traits: Good days, bad days; dispositions that were mild-mannered and co-operative, obdurate and near-inflexible. Ostensibly, they were without a soul — or were they?

It would be unforgivably negligent not to acknowledge George Hammond and Bob Fox in absentia — where ever their souls rest. Two of the finest mechanics I have ever met. They undertook to 'make a silk purse from a sow's ear', the burden borne principally by Hammond. Throughout my career I faithfully followed their dominant themes: 'Don't let it go until it's right' and 'When driving rivets, treat each and every rivet as a separate project'. The latter to be applied to whatever task was being addressed. I am confident they would not be disappointed.

Clyde Carson, a close friend, confident and boon companion who furthered immensely and unselfishly, my beginnings in aviation. There were times, during my 'growing' years, under his wing when I mistakenly questioned his theories and directions. Ultimately, though, he proved to be correct. His efforts were not in vain.

While Gail Blinde did not edit the manuscript she, nevertheless, did read the raw first draft and point out many anomalies that helped immensely. She launched me on the mechanics and deserves my thanks. Although he was paid for his work — and he earned every penny — final editing was assigned to Paul Lippman of Sedona, Arizona. I thank him for cleaning up after me.

Years ago, a fortune teller told one of my sisters she had a relative who would go far in aviation. The crystal-gazer did not clarify whether it would be distance traveled or career performance. Since I was my sister's only relative in aviation we assumed I was the relative in the prophecy. However, in spite of, or because of, the divination, in any event, I accomplished both.

Uppermost in my mind as I worked on *My Left Mag' is Out* were my children: Steve, Earl Jr., Stuart and Karen. I am grateful for the inspiration and incentive they provided — unknowingly.

However inadequate, I needed to leave them something.

CONTENTS

BOOK I

Contents

BOOK II

Contents

Preface

One day I received in the mail a twenty-eight page pamphlet with the title *Book Values* on the cover. It was one of those promotional publications listing books at attractive discounts, obviously with the intent to clear slow-moving titles from the supplier's inventory and to introduce new ones. Curious, I leafed through it and read brief reviews of the subject matter accompanying each title.

Five hundred and fifty-one books were cataloged, ranging from fiction best sellers to works on the lives of famous (and infamous) men and women. There were editions analyzing foreign-built automobiles, treatises on law, discourses concerning health and happiness, and histories chronicling great battles.

For sportsmen and sportswomen there were compendiums on shotguns, rifles and pistols. For the do-it-your-selfers, 'how-to' guide books leading readers step-by-step on how to make everything from canoes to kitchen hutches — a few even provided information on how to build a kitchen! There were a host of others too numerous to mention.

I carefully made notes of volumes devoted to aviation: Its history, use of aircraft in battle, commercial transportation and, of course, biographies and profiles of men and women who were prominent in, and influenced aviation's growth and development in one way or another. There was no work on the life and times of Icarus of Greek legend, however, if one would deem that ill-fated escapade a compelling introduction to the science of flight.

It was a revelation that in all of that inventory of books **not one** was found to be written about the men and women who have made a career of maintaining aircraft and aircraft engines. Were any written? Personally, I have never seen one. What of the aircraft and aircraft engine maintenance mechanic? [1]

The public knows little about this society of talented, resourceful craftsmen who have been steadfast throughout lifetimes of 'keeping 'em flying', to coin a hackneyed phrase. The chronicles have apparently failed to record little, if anything, about the early mechanics who ventured with pilots into a new cosmos of primitive wood, steel and fabric airplanes. How did they maintain the implausible (by today's standards) collections of pistons, crankshafts, valves, irascible magnetos and disagreeable carburetors perceived to be engines?

These men came up a difficult path from the gritty sand dunes of Kitty Hawk where the Wright Flyer's tentative flight heralded in a new age. They learned by rote, educated guess, occasional help from an aircraft or engine constructor, with inherent mechanical intellect thrown in. Their lore was gradually acquired, shared and compared with others and the information passed on to the succeeding generation of mechanics who would apply those disciplines and build upon them.

Aviation's evolution could not have flourished without the technical support provided by the thousands of men, and now women, who have gone before and are still to come. Through perseverance, dedication and, in some instances, real sacrifice, they have transcended the generic title of mechanic and matured into truly masterful technicians. They have stayed in-step with the state-of-the-art and the high-technology that has gradually infused aircraft and engine design with startling ideas, concepts and methodology.

By the time I embarked on my career the very old engines had served their purpose and been remanded to aviation's history. Unlike the planet's flora and fauna that has altered at evolution's whim over untold millennia, engine design evolved in a much more abbreviated interval.

The chronicles are replete with pre-1930 designs and their makers who sought to establish a place for their engines in the exciting new world of aviation. From the glory days of the rotaries of World War I to the second phase of development when supercharging, two-stage blowers and controllable pitch propellers increased engine efficiency, and aircraft performance and safety;. remarkably the list is lengthy with designs of hopeful distinction. Some survived, many fell into near-total obscurity, with their optimistic manufacturers. Most were air-cooled radials and 'flat' examples and some few in-line, liquid cooled types.

Out of the pitiless selection process the dynamic, disciplined designs and their procreators survived. Wright established its name with the J-5, that tireless engine that operated flawlessly for thirty-six hours, wending the design's and Lindbergh's way into the archives. Pratt & Whitney rose almost cheek by jowl with Wright, both powering aircraft to the frontier of turbine engines. They were joined along the way by Lycoming, Warner, Jacobs, Continental, Franklin, Kinner, Lambert and others. From the lengthy list, Lycoming and Continental emerged as prominent designs in both radial types and later, horizontally opposed engines. The latter by both Lycoming and Continental continue in production.

The throaty sounds of the radial engines' exhausts are like no other cacophony of tones. Even today, they still draw and mesmerize older — and younger — airmen of all persuasions like proverbial magnets. The former to relive memories, the latter from curiosity and, perhaps, a modicum of envy. The thin whine of an inertia starter still induces chills of anticipation. The sound is an eerie prelude to the power that follows the guttural, metallic thump of starter dogs engaging a crankshaft.

Sir Frank Whittle inadvertently took away the mystique of the radials with his turbine engine. But he awarded aviation with a machine that surpassed the largest radials in power output through thrust — and at less weight. The turbines were the swan song of the radials. Anyway, they had reached practical limits with the Pratt & Whitney R-4360's. It was as though the progression was pre-arranged. Probably an un-imaginable propulsion system to come is destined to replace the turbines; for now they are the ultimate.

It may shatter the common perception of 'mechanic' to know that some have become aeronautical engineers without portfolio, by designing innovative improvements and correcting design faults in airframes, systems and engines. Many have progressed to higher echelons of management by building viable aviation enterprises and distinguished, successful companies on the wealth of knowledge they accumulated throughout their maintenance years.

Given that brief profile of an aircraft maintenance technician one might be constrained to ask: "Why is it no other profession demands so much as this one, yet receives barely perceptible recognition, monetary or social?" Given public perceptions, small wonder that Charles Taylor, who built the *Wright Flyer's* engine, was denied a measure of acknowledgment for his accomplishment — and contribution to aviation's birth — until a posthumous, belated award was named in his memory. It would appear as an afterthought.

That question was answered by Ernie Gann, author of *Fate is The Hunter* when he wrote, "...people would rather read about the scouts." Gann, in fact, did credit mechanics in his book for their work — to his credit. Nevertheless, it cannot be denied that professional aircraft mechanics, the troops, have contributed mightily to aviation's growth. But, to say a scout is more important than a trooper would be comparable to arguing the old question about firsts, such as chicken versus egg.

My Left Mag' is Out is not intended as a primer of aircraft and engine maintenance and repair. Nor does it seek to establish greatness. The work is an anthology of events and commentary in one mechanic's career. Perhaps it will help throw much-needed light on the aircraft mechanic's professional life and role in aviation, be it Military, Commercial Air Transport, or General Aviation.

E.R.W.

Epigraph

Remembering The Forgotten Mechanic

Through the history of world aviation
many names have come to the fore,
Great deeds of the past in our memory will last,
as they're joined by more and more...

When man first started his labor in his quest to
conquer the sky,
he was designer, mechanic and pilot,
and he built a machine that would fly...

But somehow the order got twisted,
and then in the public's eye,
the only man that could be seen
was the man who knew how to fly...

The pilot was everyone's hero,
he was brave, he was bold, he was grand,
as he stood by his battered old biplane
with his goggles and helmet in hand...

Epigraph

To be sure, these pilots all earned it,
to fly you have to have guts,
And they blazed their names in the Hall of Fame
on wings with baling wire struts...

But for each of these flying heroes
there were thousands of little renown,
And these were the men who worked on the planes
but kept their feet on the ground...

We all know the name of Lindbergh,
and we've read of his flight to fame,
But think, if you can, of his maintenance man,
can you remember his name?

And think of our wartime heroes, Gabreski,
Jabara and Scott,
Can you tell me the names of their crew chiefs?
A thousand to one you cannot...

Now pilots are highly trained people,
and wings are not easily won,
But without the work of the maintenance man
our pilots would march with a gun...

So when you see mighty aircraft

as they mark their way through the air,
The grease-stained man with the wrench in his hand
is the man who put them there...

Anon

Book I

My Left Mag' is Out

1

Genesis in
A Dewberry Patch . . .

A fter more than fifty-years, the recollections of those two airplanes flashing overhead seem like the start of a film that had recorded the memories, still riffling through my mind like wind on water.

That first scene may be a little out of focus, but the images of those two biplanes that were a part of it, still remain sharp. If there were any doubts in my young mind that a career in aviation was in the future, they were completely erased that day in the drum of throaty exhausts of radial engines and an astonishing sight: Real airplanes flying, literally, within a small boy's stone's throw.

The day when my aviation career began to germinate was in the tenth summer of my life.

My mother had ordered me to go pick dewberries, a ground-hugging version of blackberries. She canned dewberries for an occasional delicious pie, a wonderfully delectable deliverance from our bland Great Depression diet. Hash, navy beans, eggs, salt pork, now and then a Sunday roast chicken, and fresh or home-canned vegetables from the garden were our staples. Like thousands and thousands of other families in that depressed era, practicing frugality was a way of life.

My father was steadily employed as a composing room foreman at the Donora, Pennsylvania, *Herald-American* newspaper but was paid only about one-quarter of his salary.

His take home pay was just enough to buy bare essentials and pay the light and cooking-gas bill. Employees in today's job market who object to accepting part-pay to keep a business solvent should not feel intimidated; it was common practice during the Depression.

Welfare, as it's known today, was practically nonexistent. At school, kids were given a half-pint of milk to supplement their homemade brownbag lunches; that was the extent of social benefits. My brother Dave and I dug coal from an abandoned mine for the heating stoves; one might say it was a bootleg operation, but we stayed warm. [2] In retrospect I've often marveled that aviation got off to such an impressive start considering the distressing years of the Depression.

Obediently responding to my mother's order, I found my close chum, Chuck, took two buckets, and off we trudged through a woodland to a large, open field where we knew the berries were plentiful and ripe.

On our hands and knees, under a brilliant afternoon sun, we busily picked dewberries. Overhead the garter-blue sky was sprinkled with globules of fair-weather cumulus clouds lazing, eastward under the halfhearted insistence of a light breeze.

Except for a far-off husky, metallic murmur that didn't mean anything to our senses at the time, there were the usual summer sounds: Raspy insect cries clashing with the woodnotes of birds, all competing with the strident clannish quarreling of crows in the woods we had just walked to reach the field. It was a typically lazy, late-summer day. But that odd metallic droning was beginning to creep into our senses and youthful chatter. It was getting louder and taking on a steady pronounced beat. Almost like a farmer's tractor powering a threshing machine with rhythmic insistence.

Curious about the unusual sound, I raised on my knees and searched the horizon. Two biplanes were flying low over the ground in a northerly direction. They disappeared behind a line of trees and reappeared at the north end of our berry field.

Their gleaming wings flashing insolently, they abruptly banked sharply and, losing altitude — what little they had — flew toward us. Displaying infinite skill the pilots stopped their aircrafts' descent, and with their wheels barely clearing the waist-high grass and low, scanty shrubs the airplanes bore down on us.

Foolishly we stood to get a better view, transfixed, speechless in awe and admiration. How privileged we were to witness such a display of those magnificent machines' we only read about or saw in pictures. It was not only my first encounter with airplanes, but here were two flying at us, getting closer and closer by the second. Closer! That suddenly became a horrifying realization and had to be dealt with immediately.

As they thundered toward us, our fascination rapidly changed to consternation and then fear. Abruptly we realized we could be chopped into very small pieces by the scintillating, deadly discs of the propellers. At the very least, if we were lucky, the huge, black tires would send us tumbling through the grass and berry vines. On the other hand, we could be decapitated by the thin outreach of the wings' leading edges. Seconds were flying by and the airplanes were just yards away.

Speechless with fear, we plunged as one into the questionable shelter of berry vines, grass, weeds and sparse shrubs, striving to burrow into the unyielding earth. I never thought of confronting a snake face-to-face, but worried briefly about spilling the berries. The consequences if I went home empty handed or with a paltry quantity of berries, to face my mother, would be grievous.

Our bodies quivered from the reverberations of exhausts and the dry scream of propellers as the two biplanes rumbled over us. With an awful whoosh of disturbed air and the slap of propeller wash, they pulled up and banked nearly perpendicular; we could see the pilots grinning evilly at two frightened boys groveling desperately against the ground. They were wearing helmets and goggles just like in pictures!

It looked like they were wheeling around to make another run at us. That's when an innate sense of survival surged into our senses: This wasn't right, it said. The instinct also said airplanes and trees weren't compatible and like animals that intuitively seek cover from danger, we jumped up and ran for the safety the edge of the woods offered, about three-hundred yards away. Cave people probably did the same when pterodactyls haunted the skies during the Mesozoic Epoch.

Behind us across the field the two biplanes pivoted on their wing tips and dove at us again, one behind the other. For the remainder of our perilous retreat to the trees we alternately crawled and ran in abject fear. Finally, breathless and bleeding from tiny scratches caused by berry vines, weeds, grass and bushes, we reached that leafy haven and security. The planes broke off the exercise in aerial harassment and disappeared toward a small town nearby. How we managed not to spill our berries I'll never know. It would have been difficult to appease my mother if we had.

To this day the make of the aircraft remains a mystery, but my mind's eye can still see the effortless maneuvering of the two biplanes; the bright yellow of their wings and fuselages with slender bands of black trim. There remain visions of the two pilots in leather helmets and jackets; the goggles; hearing the shattering, dynamic blare of engine exhausts. In spite of the fear that gripped me during the low-level chase, the dazzling experience only whetted my budding appetite for more of anything that was a part of aviation.

The following Christmas my parents gave me a copy of Lindbergh's book, *WE*, the account of his pioneering flight across the North Atlantic to Paris. One of my father's books, a pictorial journal of battles and airplanes in World War I, fascinated me. I devoted hours to studying and drawing the primitive fighter airplanes flown in that war: Spads, Sopwith Camels, Fokkers and several other types. They were indicative of a new idea: Using airplanes as a developing, effective method for waging war. It also set the stage for other uses to come.

Two brothers who owned a garage in the nearby town of Webster were pilots and were aware of my interest in airplanes. One day they gave me a cardboard box full of broken model airplanes, strips and sheets of balsa, rice paper, dope in small cans and other bits and pieces of paraphernalia used in building models. The gift brought untold joy with it.

I had heard the brothers owned airplanes, too, but it didn't dawn on me until several months later that they were probably the culprits who made Chuck and me grovel our way to safety across a dewberry field. Their generosity probably served to salve two guilty consciences, or they were grateful for the entertainment, Chuck and I provided. Nevertheless, I cherished that box of bits and pieces and set to work trying to make whole, one of the broken airplanes in the collection. With absolutely no idea about where to begin the reconstruction.

At the outset of the project I learned that aircraft dope wasn't compatible with high heat, let alone flames.

This product of the wizardry of chemistry had long since replaced varnish as a fabric finish. It was nitrate dope, cellulose based on highly volatile plasticizers and thinning solvents. Butyrate dope, a benign derivative with more favorable characteristics than nitrate dope, wouldn't appear for several years. One of butyrate dope's advantages is it has better penetrating qualities and can be applied over nitrate dope. The reverse application is not true. Most of all though, butyrate dope's leading attribute was that it's much more fire resistant than nitrate dope.

Years later I would, through two widely-spaced incidents, see first-hand the results of the volatility of nitrate dope versus the fire propagation resistance of butyrate dope. In any case, both types provide the means to not only tauten aircraft fabric, but to virtually weatherproof it as well.

There was a frightening revelation when I tried to melt the contents of one of the cans in the cardboard box, to useable consistency — with heat: It can't be done! You have to use dope thinner and that might not work anyway, if the dope has had sufficient time to setup to a hardened condition

The little cans held approximately one-quarter of a pint and had press-on lids, like paint cans. They were all locked shut by dried dope from previous use. It's doubtful if the lids could have been closed tighter if they had been welded shut. Anyone who has worked with dope knows it seals well, if given time to age.

Placing one can on a burner of my mother's gas cook stove, somehow. I had the sense to adjust the flame very low. After a time the lid seemed to begin to bulge ever so slightly and a tiny plume of whitish vapor began to seep from a weak spot in the old dope on the edge of the lid. The can's shape began to change — noticeably. Suddenly I became a beginning student of the properties of gas under pressure. Something was trying to tell me the situation was getting out of control and I took the hint.

Snatching up my mother's canning tongs, I clenched the can in their jaws, shut off the burner and ran for the kitchen door, holding the can behind me with an outstretched arm. Once I glanced behind me; the tiny plume of vapor had thickened and was hissing evilly as it escaped from the can. Now it resembled a jet engine's contrail or a destroyer making a smoke screen as it marked my

7

frantic flight through the kitchen and out the door to the back po-rch.

The screen door slammed shut behind me, concurrent with a mighty pop from the can as its lid blew off. I sagged with immense relief. Not only would there have been severe disciplinary action taken by my mother, had she been present, but the house could have caught fire and surely burned to the ground. In those days fire trucks weren't as fleet or as numerous as they are today. Rural fire stations just didn't exist.

I didn't press my luck and volunteer any information about what happened, for fear of post incident reprisals — my mother never knew. Later Dave and I were each awarded a newspaper delivery route in the country — through my father's influence at the *Herald-American* — and I was able to refresh my model build-ing materials' inventory — especially fresh dope — with the pitiful fifty-cents a week I earned.

In a short time, after much trial and error, I built my first model, a Curtiss Robin. It was powered by a thick rubber band and flew well — until another brother, the baby of the family, sat on it. It was the first of a litany of models to follow.

During those growing-up years between my close encounter with the biplanes and high school graduation, the genes of some mechanically-motivated ancestor gradually surfaced to influence and direct my future. The family tree gives no hint of that worthy and the ancestor remains an unknown.

On my mother's side my grandad wasn't especially mechanically-inclined but he was wonderfully adept at tying fish-ing flies, if that counts for anything. Nor were any uncles, as far as

8

I knew. My father was bound over to a family that could afford to raise him — his could not. Beyond that sparse information there is nothing. My father's known branch of the family, unfortunately, was little more than a sprig.

I became adept at reading the simple directions and plans that came with each airplane model, and there were many, all constructed of balsa wood. With each model, I learned more and more about aircraft structure. Those models were a far cry from the plastic ready-to-assemble types of today that teach little more than the fine art of using assembly cement.

Preparing for assembly of those early airplane models was tedious and it taught patience. Single-edge razor blades, a threatened species of personal toiletry tools, that followed the straight razor were highly important implements in the hobby. Wing ribs were outlined on balsa sheets to be cut out and smoothed; stringers were pre-cut into fine, delicate lengths but still had to be sized, smoothed and fitted to bulk-heads and ribs. Some kits had solid blocks of balsa from which to sculpture various major structural components.

The completed sub-assemblies, airfoils and fuselages, had to be covered with 'tissue' paper, made taut, doped and painted. When assembled, a well-constructed model was a work of art — and they flew. Model building was a valuable learning experience.

Erector sets were popular then and I was given several over a span of separate Christmases. They provided hours of amusement, building diverse mechanical objects such as windmills. When my electrician brother-in-law gave me a tiny battery-powered electric motor he built, the windmills spun grandly when the motor was rigged to drive the blades.

The Erector sets figured prominently in my growing dexterity in using tools, much to my father's apprehension and sometimes disgust. He was careful with his tools and insisted, with liberal disciplinary measures, they be returned to their proper place.

His points were quickly made; today, he would probably be charged with child abuse — then, it was discipline. From those strict lessons I learned to care for, and respect tools. To this day I abhor the sight of maintenance technicians working on an airplane with tools scattered helter skelter on a hangar floor or work stand.

After we moved to the hills of Western Maryland I was sure I would not see another airplane for a long time, if ever. But I was wrong.

There was a small grass airport where the great and near-great fliers stopped to re-fuel on cross-country flights. It is active to this day.[3] The variety of airplanes using Mexico Farms Airport, mostly biplanes, was mind-boggling — and so were some of the owner-pilots.

There was a Briggs Skylark, a J-1 Standard and a Waco 10. One well-known pilot owned a Pitcairn Fleetwing and another had a Berliner with an OX-5 engine.[4] There was also a Vele Monocoupe that was instrumental in a bizarre, dangerous stunt.

One day the Vele's pilot took off with a passenger who felt the need to impress his hometown friends and neighbors. The pair had tied a short length of heavy rope to a fuselage member in the little cabin before takeoff, with a loop fashioned in the free end.

After they arrived over the little town the passenger slid down the rope, placing one foot in the loop. The pilot flew back and forth over the little town with his passenger swinging happily to and fro under the Vele, waving to a thoroughly fascinated, admiring audience of his friends on the ground. It was an unusual event for the people and they waved back.

In a short time the amateur trapeze artist began to tire. With no directional control his body would swing back and forth, while rotating erratically. But it was one thing to descend the rope, rested and charged with euphoria, another to cling to his precarious thread, with fatigue creeping inexorably into his arms and one leg.

His high-flying exhibition of derring-do was rapidly deteriorating into a life or death matter. With aching hands, arms and legs he barely managed to struggle up into the airplane's cabin. He, fortunately, escaped unscathed, but during the escapade, between being buffeted by the relentless wind and shouting, he lost his false teeth. Unfortunately, that was before Fixodent®. The adventure was the subject of much discussion for a long time, among the pilots based at Mexico Farms.

It may seem incredulous that men and women would risk life, limb and their airplanes answering the siren call of the freedom of unlimited airspace while straining their imaginations in hair-raising aerial antics, but the stories are chronicled in literature and memory.

Typical of these free spirits was Parker, a mechanic and (then) a Designated Aircraft Maintenance Inspector (DAMI). When I met him it was after I returned from the Hawaiian Islands and had acquired my A&E license and also, a DAMI rating. He was semi-retired from aviation and had transgressed: He chose to become a city fireman.

Parker was a lanky, slow-talking hillbilly type who had a personal vendetta with an acquaintance at a small — little more than a pasture — air strip twenty-five miles from his own base. He never revealed the nature of their disagreement, but it wasn't a lethal one, he said. Both men were always alert to make life miserable, in one way or another, for the other at every opportunity.

"One day while I was flying toward his field I saw him across the field doing something," Parker told me. "He saw me about the same time I saw him and began running toward his hangar.

"I had him in the open and started buzzing him. I made the bastard crawl all the way to the hangar. Then I left — I knew he always kept a shotgun in the hangar." Parker's story activated the recall of a long-ago scene etched firmly in my memory about another buzzing incident in which I was involved as a small boy, innocently picking berries.

The venturesome aerial antics of several pilots at Mexico Farms made them legends in their time. If they were to be excused, it was an era when control by a budding Civil Aeronautics Authority (CAA), intent on exerting its domination over a burgeoning national aviation community, was being resisted. The CAA was regarded as an interloper, a threat to free-wheeling thinking and activities in the newly-discovered, exploitable cosmos of the air.

It was an era of intense learning for the CAA, pilots and mechanics.

The airplanes that evolved during the 1920s and '30s suited the growing personal flying sector admirably. They were relatively well-designed, considering the state-of-the-art, although some may not have been as forgiving as others. Some may have been ahead of their time.[5] Most were relatively inexpensive and fairly easy to maintain. Pilot-owners who learned to fly one day began to apply suddenly acquired mechanical expertise the next. The fact there were no air regulations or airplane, mechanic and pilot licenses prior to 1927 helped immensely.

Then, like the rays of the sun warming the earth, the idea germinated in Washington that just maybe, some control over what had progressed from innovation to practicality, needed to be put in place. Well, wasn't federal airspace and public safety involved? It was rationalized, therefore, that if one flew or maintained airplanes then he or she, as well as the airplane, should be licensed. Besides, the general public was becoming more and more immersed in air travel and that needed to be addressed. Still, many pilots and mechanics off the beaten path continued their independent ways, resisting all efforts toward federal — or any — control or regulating. Otherwise, the serious aspects of aviation were gradually falling in line.

If those aerial shenanigins of private pilots and the barnstormers did nothing else, they exposed an enthralled public to not only the thrill of exploring a new frontier, but also, a developing image of a practical means of doing it.

The 1930s could be considered a decade of experimentation and some would look on 1936 as the year when aviation truly began to come of age. All-in-all those years are considered by many to be the Golden Age of Aviation. Ideas and dreams ran rampant and none seemed ridiculous then.

Charles and Anne Lindbergh were busily surveying potential air routes and endeavoring to convince everyone that overseas flying would materialize; Jimmy Doolittle was keeping busy by pioneering instrument flying; Wiley Post was experimenting in endurance and high altitude flying; Amelia Earhart established forever a place for women in aviation; DC-2's and DC-3's were emerging as the springboards for reliable, commercial air travel. All of these efforts were proof that the visionaries were constantly striving for viable aircraft with progression in learning how best to use them, in support of this new dimension in public transportation and military operations.

I followed these events by radio, newspaper and in my once-a-week treat to movies and the news reels that accompanied them. These sources were the only connection available to me, to keep me going toward, what I had always felt, a career in aviation, even through high school.

The circumstances to 'hang around' the local airport and wash airplanes or insinuate myself into activities, simply were beyond my control. There was work to be done at home after school; if I failed to catch the school bus after school there was a long, long walk involved in getting home on my own. If that occurred, there was the dreadful certainty that I would feel the wrath of my father, either orally or, certainly, physically.

The otion of leniency was always an absent quantity. Although, in all fairness, his wrath subsided to an occasional admonition and all became non-existent in my late, high school years.

I liked the newsreels best of all. In that era aviation was hot news and it was covered thoroughly. And so any event that occurred — Lindbergh's historic flight; endurance flights; Roscoe Turner's and many others' accomplishments, were given top bill-ing. The wonderful thing about those films — in my mind — was they had generous footage of airplanes, either on the ground or in flight.

One afternoon when the sky was a leaden overcast and low, stodgy clouds were scudding eastward beneath it, I saw a dirigible. It was plodding westward in and out of the broken, sodden blanket, a massive elongated grey cloud itself. It seemed to fill the sky, so low and tremendously-huge it was.

It was common knowledge that dirigibles were of high interest. After all, the Germans had been building them for years and even making Atlantic crossings to the U.S. The U.S. Navy was the leading proponent of dirigibles, feeling they had promise in fleet service to ward off potential enemies and also, carrying cargo. They hadn't yet achieved the romantic image of airplanes and airplane pilots.

In the middle 1950's I chanced to meet a dirigible pilot who had made three crossings in the Hindenburg. He was in a training program arranged between the Hindenburg Line and Goodyear Tire and Rubber Company. His enthusiastic description of those flights indicated that they were the best method for crossing the Atlantic, according to him .

"It was a marvelous experience," he exclaimed. "We had excellent accommodations and dining. The passengers could relax in lounges and play cards or do whatever amused them and watch the clouds go by. I was always amazed by the near-luxury.

"You could barely hear the engines and sometimes we'd pass a ship. The ships always blew their whistles for us; it was no problem hearing them." Depending on headwinds, their cruise speed averaged from 60 m.p.h. to 70 m.p.h. and weather was never a concern, he said.

The beat of this airship's engines reverberated across the hills, pushing the ponderous bulk gradually out of sight with throaty resolve. I learned later it was the Navy's Macon, the last in an attempt to prove the practicality of the immense airships.

With its passage I recalled the cremation of the Hindenburg I'd seen on the news reels, as it was consumed in a holocaust of hydrogen-fueled flames at Lakehurst, New Jersey. Shortly after the experience of seeing it, the Macon crashed off the California coast; the Akron had already kept its appointment with destiny in 1933 in the Atlantic.[6]

It seemed that unless I made some move I would be forever relegated to standing apart from the airplanes and events that were passing by. Like a small boy pressing his nose, wistfully, against a candy store window. I had no idea what part I would have in aviation; I simply wanted to be involved somehow — to be there.

Since I had no direction and advice for getting started in aviation — my parents could offer no help because they weren't attuned to the field, not that they didn't want to — and money to attend a school was non-existent, even if I could find one.

There was only one option available: I would have to go where the airplanes were.

Purely by chance, I met a young man, about six years older than my 18-years. Dick Moyer was his name and he had returned to the rural neighborhood where I lived, after a tour of duty in the Army in Hawaii.

Dick had enlisted because there were no opportunities in the

16

area for much of anything, let alone employment that had a potential for short, or long term employment. He described the experience he had and urged me to enlist — and specify duty in the Hawaiian Islands. There were airplanes there, he said, the climate was wonderful, the scenery marvelous! It was an appealing perspective, to me. My horizon, was the tops of the surrounding hills; I had to do something, even if it was wrong.

For the remainder of the summer following my graduation from high school I continued working at my job at a service station. But all the while, I knew I was going through the motions of continuing a life there that was full of uncertainty. Answering that urge to find some answer to the dilemma, I even enrolled in a correspondence course, studying diesel engines. That, however, did little to mitigate my desires. Besides, those engines I was studying were intangible objects.

Working at the service station I was earning the princely sum of twenty-five dollars a week, full time. Although she didn't ask, I split that money with my Mother and still had enough for clothes and foolishness. The money also enabled me to buy an Indian motorcycle, the Scout model, for eighty dollars. On Sundays, it carried me with remarkable dependency to Mexico Farms airport and the Hagerstown airport.

At the former I could watch the small airplanes and associated activities but the latter was a genuine eye-opener. There, Fairchild Aircraft was building what was to me, huge twin engine airplanes in addition to smaller singles. The odor of dope was strong even from the highway where I parked, to look at airplanes parked outside the factory.

It was at Hagerstown that I stood up close and personal to a staggerwing Beechcraft in the fixed base operator's shop. The engine and the area behind the instrument panel was exposed. It was a wonder how anyone could sort out any problems in the maze of wiring and tubing.

I had no idea, as I looked that one day, I would overcome that mystery.

During that summer after graduation from high school I didn't discuss my desire to get into aviation or the decision that was building in my mind on how to do it, with my parents. Nor, with my older brother by two years, David, who was working at odd jobs on a hit-or-miss basis. As it turned out, the fickle finger of fate saw to it he became involved in hands-on activities with aircraft on a regular basis before I did when he joined the Air Corps, after I did.

Unfortunately, he wasn't active very long. His B-17 was shot down over Belgium during one of the day-light bombing raids, early in the war, that were so costly in men and aircraft.

There was no way of knowing what lay beyond those hills, except what I saw in the newsreels and read in the newspapers. Finally when I reached a decision I didn't tell my parents. I simply took action and told them that I had.

In September, three months after graduating from high school, I joined the Army Air Corps.

I asked for and was assigned to its Hawaiian Department. Within a week I boarded the train that would carry me beyond those hills. .

2

Inertia Starts
Beginners Too...

How I got from Western Maryland to Fort Slocum, New York, without getting lost or turned around I'll never know. The Army recruiting sergeant filled out a few papers and handed them to me. Then he bought my lunch, handed me a train ticket and took me to the railroad station.

"You'll get off in New York City, catch another train to New Rochelle and go to the dock and wait," he said. "Hand those papers to the non-com at the dock. Good luck!" The myriad questions in my mind went unanswered as he retreated to his car, leaving me to face an unfamiliar new world.

Some how I survived the train ride — my very first — to New York City and then found my way to Fort Slocum. It was on an island at the head of Long Island Sound — which accounted for the boat dock. It was necessary for the small ferry that plied the water between Fort Slocum and New Rochelle to tie up there.

After a week at Fort Slocum filled with indoctrination, being outfitted with uniforms and instruction in close-order drills, approximately one hundred or more of us were bundled up and taken to the Brooklyn Naval Yard. I wondered why they called it a yard when the ships were sitting on water!

The scene was utterly fascinating: Tall buildings as a backdrop to the din of shouts, an occasional ship's whistle, clatter of winches and squeak of loading booms handling cargo. Ships — big ships — were everywhere. It seemed chaotic, yet there was a semblance of order. We were deposited on a dock where a huge ship was tied up. Lettering on its bows identified it: U.S. Army Transport *Republic.*

My contingent clambered up a long gangplank to join hundreds of other enlisted men already aboard. Nearly two hours later, the Republic was freed from its bondage to the dock and we steamed out to sea. The Statue of Liberty calmly watched our passage and I marveled at the sight. At last I saw it to be an actuality rather than an abstract in a black and white photo.

Passengers weren't pampered aboard the *R*epublic, except for officers and their families — if one had a family. The usual 'class' act prevailed: Officers had the upper decks and cabins, enlisted men had the main deck and troop holds. There were about 600 enlisted personnel aboard. Many, like me, were newly-recruited, traveling to assigned stations; others returning to previous duty stations from leave or being re-assigned.

It was the beginning of a fascinating education for a teenager from the hills as the ship breasted the ocean's swells and began to plod doggedly through the sun-drenched Atlantic southward from New York to Colon, Panama. We were enthralled and lined the ship's rails to watch the huge locks of the Panama Canal raise the ship.

Then we began sailing a man-made waterway through a verdant jungle that a person could throw a rock into from the deck, and possibly hit one of the occasional iguanas we saw lying on a tree limb, was the stuff of guided tours. Actually, we were on one. By the close of day we were lowered into the Pacific Ocean by another set of locks. Here, I thought, this is a school geography lesson come to life.

We had a day's shore leave at Panama City. A recruit bought a monkey and smuggled it aboard; it promptly escaped from his arms. After several hours of futile attempts to capture it, which threw the entire ship into an uproar, the monkey was shot from the top of a mast and ignominiously tossed into the Pacific Ocean.

Not being psychic, I had no inkling that another encounter with a monkey, or more correctly, monkeys, lay in my future.

The shipboard rumor mill ground out the news we were going to San Francisco for a week and then continue to Honolulu. There was no reason to doubt the rumor. The sun arose over the starboard rail of the Republic, so we were sailing north. Besides, even I knew the Hawaiian Islands weren't situated immediately off the California coast, and my orders stated I was going to the Hawaiian Islands. But the rumor mill didn't say why the ship would stay at San Francisco that long.

The voyage, so far, had been interesting, but not truly uplifting as a tourist would find a cruise. Several hours after boarding the *Republic* in New York, I was assigned to 'kitchen police (KP)' a high-sounding phrase that had nothing at all to do with law enforcement. In the oddly formulated vernacular of armed services phraseology "kitchen police", simply defined, meant scrubbing kitchen and mess hall floors, tables, pots and pans, peeling potatoes and preparing assorted other vegetables at the behest of the cooks. It also included feeding hungry soldiers in a chow line, polishing coffee cups and any menial tasks the mess sergeant and cooks could think of. If nothing came to mind they could invent something!

After leaving New York City some bored second lieutenant must have arbitrarily decreed that thirty-nine others and I be placed in a KP company, by starting at the bottom of the troop manifest and working up. But there was a meager consolation: Another company was also formed as an alternate, so each company had one day on, one day off. One company couldn't have survived continuous duty.

Fate must have decreed that with five others I was assigned to wash silverware, meal trays and pots and pans while the ship sailed through the sunny Caribbean to Panama. We had a short break there and went ashore, but resumed KP duties when the ship sailed to San Francisco. The odious work was done by hand in three huge, deep, elongated tubs.

Every item was first washed in a veritable cauldron of unbearably hot, soapy water followed by a rinse in succeeding tubs. Steam formed a hoary, sweltering, searing cloud over the three tubs to ensure that not only were our hands and arms boiled raw, but our heads and shoulders were steamed like lobsters.

22

Sweat streamed from our bare torsos in torrents until, it seemed, we were vertical extensions of the mass of seething water much like water-spouts on the ocean. No one can fault the Army for its concern about food poisoning and dysentery. Its method of hot, hotter and hottest full-filled the search for the ultimate in sterilization.

After leaving Panama I was assigned to dishing out food to the troops, a truly exalted position. The chief cook made sure the chow line moved along smartly and would stand ever alert, arms akimbo, in command of all he surveyed, to make sure it did. On occasion a man would ask for a second helping and be rejected out of hand.

"Move along," the chief would growl. "We're here to only keep you alive, not fatten you." Ironically, we K.Ps could eat more but we barely had time to eat our regular meal.

Fate further decreed that my education as a kitchen policeman be continued. While the ship was docked at San Francisco we were billeted at Fort McDowell. I worked from 04:00 to 20:00 (4 a.m. to 8 p.m.) daily, in the most immense mess hall imaginable. But fate relented somewhat in my duties there: I escaped the dreaded wash tubs.

Mysteriously, when we reboarded the Republic, I never pulled another day of KP. I whiled away the days of the ocean crossing to Honolulu, watching the Pacific Ocean slide by the ship's rails. I felt almost like a tourist, lounging on deck and gradually acquiring a tan.

It was beginning to feel like this was becoming an endless voyage that might stop somewhere in an uncertain future. Then a bright spot, or rather three, appeared suddenly one glorious morning about fifty-miles from the coast of Oahu.

Three B-18's, the latest bomber type in the Air Corps bombing fleet, roared by the *Republic* in a tight 'V' formation at mast height. Their Air Corps markings stood out in bold relief against the bright aluminum fuselages.

The glimmering discs of their propellers, the reverberation of six engines against the ships sides and superstructure. They were the largest airplanes I had *ever* seen. They banked around well in front of the ship and flew by once again, then disappeared toward the island that was looming larger and larger on the horizon ahead of the ship. The sight of those airplanes was absolutely thrilling, and they imparted hope.

They had to come from somewhere ahead and that's where I was going. I took the welcoming fly-by personally, with brightening spirits, turned my attention to the island, seldom leaving the rail, except for chow. The last meal of the trip.

Oahu was becoming more detailed as the ship neared. Now the sharp spires and peaks of a mountain range, tops swathed in cottony clouds, sides verdant with forests and vegetation, stood out. So this was the island of Stevenson and Captain Cook, who had discovered the islands. Finally, there ahead of us was Diamond Head, just as in pictures, as was the Statue of Liberty. Now, sliding past Waikiki Beach and the Moana and Royal Hawaiian hotel — the only hotels on the beach at the time — the *Republic* began to slow as it neared the entrance to Honolulu Harbor.

Honolulu itself lay spread between the first rise of the mountains behind it and the island's shore. Mostly the residences and buildings appeared to be one story with a sprinkling of two story structures. Stately coconut palm trees were scattered in profusion through out with the venerable Alexander Hotel in the downtown sector lording it overall. There was, at that time, a sprinkling of more expensive residences perched high above all else on the slopes of the mountains. Obviously owned by moneied people.

Since everyone aboard knew our arrival would be the end of the voyage, all of the enlisted men had quietly collected their belongings, packed their barracks bags and began to line the ship's rails to watch the end of the voyage.

At the harbor's entrance, a small boat laid alongside the *Republic* to discharge the pilot who would guide the ship to its mooring.. With minimal speed, the ship crept across the harbor and finally, with the aid of two tugboats that bustled importantly around the ship, the *Republic* was finally tied to the dock and the gangplank lowered.

With the usual Army controlled confusion, men were sorted out according to their final destinations. My contingent of Air Corps recruits and those bound for duty at Schofield Barracks were directed to board a train. It was a narrow-gage train, used mostly to haul sugar cane and pineapples to respective mills. But we were seated in passenger cars, not stuffed in like those two commodities. As we chuffed out of Honolulu, I thought it a remarkable coincidence that I had begun my excursion into the outside world from the hills, and it would end on another train!

But the train ride was interesting: Everything was different. The geography, the pineapple and cane fields we rode through, the vegetation and even the color of the earth. That was reddish and, apparently, very fertile.

The train ride was about an hour and at approximately 16:30 hours I stepped off with my companions, all new members of the U.S. Army Air Corps. I was at Wheeler Field.

There, before my very eyes, was a line of solid, brick hangars, with airplanes parked in front of them. My misgivings aboard the *Republic* were without foundation. At last, I was where the airplanes were. Except for the Boeing P-26s parked in front of the various squadron' hangars, I had no idea what the others were.

On the night of our arrival at Wheeler Field the Air Corps recruits were housed in the end of one squadron's hangar on canvas cots. In the other end, several P-26s were parked.

My sleep was sound and restful that night knowing that there I was: Not only arriving where the airplanes were, but virtually surrounded by them!

2a

Inertia Continued....
And a Home at Last!

Wheeler Field was like a scene from that early movie, *"Dawn Patrol"*, except for the aircraft, hangars, vehicles and Air Corps uniforms. Indeed, dawn patrols were standard operating procedures. The field itself, had long since established its place in Air Corp — and, indeed, aviation history.

It was here on June 28, 1927, that Maitland and Hegenberger landed a Fokker C-2 trimotor, the *Bird of Paradise*, after a 26-hour flight from Oakland, California. In the Dole air race to the Hawaiian

Islands, Gobel and Davis in their Travel Air, *Woolaroc,* landed there to win the race and Jensen Schluter followed in the Breese mono-plane, the *Aloha*, to place second.

In 10-years Amelia Earhart would land there, first as the first woman to fly between Hawaii and California and then to experience an aborted attempt to fly around the world, from a different departure point.

There were also activities for which Wheeler Field was intended.

Daily — weekends generally were excepted — just when the first dim light of a new day began to silhouette the ragged profile of the Koolau Mountains against the sun's faint glow, a squadron of Boeing P-26's would take off.[7] Two by two they would race across the grass field, their exhausts snapping in the day's dim first-light in steely-blue banners of flame that proclaimed satisfied engines fed by well-adjusted carburetors.

When the duty squadron was airborne the little fighters would form up and disappear into the new morning. It never found an enemy to repulse. Regrettably, the peace-time habit of standing down on Saturday afternoon and all day Sunday would come back to haunt Air Corps commanders in the not-so-distant future.

Because Wheeler Field's barracks housed full complements of personnel of the fighter and attack squadrons based there, our group of Air Corps recruits was housed in one end of the cavernous hangar.

The remainder of the hangar was reserved for a squadron of fighters: Boeing P-26's. RKO Pathe News always showed a flight of them in the introduction to its news reel films. The sight of them squatting demurely in the hangar's subdued light belied their true intent.

In the light of day these fighter planes exuded an air of feisty belli-gerence. The nimble picturesque Boeings and Curtiss P-36's, tiny by today's standards, were the first line fighters in the Air Corps' Hawaiian Department when I arrived at Wheeler field. They would be replaced with P-40's in a matter of months.

The Boeing's powerplants were Pratt & Whitney R-1340, 600-horsepower engines. These P-26's were capable of 235-miles per hour and had a range of 635-miles. Service ceiling was 27,000-feet. Armament was versatile: One .30-caliber and one .50-caliber machine gun or two .50-caliber machine guns. They could also be fitted with two 100-pound bombs. The prototype first flew in March of 1932.

There were aging Martin B-12's at Wheeler Field, as well. They were a trim mid-wing, twin-engine bomber with the distinctive feature of having corrugated fuselage skins. They also had two other outstanding characteristics: Hand-operated, retractable main landing gear and a Plexiglas, rotating nose cupola. Its movement was limited: About ninety-degrees, left and right. The bombardier-nose gunner occupied that position.

Powered by either Wright Cyclones or Pratt & Whitney Hornets, the B-12's had a remarkably high performance for their time. They were somewhat faster than, but incapable of the load-carrying ability of their successors, the Douglas B-18's.

There were also Curtiss A-12's, a low-wing, single-engine attack aircraft powered by a nine-cylinder Wright Cyclone with an adjustable-pitch propeller. Designed primarily for ground support, its purpose was to harry troop and supply lines with machine gun fire and a store of small bombs. They had a two-man crew: Pilot and rear gunner. Maximum speed was 202 miles per hour at 6,800-feet.[8]

Because we had time on our hands while awaiting permanent assignment, several of us were detailed to help push the P-26's out of the hangar into precise parking alignment on the warm-up apron in preparation for the day's flying and maintenance activities. If the P-26's were destined for dawn patrol, we worked in the pre-dawn darkness. Otherwise, we began the day more sensibly at six o'clock.

After breakfast on one such morning I was introduced to a fiendish device that could only have been spawned in the warped mind of a born sadist. It was an inertia starter.!

The introduction also contained the law of inertia: "The property of a body which causes it to tend to continue in its present state of rest or motion, unless acted upon by some force." The experience imbedded the fundamentals of inertia in my mind forever. As it developed, I was the lead actor in the soon-to-be drama of enacting the 'some force' production.

"What's your name?" a voice behind me asked. Startled, I turned from sweeping the hangar floor and saw the voice's owner: One of the sergeants of the squadron. From his activities around the P-26's I judged him to be a crew chief. Whatever...he had to be obeyed.

"Wilson," I answered, and at the same time wondered what I had done, or not done, to warrant the attention of the sergeant.

"Come with me, I need some help."

I leaned the broom against a workstand and followed him out the hangar door. If someone — anyone — with stripes or higher rank issued an order you obeyed it, especially if you were a recruit. We strode up to a P-26 parked apart from four others on the small ramp.

The sergeant picked up a ponderous crank lying next to the airplane's left wheel. It had a long shank with a slot cut across the diameter of one end, at an angle. At the opposite end was the handle: Two hand-grips that rotated independently of each other. They were rubber-covered so as not to create, I assumed, more blisters than necessary on one's hands.

4

That should have been my clue that I would be the operator of the device and would grip the handle for extensive periods of time. But I had no inkling why. Automobiles were once equipped with similar cranks, in case the starter or battery failed, one of the many sensible accessories and design features that have flown in the face of advanced thinking.

"You see this hole?" the sergeant asked, pointing to a small opening in the engine's side cowling. It was a tad larger than the diameter of the crank's shank. "You slide the crank in this hole until it stops. Then you turn the crank until it engages the starter, and then you start cranking.

"Now, when you get the starter turning you have to keep pressure on the crank," he continued. But he didn't volunteer any information about what would happen if I didn't. "When you get the starter up to speed I'll yell 'contact'. That's when you pull the crank out and pull on this ring. It engages the starter. When the engine starts, get back out of the way!"

Then as an afterthought, he added, "You'll have to stand on that main wheel fairing, but don't fall into the propeller."

He walked around the wing and climbed into the cockpit, leaving me with the ponderous crank hanging in my hand. I glanced fearfully at the gleaming propeller and recalled others in the past that had caused me concern. It was silent, ominous, poised, as if waiting to pounce. Surely it was a rotary guillotine. If the first blade didn't decapitate me, the second would. The thought sent a chill of appr-ehension up my spine.

I stepped up on the wheel's fairing and slid the crank's shaft into the hole until it stopped. Then I tentatively rotated it and engaged the starter. Fortunately, the handle stopped at about the eleven o'clock position, the best possible place for beginning the cranking exercise, I would learn.

An inertia starter operates exactly as its name implies. The unfortunate crankee has to spin-up the internal system of planetary gears until their rotational speed stores energy at maximum peak. When the engaging ring is pulled, the starter's drive meshes with the engine's starter dogs. Crank shaft rotation begins — hopefully. If ignition is on, then engine start is almost immediately accomplished — also hopefully — all things being in harmony.[9]

As I waited patiently, muffled sounds came from the cockpit. There were some subdued, metallic clicks and mysterious, muted sliding noises as the sergeant prepared for engine start. Finally he raised his head and looked out the side of the cockpit. "Aw' right...start cranking!"

Resolutely I grasped the crank handle, one hand on each rubber grip, pulled down — and nearly chinned myself on the handle. It seemed to be stuck. I put more weight on the handle and ever so slowly the crank began to turn. At the bottom of the crank's swing the rotation picked up to a snail's pace, but then my efforts were reversed: I had to push up.

It was as though the crank suddenly gained one hundred-pounds or more and my back immediately protested. Standing on the left main wheel's fairing instead of the ground directly under the crank reduced my advantage: I wasn't directly under the crank. On the other hand, if I was, I couldn't follow through when the crank was at the top of the turn. When I pushed up, the fairing protested with a distinctive creak.

Over the top of the swing and starting down again it was gratifying that the crank gained a little more speed. Ever mindful of the sergeant's warning to keep pressure on the crank I strained mightily through the bottom and up again. At the top I lagged slightly as

6

anyone is wont to do when cranking in a circle, but caught up quickly and continued down.

The starter's gears began to produce a perceptible dry metallic whine and the pressure on my arms, shoulders and legs seemed to ease off a trifle. Through several more revolutions the whine reached a feverish pitch. I was hard put to maintain pressure enough to keep the crank engaged with the starter. Without the dis-engaging slot at the end of the crank the devilish thing probably would have pumped me up and down like the sucker rod on a windmill extracting water from a well.

My muscles began to protest vigorously from the cruel and unusual treatment when the sergeant suddenly yelled "Contact!", not a breath too soon. The starter's interplanetary gears were screaming by now and my arms were a circular blur in front of my face. Besides, they seemed to have suddenly gained weight.

As suddenly as I stopped cranking the crank dis-engaged itself and I pulled it free of the cowling. The starter engaging ring pulled easily enough, and a solid thump followed as the starter's dogs engaged the engine's starting dogs. The propeller jumped abruptly into motion and spun energetically through several revolutions, then slowed with sickening languor to a dead stop. Except for the faint whine of the starter's gears slowing to a bare whisper, there was dead silence.

There was a muffled, heartfelt curse from the cockpit accompanied by more subtle sounds of things moving.

I studiously contemplated a row of rivets on the P-26's fuselage and waited in silence for the sergeant's next move. My arms and shoulder muscles tingled with alarm; until now, they hadn't been called upon to do anything more strenuous than washing pots and pans and sweeping the hangar floor. It seemed interesting that a tiny stream of gasoline dribbled from under the engine cowl to form a small, shallow pool on the apron.

"Well, don't just stand there. Crank again." My education had advanced remarkedly, I thought. Now I'm a mind reader.

"Sergeant, there's gas dripping on the ground." I offered the information tenuously, well aware that my boldness could result in a scathing denunciation of my mentality and right to life. It was also possible any that could include my ancestry. All recruits suffered a lowly status. Sure enough it came, but not as demeaning as I thought it would be.

"Well hell, why didn't you say so?" Probably it didn't occur to him that I couldn't have until the gas appeared, but I took heart. Apparently my volunteered information shed a modicum of light as to why the engine didn't start because the sergeant's voice was about ten decibels lower when he yelled again: "Start cranking!"

I inserted the crank, but couldn't engage it at any better than about the seven o'clock position. Pulling mightily I urged the crank to creep through the bottom of the swing. The exertion of the upward push again surged through my shoulders and back, then to my feet.

I thought of Atlas with the world resting on his shoulders and empathized. Gradually, the muttered whine of the starter's interplanetary gears achieved their grinding scream and I was back to being the sucker rod on the windmill again.

I engaged the starter on command, the propeller started turning on cue and this time, there were several faint pops from the exhaust accompanied by dense, whitish billows of vapor. For just an instant the propeller seemed to gain speed, but then slowed to a disgusting stop.

Naturally, the starter had lost its will to continue cranking the engine. Horrified, I resignedly called on my tiring muscles for another effort. The curses from the cockpit were more audible and lucid.

"Sergeant, it seems to me that electric starters would be better," I brazenly remarked.

"No one needs your opinions!" came the scathing retort. "Just shut up and get your skinny ass to cranking again." Obviously I had touched upon a sore spot that may have had something to do with the sergeant's manipulation of the engine controls. Or maybe he had a hangover, as sergeants were known to have on Monday mornings. Anyway, I inserted the crank yet a third time.

Energizing the starter was smoother and why not? I was rapidly becoming more experienced and, therefore, more skillful in winding it to peak energy storage. My muscles, furthermore, were becoming more attuned to the workout. But they also were becoming steeped with severe stiffness in the bargain. I'd seen wild rabbits run until their leg muscles locked, iron-hard, immobile, and wondered if arm muscles could be atrophied too.

A question arose in my mind: 'Where was the airplane's regular maintenance crew?' I wouldn't dare ask, though.

On the next attempt to start the engine I was thrilled that several cylinders actually fired vigorously. The exhaust vapor swirling over the wings to drift away behind the airplane was encouraging.

Momentarily I thought about falling forward off my dubious foothold on the left wheel fairing into the deadly disc. But the results, if I did, were horrible to contemplate and I became all that more careful about maintaining a firm foothold and grip on the starter handle.

The thought occurred to me: If the starter was wound up and I did lose my footing would it pump me up and down? I cast that thought aside quickly!

9

By now there didn't seem to be any more room for ache in my arms; I felt it was overflowing into my rib-cage, in concert with a stinging, burning sensation.

Wearily, I engaged the crank once more after the engine lapsed into a series of half-hearted snuffs and finally stopped altogether.

The next attempt to start was successful. The engine, having cleared itself of its overdose of gasoline, sputtered into a delightful, steady roar; the propeller spun grandly and I congratulated myself that I had not gotten tangled in its gleaming disc.

From a safe distance at the left wing tip I leaned and rested my muscles, watching intently while the sergeant ran the engine through an operational check. After a time he seemed satisfied it was running as it should and shut it down.

"That's all, Wilson," he said in a voice that hinted at what I thought was a reluctant attempt to regard me as a human being, after all. "Go back to your sweeping." I handed him the starter crank and returned to my broom. It seemed to have gotten heavier since I leaned it against that workstand.

The following year I chanced to be at an airstrip on the North Shore of Oahu that was used by the Air Corps and the Navy for practice. The Navy had marked off the one grass runway to simulate a carrier deck so pilots could improve their landing techniques. For some reason, probably engine trouble, an Air Corps P-26 was being attended to by a sergeant and a crewman. I watched, as they tried to start the engine. It required no less than eight attempts.

I felt sorry for the private doing the cranking, but it never entered my mind to volunteer to help. For one thing, I learned one never volunteers, unless he's dead certain doing so would be an advantage. On the other hand, I didn't need to go through that exercise again.

10

When I joined the Army Air Corps I'd heard the adage among various Army services that indicated recruits would do everything, except being assigned to maintain aircraft in a line squadron. Or lucky enough to becoming a gunner or other aircrew member. Hearsay had it that mostly recruits would cut grass, and Wheeler Field had a surfeit of grass. I was determined to try and escape menial assignments like that, if at all possible.

While at Wheeler Field I helped in the hangar where we slept, by working at minor jobs I was ordered to do. There were airplanes to wash, push out and back into the hangar; the hangar itself and the ground equipment needed to be kept clean; errands had to be run for anyone who had a higher rank than I did.

There was an attempt to convert me to being a truck driver and I began to take training. But, after three days the attempt by the motor pool failed after the sergeant-in-charge experienced my deliberate, but subtle, ineptness. He finally decided he didn't need another truck driver, after all. To my relief he sent me back to the fighter squadron I was temporarily assigned to.

To me, driving a truck would have been as satisfying as making love to a hungry woman on a cold floor. Besides, I knew how to drive; I didn't know how to maintain airplanes or airplane engines.

In retrospect, that time at Wheeler Field was somewhat enjoyable and educational, as far as being exposed to military methods, thinking and chain of command. But we were kept busy to keep from fretting. The Army had the policy that an idle mind was the devil's workshop.

Therefore, if the troops were kept busy, the troops wouldn't have time to think of anything pleasing to them — or cause trouble of some sort.

While we were awaiting permanent assignment we ate in the

squadron's mess hall, that was logical since we slept in its hangar.

That alone was a vast improvement, in all respects, over eating in a transient mess hall. It was unusual being asked how one liked his eggs! The squadron's cooks were extremely efficient in turning out tasty meals since they — and the other squadrons' cooks — took great pride in out stripping each other.

The period of waiting for permanent assignment was boring to some degree, although we were kept mildly busy during the day. It was a good time for the squadron to tidy up its hangars and grounds and the squadron commander made use of us. Between those duties and occasional work around Wheeler Field itself — including cutting grass — we managed to stay occupied.

There was a general, unwritten rule in the Army: Keep them busy. That will exclude boredom and thinking un-soldier-like thoughts. In other words, the idle mind is the Devil's workshop.

There were approximately 40 of us so we became acquainted in a short time. That was another education for me: Acquiring knowledge of where the men I talked with came from.

There was an excellent representation of various geographical areas. Several were from the South, hill people as I was. They had joined the Army for various reasons, chief among them to get out of the hills where there was little employment. The Army did offer housing and meals and a wage, as paltry as it was. Twenty-one dollars a month, a private's pay.

Wheeler Field itself, and the environment and landscape, was almost bucolic. There were no runways; no concrete except for the small warm up pads at the hangars and, of course, the streets. All else was grass whether because the Army Air Corps apparently felt there was no need simply because the aircraft based there were light, as

12

compared to those at Hickam Field: The heavier B-18s and DC2s and DC3s. Hickam Field, therefore, had concrete runways. Wheeler Field and its B-12s, A-12s and P-26s fit the overall scheme, if an observer were considering the picturesque aspect.

There was one, important feature of having a grass field: When the prevailing wind changed, landings and take-offs could be accomplished according to the direction of the wind sock. Also, there was very little maintenan except for keeping the grass mowed.

I envied the air crews and their flying paraphernalia. There was the roar of engines on takeoffs and on the hangars' ramps that never failed to stimulate my interest. Now and then a DC-3 (C-47) would land on some errand, or maybe a B-18. It whetted my appetite for more exposure to airplanes and, after three weeks at Wheeler Field, the term loose ends was apropos and impatience set in.

I couldn't understand why one of the squadrons based there didn't need a replacement for some reason — any reason. Or even some squadron at Hickam Field.

One day, to my vast relief, from somewhere in the mysterious depths of the inner sanctums of the Air Corps, an order was issued. I was suddenly posted to permanent duty in a support squadron at Hickam Field, adjacent to Pearl Harbor.

The very next day after breakfast a truck stopped at the hangar and waited while me and several others packed out barracks bags and boarded it. It wasn't difficult to try to imagine what would be. But we had been in the Army long enough to get a sense of the machinations of our beginning service life and the manner in which the Army operated.

However, we all enjoyed the ride to Hickam Field, adjacent to Pearl Harbor.

At long last, I would at least have a home even though, as I learned very quickly, it was an air base squadron. But it had solid, comfortable barracks and each man had his cot, footlocker and wall locker. Even dogs don't feel secure unless someone places a collar around one's neck. It's then that it feels as though it belongs.

I found that being a transit and not belonging to a section with a name induced the same feeling. More than that, across the base street was the hangar line where bombers were based!

3

Fundamentals In
Cleaning Vats...

C early something was in the gentle trade winds other than the soothing coolness they blew over the Hawaiian Islands from the Pacific Ocean.

The signs were ominous: Honolulu's two daily newspapers were running more and more news items about the diplomatic maneuvering between the U.S. and Japan over Japan's increasing military incursions in China and the Far East. Air Corps personnel were being trained, or at least familiarized, in the use of infantry-type weapons, a radical departure from .45-caliber pistols. Vital installations, including the bomb dump, were being guarded more closely.

The Air Corps was quietly assuming a new appearance with the coming of B-17's, and the new P-40's were arriving on what seemed to be regular schedules. They were a fascinating departure from the P-26's and P-36's. They were more streamlined, by virtue of their in-line engines, retractable landing gear and cockpit canopies. Except in trainers, open cockpits were history. New fighter squadrons blossomed.

The venerable Douglas B-18's were being phased out. Some departed to the Philippines, others to the States.[10] A couple were held over with a few P-36's but the P-26's and B-12's quietly disappeared. It was a relatively swift and decidedly dramatic end to an era.

At the Air Corp's overhaul depot on Hickam Field more civilian employees were arriving from the States to overhaul engines and repair aircraft.[11] They were in Civil Service and destined to increase the staff to meet the needs of increasing numbers of Air Corps aircraft. Logistically, it wasn't practical to ship aircraft and engines to the Mainland for repair. Air Corps mechanics were needed in their squadrons, although a few worked at the Hawaiian Air Depot; it was therefore necessary for the bulk of the depot's staff to have civilian employees. Meanwhile, the war in Europe had since begun.

At Hickam Field I settled in with my squadron, got acquainted and acclimated to a new life: My own bunk, footlocker and wall locker. The barrack was spacious and airy, in spite of the many cots and appurtenances. I haunted the orderly room bulletin board for a notice that men were needed in a line squadron, but none appeared. They were at full complement since the aircraft arrived with their air crews followed by ground crews and squadron staff.

For the first couple weeks, duties were varied and without a future. Mostly, they were simply an exercise in keeping busy. Then one day the First Sergeant called me into the orderly room. "I see from your records you can type," he said. "Operations needs a clerk/typist. How would you like that?"

"I've been hoping to get into a line squadron. I'm not much for that sort of work," I replied.

"Well, it's better than what you've been doing. Anyway, I've already told them I'd assign you to them. Report tomorrow morning."

There was nothing more to say, since he was the sergeant, so I dutifully reported to field operations. It was located in the base of the control tower.

The work consisted of typing various documents: Orders, memos, schedules and whatever else was required. There was filing to do, too. I was beginning to feel as out of place as a turd in a punchbowl. But the job had its compensations: I could watch airplanes come and go and the pace wasn't hurried. And, at least, I knew what I was going to do from day to day. One morning I checked in to operations and was pleased to see a P-36 parked on the ramp just outside the office windows. And then I was given a surprising lesson.

After about an hour a pilot walked out to the airplane and

clambered into the cockpit. He busied himself with whatever he had to do to prepare for flight while I watched. Suddenly there was a **Bang!** from the engine that startled me. I immediately suspected something had blown up and half-expected the airplane would start burning. But it didn't. Instead, the propeller began turning straight-away and the engine started. The engine, I found out later, was equipped with a shotgun starter. I wondered, if such a device worked so well, why weren't the P-26's so equipped?

After several weeks I was promoted to Third Class and a short time later to Corporal. Third Class privates were paid a few dollars more than corporals were, consequently I lost money but it was a decided increase from twenty-one dollars per month, a private's pay.

So far I was fortunate to have two rides in aircraft. The first was in a DC-2, captained by a Master Sergeant. I don't know how he became an enlisted pilot, or did anyone I talked to know. He was the envy of every enlisted man who knew what he did, though. Not only was he drawing master sergeant pay, but flight pay as well. That put him in about the five-hundred dollars per month bracket, a monumental salary in those days. I suspect he was the envy of every junior officer at Hickam Field. Not only that, he was exempt from the usual duties of master sergeants.

I stumbled into that flight, my very first in an airplane, somehow and it was an entirely new experience. The airplane was lightly loaded with a variety of equipment and boxes for Bellows Field, across Oahu. It was delightful to look down on everything I'd been walking on. The wing tips flexing up and down in some mild turbulence first caught my eye. I wondered if they should, but they didn't break, so I guessed it was all right and the structural engineers at Douglas knew what they were doing.

The second flight I scrounged was in a B-18. I didn't know why the flight was scheduled, since no practice bombs were dropped. It seemed we were merely taking a tour of Oahu and across the channel to Molokai. I didn't question it; it was enjoyable sitting at one of the waist gunner positions watching the scenery and ocean pass by beneath us. Why question anything? The work in operations had its fringe benefits, after all, and my emergence from the rank of private must have helped in getting those airplane rides.

During that time in operations, after hours and on weekends I went to the Hickam Field dock, immediately inside Pearl Harbor's entrance channel. It was a good place to swim and fish. There was a boat house, too, that housed two air-sea rescue boats, operated by Air Corps personnel.

I became acquainted with the sergeant in charge, Staff Sergeant Bossert, and would watch the comings and goings of the boats and even go inside to look them over more closely. I always liked reading about boats and ships and the sea, but had never been to sea except on the *Republic*. This duty, I thought, would be more interesting than what I was doing.

"Sergeant Bossert," I asked him one day, "do you have an opening for another man?"

"I might have. Do you know anything about boats?"

"No, but I'm a fast learner and I don't get seasick." There was no point in lying, since he could always look at my records.

"Is it worth a box of cigars to you? I smoke White Owls."

My first lesson in politics, I thought. The common saying among the troops was true, after all. "It's not *what* you know but *who* you nose," was blunt and to the point. I allowed that a transfer would be worth a box of White Owls, although the price would have an awful impact on my meager pay.

Two days later I presented Bossert with the box of cigars; the following week I was relieved of duty at operations and re-assigned to Bossert.

Although it was good duty, there remained in my mind the airplanes. After nearly two-years of service with the air-sea rescue group I applied for duty at the Hawaiian Air Depot; it was still short of men in the face of increasing work loads. Through a service proviso I was discharged "...for the convenience of the government..." I became a civilian to the extent I lived off base, but I belonged to the air depot. In any case, it was an opportunity to start an aircraft maintenance career.

I reported to a civilian foreman, George Hammond, who managed overhaul of engine sub-assemblies. I had become acquainted with him when he supervised overhauling the engines of the crash boat I commanded.[12] Occasionally I would visit his department in the overhaul depot and watch him and his mechanics at work on engine components. His expertise was obvious.

The boat's engines were massive Wright Tornados, liquid-cooled V-12 designs rated at 600-horsepower each. They were fitted with reduction gear boxes to drive the boat's propellers and converted to sea water cooling for use in boats. These were the biggest in-line engines — or most other types — I'd seen up close. Physically, they were more bulkier than the Allisons and Packard-built Rolls Royce

32

engines of the P-40's, and of lower horsepower.[13]

It was after Hammond had finished with the engines and they were re-installed in the boat that I realized the extent of his uncanny sense as to how well an engine was operating. He seemed to absorb the engines' vibrations and sounds into his body and mind and translate them into projections of his perceptions of what events were taking place in the engines— from the bridge of the boat! It was extraordinary. But my observations of him may have been a bit exaggerated, since I knew little if anything about engines — any engine. Later, after I knew him better, I learned my concerns were also exaggerated

During sea trials he stood near me on the bridge, his head cocked toward the engine room hatch, listening intently to both engines' sounds. He seemed to be in another world, oblivious to the ocean, sun, wind, the sounds of the boat moving through the water. He totally ignored everything and everybody. He seemed to have projected his inner self into the engine room where it could better analyze the engines. He was uncanny!

Now and then he would issue instructions to the engineer through the speaking tube, apparently for some adjustment to the carburetor on one or the other engine — or perhaps both together. It would have been impossible for Hammond to squeeze through the engine room hatch to make any adjustments personally. He was simply too massive to get through it, let alone clamber down the narrow ladder to the engine room deck.

Finally he asked me to make a high-speed run. I opened both throttles to their limits and the boat surged forward, planing over the water at thirty-five knots. After five minutes into the run

Hammond tapped me on the shoulder. "I guess we can go home now," he said. Hammond's performance rendered me forever impressed. I was further impressed because he didn't get sea-sick!

Through that previous relationship Hammond was instrumental in having me assigned to his department. He, more than any other, would give me direction and mold my future, as one would direct the shape of a growing twig. And he would begin by placing me at the very bottom of the maintenance chain: Cleaning engine parts.

Hammond had come to the overhaul depot when it began to expand to meet the increasing maintenance demands of the growing fleet of combat and transport aircraft assigned to Army Air Corps operations in the Central Pacific. I learned very little of his background other than the bits and pieces his close friend, Bob Fox, gave me. Fox was assistant foreman under Hammond; both had worked on rotary engines, and they were the only men I have ever known who did so.

"You didn't install or remove anything from one side of those engines without compensating for the change on the other side, even if it meant adding a weight," Fox sternly informed me. "You always had to be aware they must be balanced." I was dutifully awed by the revelation and knowing two men who had actually maintained rotary engines. I had studied pictures of them and to know someone like these two was almost like meeting Eddie Rickenbacker himself. Rotary engines were being phased out just before I was born.

I sensed that Hammond had such a wealth of experience he could cure the ills of any engine built or on the drawing boards. He certainly had overhauled the old Tornados, as a matter of course.

Heavy almost to the point of obesity — he must have weighed

over three-hundred pounds — Hammond's shaggy, lion-like head probably held more knowledge than most maintenance textbooks written at that time. He didn't like the tobacco chewing habit of two men who worked under him. They would aim a stream of juice at their makeshift cuspidor and invariably dribble across the shop floor although the main body of tobacco juice would unerringly hit the receptacle.

"I'd rather have a congregation of ducks walking around," he would grumble. He never stopped the practice, although he insisted they clean the dribs and dabs of spit from the floor.

Because of his weight, extended walking was challenging, so he had been issued a two-wheeled Cushman motor scooter which was always parked close by. He would buzz through the huge main hangar of the depot on the little machine, his formidable butt draped on either side of the scooter's tiny saddle like the sagging jowls of a Basset hound.

Privately, I marveled that the little one-cylinder engine could contrive to propel Hammond's considerable mass so effortlessly. The hangar's level floor gave it an advantage; otherwise it probably couldn't have negotiated a two-percent grade with him on it.

Hammond's right elbow was permanently locked at an angle and his forearm was set in a grotesque twist from the elbow to the wrist; that set his hand in a reverse oblique position. The fingers were distorted so badly his right hand appeared to be a claw. I was impressed at the ease with which he manipulated the scooter's throttle, used a wrench or even wrote. He seldom rolled up his shirt sleeves, but once when he did, in a fleeting moment I caught a brief glimpse of wrinkled, angry-red skin above his wrist, an indication his withered right arm had been horribly burned.

"He got that in a crash some years ago," Fox said when I wondered about it. "The airplane burned." He refused to elaborate and I didn't press the issue.

Although Hammond's chubby face and deep-blue eyes were capable of exuding a friendly warmth he, nevertheless, ruled the crankshaft, crankcase and cylinder sub-assembly overhaul section with the iron hand of a perfectionist. When someone was struggling with fitting one part to another or determining a correct replacement part he hastened to help.

Stopping whatever he happened to be doing, he would carefully and patiently explain how to arrive at a solution, apparently unperturbed by the interruption. But he had a personal, unwritten law that never again should the same person ask the same question.

As the sergeant at Wheeler Field did, Hammond immediately squelched any illusions of grandeur I might entertain. He accomplished that by putting me to the drudgery of cleaning engine parts.

The work was the lowest of the low; even janitors and floor-sweepers enjoyed higher respect. Men who were tearing engines down for overhaul were a cut above the salt, too. They displayed a haughty disdain for us parts cleaners when they would deliver their loaded carts, bursting with an assortment of parts to be cleaned that were once an assembled engine.

The unknown can be either a joy or grievous, depending on what you find when the options are manifested. My feelings were mixed until I first saw the cleaning shed and then two surfaced: Depression and resignation.

Parts cleaning was done in a low wooden building approximately forty-feet long by twenty-five feet wide. The roof was tar papered and drooped slightly over sides that were open four-feet at their tops. Both ends were closed except for a door in one end, wide enough to admit the parts racks.

It was absolutely dreary; even the wood appeared tired. Perhaps it had been shamefully and secretly constructed and then stealthily, sheepishly set down in the dead of night, on the concrete ramp. It was as though the forlorn building was a diseased object, forever put in quarantine.

'The Shed', as I came to call it, had benches, buffers and assorted cleaning equipment and racks along its walls with space for the parts racks in the center. There were deep, metal soak tanks containing dark thick, ominous liquids that emitted acrid, cloying odors.

The only bright spot in The Shed was a huge owlish clock with grand, black numerals. It hung in pompous solitude on the completely closed south end wall. Otherwise The Shed was an utterly depressing, characterless place — but the die was cast. My education and pride were at stake. Besides, I couldn't have changed my situation even if I wanted to. Under martial law, which had been imposed, there were no allowances for changing jobs at will. The system had me locked in. I couldn't even quit to go back to my squadron. I set to work, relying on the hope that somewhere in the future there was bound to be relief of some degree.

Engines kept arriving, as they had been before I started to work in The Shed, in a seemingly endless procession from the tear down section, their parts showing severe use. Cylinders were cast in shades of weary grey, their heads and barrel cooling fins stained with red dust. It was the same hue of island soil. Piston heads, scorched in the awful fires of combustion, were crusted with carbon so stony hard it would have registered high on the Rockwell hardness scale.[14] It defied chemical cleaner soaking and hand removal, to the point of frustration. But they had to be cleaned.

Piston ring grooves were inlaid with the same un-yielding material. Gears, link rods and piston rods, piston pins, link pins and other internal operating parts were always discolored with varnish, gums and ebony-black oil stains, well-baked on the metal.[15] I'm convinced that engine oil when subjected to a period of time in that most efficient of oil refineries, an internal combustion engine, is reclaimed, re-refined and filtered, it has as good as, or better quality than when it was originally refined.

In that dreary cosmos of the cleaning shed the most dreaded task for me was cleaning piston ring grooves. It was exacting, detailed work using broken piston rings, sharpened at an angle on one end. The opposite end and several inches of the ring's curvature were wrapped with friction tape to provide a 'handle'. That protected our hands from being cut by the sharp cross-section of the rings. Piston rings were discarded so there was an ample supply of rings from which to fashion our tools — on a grinder. The ring grooves had to be completely cleaned without destroying their walls and, especially, the finely-machined radii at the base of the grooves. Sometimes it was virtually impossible not to gouge a groove considering the diamond-hard carbon that had accumulated at groove bases. It seemed a thousand or more pistons passed through my weary, seamed hands in The Shed. When my education progressed I wondered how many pistons were rejected by inspection after they had been cleaned!

My cohorts in The Shed helped me through the rough spots when I first entered it to begin my education. I asked questions but not too many and, as Hammond later told me, not too many and never the same one. That admonition remained imbedded in my mind for all time.

The soak tanks reeked vilely of degreaser; my clothes stank constantly, the odors even creeping into the pores of my skin. My hands quickly became rasplike, permanently colored angry red, complete with skin cracks, in spite of using rubber gloves whenever possible. The three local people I worked with — all Philippinos — were unaffected. I often wondered why their skin was obviously different and could withstand more abuse than a 'haole's',[16] a non-complimentary term Hawaiians reserved for us Mainland 'intruders'.

We scrubbed accessory drive gears, link rods, piston pins, master rods and other steel parts until they glittered with a near chrome-like sheen. I didn't mind cleaning steel parts, since their finishes resisted carbon and stains unlike the porous surfaces of piston heads. But everything had to be impeccably cleaned for the gimlet eyes in the inspection department.

Days turned into weeks, weeks to months, as I labored in The Shed. Its open sides were a salvation: I could look out and see another world with airplanes in it. Many were parked on the ramp between The Shed and the main hangar awaiting repair. The open sides also allowed gentle breezes to flow through The Shed, giving some measure of comfort to weary mind and body.

It's impossible to know or remember how many parts I cleaned, but what would be the point? I only remember that disassembled engines kept arriving in a seemingly endless procession. Except for the obvious parts, pistons and rings, cylinders, link and master rods, I couldn't identify the various gears and their functions — that would come later. But, on the other hand, I didn't have any idea when 'later' would take place. Hammond rarely appeared to visit The Shed. When he did, he never spoke or dismounted from his trusty Cushman, merely sitting and scanning The Shed and its occupants. Then he would scurry away, the little scooter's exhaust snapping spitefully. It seemed strange, to me, that he didn't at the very least get off and visit with each of us in The Shed. He could have said "Hello" or "Go to hell" — or something. Well...if he didn't like my work he could fire me and I'd go back to my squadron and try again after the war.

It seemed an eternity had passed and I was beginning to inwardly question the wisdom of setting goals. Is this, I asked myself, all there is or I can expect?

In retrospect, the toil I experienced in The Shed was planned by Hammond and I didn't have the sense to realize it. In his wisdom he probably sensed my eagerness to leave The Shed, and he deliberately held my feet to the fire so I could sweat it out. It was a major lesson in Controlling Impatience 101. Simply handling and gradually learning, by way of countless questions of the men who brought disassembled engines to The Shed, was invaluable in identifying various gears, bearings, bushings and the very design of cases and other items that are a part of the total engine.

There was, after all, a purpose when he scooted up to The Shed and sat there, silently, detached, observing. Even today, I realize not every mechanic starting out on a career has an opportunity to begin learning the very guts of engine work, although it means cleaning parts. Nor, I am positive, does every beginning mechanic relish the idea, as the initial step in the learning process. Over the years, though, I've become convinced that any mechanic – and I've met several – who was exposed to such an onerous start, never regretted the experience.

Hammond was a wise old pelican indeed.

During those dreary times in The Shed it seemed the nights became shorter and shorter, and my weary body complained in concert with the ticking of the clock – and protested bitterly when the alarm blared each morning. After-work hours consisted of driving to Gibson's house, in Pearl City, — he was a squadron member and took his discharge there — washing thoroughly to attempt to rid the pores of my skin of the loathsome odor of the cleaning vats; then eating supper with him and his wife, Barbara, and relaxing. Next, it was off to bed, to repeat the same process the next day. I had Sunday off but that *could* be eliminated in view of the increasing activities of the Air Corps and its gradual upgrade in aircraft. Activity was escalating in Pearl Harbor.

Gibson worked there and kept me informed of the increased bustle of ships moving in and out of the naval base. I saw a like increase of aircraft and flying when driving by Wheeler Field on my way to Oahu's North Shore. It was a Sunday habit to visit friends, when I was off. Then, it was back to The Shed, after the rejuvenation of a day off. I managed those brief excursions by borrowing an acquaintance's car. Gibson managed to slip me a gasoline chit every now and then since he managed a station within Pearl Harbor's gate.

It began to seem as though my personal *'Pilgrims Progress'* would never reach its conclusion and I was destined to become a professional engine parts cleaner. I began to think of the futility in beginning to assemble a collection of hand tools — at considerable expense. The dollar, then, would buy a considerable amount of merchandise but it was important one had a generous supply if one wanted to upgrade.

Meanwhile the local newspapers published more and more news of the diplomatic maneuvering between Japan and the United States. There were also more and more in-depth stories of Japan's conquests in the far east — and its building record of atrocities. It seemed that the balmy Hawaiian air was subtly being charged with unease and uncertainties. There seemed to be an undercurrent of a sense that war was a threatening potential.

Then suddenly, abruptly, emancipation finally came — three days after the Dogs of War slipped their leashes with ferocious, bloody fury!

We became, in fact, immersed in total war!

This photo', taken in 1931, illustrates the variety of aircraft that emerged in the late 1920's and in the 1930's as the Golden Age of Aviation materialized. It was a time when the public was seized with the thought and thrill of flying in a world where birds prevailed. It was also a time when imagination and motivation began to influence the development of aircraft that has never ceased. Although these proud owner, poised with their aircraft - the hundreds like them - didn't realize it, they played a large part by buying and flying such aircraft, and proving or disproving the designs, albeit inadvertently.

From left to right: Standard J-1, Driggs Skylark, Challenger K-R31, Waco 10 and PA-4 Pitcarin. The Pitcarin remains active in a wonderfully-restored condition.

The setting for the photo' typifies the airfields the majority of privately-owned aircraft operated from. Many were no more than glorified pastures. typical were wooden-framed hangars, little more than sheds, covered with corrugated metal sheets. In most instances the little airfield were located close to small towns and some cities. The field in this photo' was called Mexico Farms.

Photo' by Gene Kelley (deceased)

1929 CESSNA DC-6A -- FIRST AIRCRAFT PRODUCED BY CESSNA PAWNEE DIVISION

1929 CESSNA DC-6A First aircraft produced by Cessna's Pawnee Division. Cessna Aircraft's influence on the growth of aviation is undeniable. By early 1930's 49 DC-6s, 300 gliders and numerous racing aircraft were produced in the Pawnee Division. This example was the first in a long series of four-place cabin models that continues to this period. One example was built. It cruised at 105 m.p.h., maximum 130 m.p.h.

       Photo by Cessna Aircraft.

4

Interlude and
Deliverance....

It's safe to assume most of the inhabitants of the little village of Haleiwa on Oahu's North Shore were asleep. After all, what need was there to get up early on a Sunday morning if you weren't going fishing, or the hangover from last night's party demanded an extra hour's rest.

Probably an occasional vehicle pottered quietly along the highway through the hamlet, its driver intent on some early morning activity. Otherwise the sea, soft and spicy with seaweed smells, washed through the narrow opening to Haleiwa Bay, its subdued surge degrading into tiny wavelets that skittered along the sandy, curved shore. By any standard, Haleiwa was a quiet place most any day of the week, but Sundays were reserved for doing absolutely nothing in particular or, at least, as little as possible. Fishing, of course, was accepted.

Haleiwa was a favored settlement of mine. It was there in the bay where we anchored my crash boat for North Shore patrol duty where the Air Corps trained over the area and the adjacent Pacific. We were always dispatched for summer duty there when the seas were relatively calm, living up to Magellan's decision to name the ocean 'Pacific' during his exploration. We were 'adopted' by the inhabitants of the North Shore and made many friends there. In retrospect we did more Coast Guard operations than Air Corps work, plucking hapless swimmers that were overcome from the sea's sometimes vigorous surf and searching for lost boats. But we had our share of rescuing pilots from bail-outs when their engines ceased to function, or there was a rare collision with another aircraft.

On our patrols at sea, there was opportunity to fish, by trolling a stout fishing line with large, feathered lures. We were often successful catching tuna in the sixty to ninety-pound range. There was a ready market for the fish and we gladly sold them. The money supplemented our meager service pay. Just as often, we shared with our immediate friends in Haleiwa. This intelligence, of course, never reached our home base at Hickam Field.

There was a Japanese fellow who owned a popular restaurant situated along the highway with a full view of the bay and ocean in the background. It was said he was a colonel in the Japanese army before coming to Oahu. How true that rumor was I do not know. But I know he had a magnificent, brass telescope, complete with a tripod, which he used to scan the ocean view. Thus the rumor that he was a spy wafted through the community. Was he? It was possible but I never heard of him again after the war started. He *did* have a front row seat to Air Corps air craft that flew regularly in the area.

Approximately forty-five-miles across Oahu, Honolulu's atmosphere was much the same, except more people lived there. There was bound to be more activity; in any sizeable city there are always people moving around on errands, even on a Sunday — or simply moving with no purpose or goal.

Out at the sprawling Hickam Field-Pearl Harbor complex some servicemen were going about essential duties. This was Sunday, a normally relaxed, stand-down day on a peacetime weekend. In fact, hundreds of servicemen were on pass, which meant fun and games in Honolulu. Up on the middle height of Oahu, Wheeler Field and Schofield Barracks personnel were enjoying the same laid-back mood.

Sunday, December 7, 1941 was ushered in by a lovely, fresh morning with small cumulus puffs scudding across the verdant Koolau and Waianai mountains that formed a near-vertical skirting on both sides of central Oahu.

The land sweeps upwards from Haleiwa to Wahiawa, forms a broad plateau and then slopes gently toward Pearl Harbor. On either side, the upland's edges wash against the two mountain ranges and become captive to thick, densely-green forested ramparts. Except for widely separated clumps of plantation buildings, Wahiawa and the two military reservations, the landscape was given over to pineapple and sugar cane fields. The morning sun, bright and warm, promised another delightful island day. Unknown to many, there was a radar installation smack on top of a high ridge of the Waianai Mountains at their extreme northern edge where the mountain's profile turned and progressed west by north and sloped into the sea. It was in an advantageous position to scan the northwestern expanse of the Pacific Ocean. The radar itself was crude in the extreme, by today's standards. But it did work.

They came from the brightening, far away sea horizon to the northwest and there were many of them. The drone of their engines probably caused some idle curiosity when part of the air armada overflew Haleiwa. There were so many the sky seemed to be satiated with them. The carriers that brought them were surely empty wherever they were. Somewhere out there they waited expectantly. The throb of radial engines was an obscenity in the early morning peace.

There was nothing new about aircraft flying over; the Air Corps and Navy always had some airplanes flying over the area, for one reason or another, but never hordes of them.

The few people awake may have wondered a bit about the markings on the fuselages and wings; a plain red ball? There, undoubtedly, was considerable speculation about that oddity, but by the time thought processes began to form a reasonable explanation, or any answers at all, the small, trim aircraft had passed on toward Wahiawa.

Overflying Schofield Barracks, aircraft identity was firmly established, but the planes didn't waste time there; they were intent on larger game. Besides, Schofield Barracks, unlike its neighbor, Wheeler Field, had infantry and artillery, not airplanes. A sizeable number of the intruders did pause and thoroughly strafe the P-40's at Wheeler Field. It was a wise move, in order to decimate the opposition the fighters represented.

The attack was highly successful, but four fighters *did* manage to arm and get airborne. Meanwhile, the bulk of the air armada of Japanese planes continued on and pounced on Hickam Field and Pearl Harbor. Others overflew and attacked Bellows Field, on the southeast shore of Oahu.

Carl Gibson's urgent shouts shook me from a deep, restful sleep. He was a sergeant in my squadron until taking retirement. He had moved from Pearl City to a house on the west side of Honolulu; I had spent Saturday night with him and his family. Scrambling into my pants I scurried outside to find him in the yard. He was gazing anxiously toward Hickam Field and Pearl Harbor. Huge many-fingered swirls of dark smoke saddened the bright morning sky over both places.

"The Japanese are attacking Pearl Harbor!" he exclaimed, in disbelief. "I just heard a bulletin on the radio!" He gestured toward a little portable Zenith laying on the grass at his feet. I looked west in the direction of the two installations. The dull, hollow thud of anti-aircraft guns rolled forlornly across the few miles, to us. There were scattered, ragged dirty gray clumps of bursts high against the bright sky. Above them were airplanes — many airplanes. The two Honolulu radio stations were frantically broadcasting the news that Pearl Harbor and Hickam Field were under attack by Japanese aircraft. "All servicemen and defense workers are to report to their stations!" they blared out.

Dressing hastily and snatching a baloney sandwich Gibson's wife

Barbara quickly made, I left. At Kamehameha Highway I tumbled into a convertible that barely slowed its pace in a line of vehicles strung out on the highway, servicemen and defense workers all intent on getting to Pearl Harbor and Hickam Field.

A Japanese torpedo plane appeared unexpectedly from the direction of Honolulu behind us and growled along the highway at telephone pole height, parallel to the traffic.

Having relieved itself of its ordnance against the hull of a tethered ship in Pearl Harbor the 'Val' became a roving predator, but there couldn't be any real value in the cars its rear gunner gleefully strafed. There's one characteristic about shrieking, errant bullets: The memory instantly identifies the sound if ever heard again. A P-40 suddenly materialized in pursuit of the Val, its engine raging with a deep, throaty resonance that only an in-line engine produces at full power.

Both aircraft disappeared toward the thick, roiling death of the Arizona and the devastation in Pearl Harbor and at Hickam Field. I never learned the outcome of the chase.

At the Hickam Field gate I jumped into another vehicle that stopped near my former barracks. The shambles was a tribute to improvident laxity. B-17's lay shattered in heartbroken disarray on the hangar ramps of the bombardment squadrons. The broken, battered hulks had transfigured the expanse of parking ramps, where whole airplanes had been neatly parked, into a stark, bleak battlefield. That weekend custom of neatly parked aircraft presented an unmistakable target, nearly impossible to miss. The base fire house suffered severe damage, rendering it useless, for all practical purposes.

At the corner of one bomb squadron's hangar, I nearly stepped on a fragment of what once was an airman. The splash of crimson blood on emerald grass was like the scrim of a careless brush on an artist's canvas.

There was a gaping, ragged hole in the window line of the second floor of my squadron's barracks where a small bomb had hit. On the inside several airmen lay wounded — St. Germaine, a buddy in my squadron, lay dead.

A shipboard variant of a Zero was taken virtually intact when it landed in despair from its wounds. The pilot had taken the sensible course and landed it — Kaimakaize pilots would come much later in the now beginning war. The red data plates on the engine's magnetos bore the legend: 'Bendix-Scintilla, Red Bank, New Jersey'.[17] This brought to mind how Japanese merchant ships made it a practice, if returning home lightly loaded or empty, to buy scrap iron in U.S. ports and load it as ballast.

Plainly seen, at nearby Pearl Harbor, the spire of the Arizona's death knell was more intense, a hideous thick plume of dense-black, roily smoke blotting out a serene sky. A Japanese airplane struggled up across it, desperately trying to gain altitude. Its form was trailing a rope of grayish-white smoke from damage. A cruel slash against the dismal backdrop of the Arizona's cremation — like a mark of omission on a shopping list.

Late that afternoon when we had done everything we thought could be done under the circumstances, I went back to Gibson's little house. On my way, I stopped on a rise at the west side of Honolulu, where sprawling Pearl Harbor was plainly visible. The Arizona was still burning, and other damaged ships were crouched mutely at their moorings. The Ogalla, and others, lay like wounded whales, their hulls' long, round bottoms exposed to the dwindling sunlight.

The repair depot had survived the attack, but not without suffering moderate damage.

A few machining tools in the shops off the main hangar were damaged and would require replacement. We extinguished some fires. Miraculously, the few airplanes that chanced to be in the hangar escaped with minor damage. I picked up several fire-blackened hand wrenches scattered about the floor. I have managed to retain a few through the years.

With disgust I saw that the 'institution to higher learning', The Shed, had withstood the attack, smugly intact, ignorant of the apparent disdain even the Japanese pilots held for it. The clock had stopped at 07:55 hours.

On the whole, the shops were remarkably workable. Damage and fire control had been effective. The prime targets for the Japanese pilots were the B-17's; they had successfully reduced them to a veritable boneyard of twisted, broken hulks. The few that escaped the carnage amounted to a token force of what was once a potentially formidable bombing capability.[18]

It was an eerie feeling that Sunday night: A blackout was ordered immediately and martial law was declared. Sole movements on the highways were Army trucks, carrying troops to set up defenses at strategic beaches around Oahu. The radio stations became silent to deny radio paths to the island, in the event of another attack. A wholesale sense of nervousness seemed to permeate the darkness. The only news available came via radio from the Mainland, for those who had radios capable of picking up broadcasts over 2,000-miles of

Pacific Ocean. But those broadcasts merely confirmed what everyone on Oahu and the islands knew!

With martial law a series of edicts were broadcast and printed in the newspapers. Chief among them concerned rationing, especially gasoline rationing. This was critical since, unlike on the Mainland where train tanker cars carried fuel in safety, ships were required to transport fuel to the islands; fortunately, no submarine attacks were reported. The ships did carry commodities essential to normal living, not produced throughout the islands, including fresh fruit and beef. Since fishing boats were severely restricted from plying island waters, for a year or more, the people were sorely tormented by the scarcity of fish. To them, it was an essential staple. The island people dearly relished the latter commodity.

Insofar as recovery from the attack was concerned, it was incredibly swift. Thousands of irate defense workers, men and women both, began to work with determined resolution. For the Hawaiian Air Depot there were damaged aircraft to repair, useable parts salvaged from aircraft beyond salvation and more engines to overhaul. At Pearl Harbor, the Navy had its hands full getting damaged ships seaworthy, and the soft, night skies were splattered erratically with the brilliance of arc welder bursts. It was a time of an all-out recovery effort and both the shipyard and air depot went to second shifts.

On several occasions I have been asked: "What happened? How could we have been so unprepared?"

The answer to that question may never be completely or, for that matter, truthfully answered. If Diogenes walked the streets of Washington, D.C., his search for the truth would be difficult indeed. Some suspicion it was a deliberate move on the part of the White

House and State Department to provoke Japan into a first strike. That would have been an expedient reason to enter the war in Europe. International politics sometimes use direct and pitiless means to achieve an end result, or influence arrival at one.

On the other side of the coin, the Army and Navy high commands in the Pacific, being intelligent men, should have interpreted the warning signs as indicators of impending trouble. Certainly the press was diligent in covering the activities of our state department. In that time news coverage was done with objectivity as opposed to present reporting. And so, readers could assume a high degree of accuracy in news reporting. At the very least, minimal steps could have then been taken to make preparations to counter any perceived threat. But then, this is not a coldly perfect world and we're all richly endowed with hindsight.[19]

History may some day reveal the truth but the facts remain: There was a noticeable but not massive buildup of service personnel; newer, more capable combat aircraft were arriving; training activities increased in front line infantry and artillery combat units; Air Corps personnel were learning there were more weapons than their standard personal armament, .45-caliber pistols.

The overall atmosphere, however, didn't reflect impending conflict or even sincere preparation for one. Why was the bulk of the Pacific fleet, except for the aircraft carriers, snugly berthed in Pearl Harbor? And the B-17's parked so neatly on the hangar ramps at Hickam Field, the P-40's at Wheeler Field?

The one saving grace was that the carriers escaped devastation. But a blind hog roots out an acorn now and then. Given those realities, were the ships held out as a carrot to entice the Japanese? If so, that would give some credence to the opinions of those who thought the worst. That thought didn't make any sense at all. Even in a worse case scenario why would anyone hold out the carrot of military might that would be needed to fight with later. Such an absurdity is beyond all comprehension. The fact remains, however, that in any situation of such magnitude as the Pearl Harbor and Hickam Field attacks, pundits searching for cause have a field day.

In any event, there had to be a 'fall guy' or 'guys', so Admiral Kimmel and General Short were awarded that dubious distinction. But isn't that the way of things?

A sports team coach is fired at the end of a bad season. An executive is fired because the books don't reflect a good year and the footing is shaky. Nevermind that there could be an insufficiency of support for a coach or executive or manager. Although blame could be shared.

The troops, however, in their inimitable, basic logic analyzed the reason for being caught flat-footed. Succinctly and bluntly, in the pungent, straightforward vernacular of armed forces personnel blame was established. The ultimate conclusion was: "Someone in Washington simply fucked up!"

Never mind though. Suddenly a world of sunshine, security and the good life of islanders and peacetime routines of servicemen had been drastically modified.

Passes to the civilian world were instantly and drastically reduced; uniforms, instead of 'civvies', were mandatory off-post — when passes were issued; the atmosphere, both military and civilian, took on a sense of urgency. There seemed to be an underlying sense of guilt that we could have been so totally surprised.

Pearl Harbor's night skies' darkness became stuttered with white-hot bursts of arc welders on a regular basis, as the civilian shipwrights immediately began to heal the awful wounds of combat ships; work became a virtual 24-hour routine. A submarine net appeared at the entrance of Pearl Harbor, almost miraculously it seemed. Naval traffic took a dramatic upturn through that same entrance as destroyers and submarines bustled in and out to sea, presumably on patrols and ultimately, combat. Capital ships followed as quickly as their injuries were mended. To return weeks later to mend battle wounds or refit to return to the task of hunting enemy ships.

At Hickam Field, and Wheeler Field, 'routine' became a forgotten word, to be replaced by 'urgent', as ground and air crews worked frantically to salvage what they could from the air fleet that had been so decimated. It was astonishing to see the arrival of replacement aircraft with their crews. Not only bombers but fighters too, and newer designs at that. Training was intensified to the point that air cadets, presumably about to graduate from Mainland airfields, were arriving to complete their training in combat aircraft, they would fly anyway.

I had 'painted' myself into a corner: I couldn't return to my squadron. Martial law had instantly been imposed and labor was frozen, and many other conditions were set. This was manifested in the appearance of more Military Police on the highways and, streets of Honolulu. Also gasoline rationing and painting vehicle headlights and a host of other regulations. Civilian activities had been severely curtailed so it didn't matter anyway.

There was nothing else to do, or could be done, so it was back to the cleaning shed. Then, 'Deliverance' came one morning a few days after the attack.

I had barely begun to clean an accessory drive gear when Hammond putt-putted out of the inner sanctum of the main hangar. He skillfully threaded his faithful Cushman through a number of airplanes damaged in the attack, patiently awaiting their turn for repairs. He stopped in The Shed's open doorway and waved me to his side.

"Think you've had enough?" he asked in his usual blunt manner. "If you don't think you've learned anything I'm not going to take your ass in there." He nodded toward the huge, main hangar that housed the shops, with adequate space for aircraft. "I've got enough bubbleheads to worry about."

Momentarily taken aback I could scarcely quell the quiver of excitement that surged through my body. I would have sworn to anything to get out of The Shed. "I think I've learned enough to at least get a good start, and I won't cause any trouble." I also hoped I sounded properly casual.

"All right then, see me tomorrow morning; you know where I am."

Without a response to my faint thanks, Hammond putt-putted away on his staunchly obedient scooter as abruptly as he had appeared.

The balance of the day trudged by like a snail on a leisurely stroll. No matter how intensely I stared at the clock, or how often, its hands didn't rotate any faster than they were supposed to. I truly learned the definition of patience that day.

When the clock's hands at last reached the magical 17:00-hours, I packed the meager variety of cleaning tools I had fabricated — that's when I began learning to never discard a tool made for a specific purpose, no matter how crude. Bidding my two Filipino cohorts goodby I left the cleaning shed. They good-naturedly wished me well, and I them. I'm ashamed to admit I didn't know their names!

My last act, when I closed out the last day in The Shed, was to hang my shabby, smelly, dirty worn coveralls hanging on a nail. They were the symbol of an immeasurably-valued education that figured prominently in my career.

Perhaps that's why I still remember them.

I left them hanging directly under that icon of Time's passage, the clock. Limp, forlorn, bedraggled! Never, during my time at the Hawaiian Air Depot, did I enter The Shed again.

4a

Beyond The Bend,
A Wise Old Pelican....

The abrupt change that came with being suddenly introduced to that new world of Hammond's overhaul department was almost staggering.

There were clean work benches, clean floors, strange tools with strange names and gleaming engine parts. Since Hammond's bailiwick was power section sub-assembly there were racks for valves and cylinders, holding fixtures for radial and in-line engine crankshafts.

The latter were for Allison V-1710s and Packard-built Rolls Royce.

There were machining tools and trays of gleaming nuts, bolts and special fasteners peculiar to the insides of engines. And there were overhaul manuals, parts manuals, parts lists, overhaul forms and other elements important to the process of making tired engines whole again.

In that exposure to the very guts of engines it gradually became clear why and how they did what they were designed to do: Produce horsepower. I learned the intricities of using and reading micrometers, depth gages, dial indicators and other devices to determine delicate fits and clearances.

The first radial engine master rod bearing I machined to a precise fit to the crankshaft journal was a thrilling achievement. It was also a revelation as to the mammoth vertical mill's uncanny ability to follow the instructions I dialed on its controls.

However, with the ecstasies of my progressing education there were occasional agonies and frustrations Fitting oil retaining plugs in the rod bearing journals of Allison and Rolls Royce crankshafts was as disconcerting as trying to untangle a handful of wire clothes hangers.

The plugs were aluminum cups with a machined surface on the large diameter that mated with an internally machined surface of the journals. There were two cups to each journal. A through bolt connected each pair of cups and tightened them against a retaining ridge inside each journal.

Ideally there was a .0015" interference fit. But, since they were used over and over, the fit was reduced from wear or they became galled, warped, or out-of-round. The procedure was a repetitive exercise in install and test, until the worn ones were eliminated. There could be no oil leaks. That would have robbed the connecting

2

rod and main bearings of precious oil. Another exacting operation was aligning crankshaft dampers with crank cheeks of radial engine crankshafts, both single and double-row engines. It was one that tried perseverance to where it spilled over into applying temper control. repeatedly.

The strain of tightening the bolt to its specified stretch would throw the damper out of alignment with the crank cheek by a mere hair's breath. That, of course, was unacceptable since an out-of-balance condition in the crankshaft assembly would result in fearful vibration throughout the entire engine. It was amazing how easily alignment fell into place when I returned from those soul-searching walks around the hangar.

I had a dramatic lesson in non-interchangeability of parts between like models of Allison engines, but with different dash numbers. Fortunately I wasn't kicked out of class later.

The massive thrust bearing had lain in the scalding-hot oil bath for thirty-minutes. The hot soak would expand the bearing's inner race sufficiently to slide onto its seat on the prop shaft section of the engine's crankshaft, on the front. When the bearing cooled and shrunk it would lock onto the seat. Thereafter, nothing would budge it unless it was pressed off with hydraulic power — lots of it!

I slipped my hands into the thick asbestos gloves (It's amazing: I'm still alive after being exposed to asbestos!) we used to handle fire-hot parts from the bath. Using a heavy wire hook I pulled the bearing from the oil, grasped it with both hands and turned to the crankshaft, all in one motion.

The procedure had to be accomplished swiftly before the bearing's inner race began to cool and ones hands began to heat. I had barely started sliding the bearing onto the crankshaft when it abruptly stopped. It threatened to lock there without being seated against the shoulder of its seat, a considerable distance from where it stopped.

A horrible feeling nearing panic engulfed me: It was going to lock onto the crankshaft where it wasn't supposed to. That would require only a fraction of a degree of temperature drop and the process would begin immediately, when the bearing's inner race touched the cooler crankshaft.

I don't know to this day why I instinctively, instantly, grabbed a heavy brass drift punch and a hammer and bumped the bearing back off the crankshaft. My relief was indescribable as I laid it on the wooden work bench to cool. Obviously, it wouldn't fit because it was the wrong bearing.

"You want to step outside?" Hammond's question was an unmistakable command. He'd seen the entire episode.

He preceded me into the cool, dark Hawaiian night. I lit a cigarette as solace for what I knew was coming. He didn't hesitate when he entered a lengthy, pointed discourse in chilly biting tones, his blue eyes as unfeeling as glacier ice, and just as cold!

Among the subjects he addressed was my apparent mental ineptitude, while pointing out the possibility of re-working a crankshaft — or total loss thereof — that was only steps away from installation. He also launched into a scenario of potentially lost time with signs abounding that could mean I was a lost cause. Being somewhat of a gentleman he didn't include any detrimental reference to my ancestry in his diatribe.

"All you had to do was get the correct part number and measure the inside diameter of the inner race against the crankshaft diameter to be sure," he pointed out with considerable heat. "That would have been the final answer if the fits and clearances chart was read correctly.

"The only thing you did right was to immediately bump the

bearing off and, damned if I know why you thought of that," Hammond concluded sarcastically. "Especially as fast as you did."

With that stinging remark he dismissed me, shaking his head sorrowfully. My ears scorching from the fury of his harangue, I went back into the shop and installed the correct bearing.

Under Hammond's firm tutelage my experience and education prospered. Occasionally I was assigned to help with airframe repairs, working with civilians imported from the Mainland. Some — by their admission — signed for the work to escape the draft; others were transferred from Mainland repair depots. The latter were well-experienced and helped me immensely in the nuances of general airframe maintenance.

I liked the variety of work: Sheet metal repairs, control surface rigging, hydraulics, engine changes and engines and systems troubleshooting. In retrospect that experience influenced my preference for line maintenance and airframe heavy inspections.

I was completely surprised one day to be told I was transferred to Wheeler Field. More help was needed to prepare engines for installation and to install them on aircraft wherever required. A small depot had been set up there to support a myriad of new fighter and bomber squadrons located on and near Wheeler Field, also on the North Shore of Oahu.

Wheeler Field had changed dramatically: Paved runways now, swarming with new aircraft and personnel. There were B-17's, A-20's, P-40's and a few B-26's, where once P-26's, B-12's and A-12's reigned. At newly constructed Kipapa Airstrip, B-25's; on the North Shore, B-24's, P-47's and more P-40's.[20] P-38's would follow soon.

Our crew at Wheeler Field was small. We were kept busy building engine installations from core engines. This meant installing accessories, fittings, wiring, fluid lines and all the elements necessary to connect engines to air frames and cockpits to give the aircraft life.

It was necessary to remove failed or out-of-time engines when a squadron called for help, and install a replacement. There was other work as well: If a landing gear needed to be replaced, or a damaged structural element repaired, were some examples.

By that time the war in the Central Pacific had heated to the boiling point. During the determined push toward the Western Pacific someone in the high command decided that close-in air support of ground troops needed to be more effective.

Engineers chose the B-25 for that role; in doing so they unknowingly produced the ancestor of the gunships used in the Vietnam War years later but with a different airplane: The venerable C-47. Some, I don't know how many, B-25's were modified by installing a 75-millimeter recoilless cannon to fire out the nose. I looked at one installation and marveled at the engineering. It was mounted below the cockpit, the breech chest-high to a stand-up loader. Shells were stored in a rack on the opposite side of the cannon so the loader had to reach across the breech to get a fresh round and re-load.

A gunner told me that when the gun was fired the meager recoil thrust the breech past his chest, within inches, space was so limited. It was prudent, therefore, to stand practically at attention, back pressed against the fuselage wall, to prevent being bashed in the face or head, or suffer a scraped chest. He added that a slight hesitation was felt in the aircraft's flight when the cannon was fired.

Apparently the idea lacked merit and a subsequent program was started to fit B-25's with eight nose-mounted .50-caliber machine guns. Four were mounted outside in pods on the nose, two to a side. An additional four were mounted internally, firing through the nose. The plex noses were replaced with aluminum skin. I was assigned to help in the modifications and worked over a month installing firing solenoids on guns.

The conception was effective in combat. We were shown a combat film taken from a B-25 attacking a Japanese freighter, about two-hundred-feet long, and it was an awesome spectacle. A veritable sheet of .50-caliber bullets sprayed the ship's bridge and practically disintegrated it. Subsequent attacks left the freighter dead in the water and burning.

Wheeler Field was a different world in which we were constantly exposed to airplanes coming and going. There was also the antics of young pilots.

Once, while changing the number one cylinder on the number one engine of a B-17, a P-40 squadron 'attacked' Wheeler Field. The fighters came from all directions, fearfully low and my memory rang an alarm. I retreated to questionable safety under the wing until the pilots exhausted their exuberance and disappeared as suddenly as they had arrived.[21]

In another incident, involving a P-47, the pilot decided to 'buzz' one of my squadron's outlying boat bases on the North Shore of Oahu. In his exuberance, he underestimated his height above the tops of three Norfolk pine trees growing on the little base. The trees were approximately 70-feet high. He pulled out of his shallow dive but not soon enough. It was a tribute to the integrity of the P-47's wing structure when about 10-feet of the tree's top was sheared off, leaving a very prominent dent in the left wing's leading edge.

I recall plainly seeing the engine's turbo-charger compressor wheel as the airplane roared overhead after pruning the tree. We later learned the young pilot was grounded for three-days in a half-hearted reprimand by his CO.

For anyone who has never seen or experienced a massive buildup in airpower the perception is memorable. At the height of arming for the push through the Central Pacific the number of aircraft overwhel-med existing Air Corps fields. They consisted of Hickam Field, Wheeler Field, Bellows Field; expansion was necessary. A strip at Haleiwa, once used for practice, became the home of a fighter squad-ron of P-40's, the 47th.

Two more were hastily constructed: Kipapa, a few miles south of Wheeler, another near Kaena Point on the North Shore. There was — and still is — only one runway. A B-24 squadron was stationed there. Today, glider flying dominates flying activities. There was another field at Kahuku Point at the north end of Oahu where more B-24's, and P-47's were based.

After the battle for Tarawa a subtle change in over all activities at those fields was manifested.

The battle assured the establishment of forward air bases — at a horrible cost in lives and wounded — in the Central Pacific atolls to carry the fight with a vengeance to the enemy. Combat aircraft were gradually moved forward, so maintenance pressures began to lessen. Now and then, we actually had a weekend off. Still, there remained much to be done: There were the resident aircraft and engines to maintain. Also, engines shipped from combat zones for overhaul and occasional transports to repair. The push became more accelerated against the Japanese, far from Oahu. It was an appropri-ate time for me to pursue my goal.

I redoubled my efforts to be recalled to my squadron. Finally I succeeded, but had to go through six-weeks of jungle combat training, before rejoining my squadron.

The time at Wheeler and Hickam fields was filled with invaluable experience. I had accumulated a wealth of knowledge in aircraft and engine maintenance and overhaul. My tool collection, meanwhile, although not extensive, had grown. It would be the basis from which to cultivate my future, I thought, when I placed it in storage; I was rejoining my squadron!

I served on my former air-sea rescue boat for a time on island waters and then was posted to the Western Pacific, based on Guam, with the 20th Air Force, in command of another boat. By then, the Mariana Islands had been militarily secured. There were still some die-hard Japanese hiding out, but not posing any semblance of serious resistance.

. Runways were rapidly constructed on Guam, Tinian and Saipan; B-29's and B-24s were there in force. Operations would be long range and it wasn't likely there would be no Japanese air attacks. Fighters, therefore, weren't thought to be needed.

It was an impressive sight to watch a strike force of upwards of 200 B-29's take off — a sight seen only in that war, and never to be seen again — as we watched from the boat from our stand-by position on the ocean.

Duty in the waters around the Marianas was relatively light, consisting mostly of stand-by and taking 20th Air Force staff on fishing trips. Not once were we called to answer a distress call from an aircraft that was ditching or in danger of ditching. But the boat provided some sense of relief from running the 20th Air Force for the higher ranking officers.

General Giles and General Spaatz and some members of their staff's weren't highly successful as anglers but they enjoyed the sea trips. Rank, indeed, has its priveledges. The two generals were gentlemen and asked very little of me and my crew. They appeared to appreciate the luxury of merely relaxing and enjoying the swish of water, hum of boats engines and the sun and wind, their conversations meager when others of their staffs were aboard. Which, I thought, was sensible considering the actions of some of the staffs.

On one occasion a brigadier general on General Giles' staff decided he would like to be towed behind the boat. By definition, body surfing. We obliged him by tying an inch-thick rope around his torso; that done he dove overboard.

I started the boat forward and with the general approximately fifty feet behind it, increased speed to ten knots. The exercise came to an abrupt conclusion when the general started to submerge. After I stopped the boat he clambered aboard, frightened and subdued. After that the members of the staff dubbed him "Kamikazi McNaughton, the human torpedo."

After leaving Oahu for the Western Pacific and finally leaving there when the war ended, I never saw George Hammond again. I have not since, seen his equal!

5

Magnetos and Migraines....

Mounted on the accessory cases of some piston engines, the nose cases of others, magnetos aren't especially attractive, physically. But then they aren't designed to be entered in beauty contests.

Their sole purpose for being is to operate steadily and dependably for hours on end, manufacturing and delivering life-giving high voltage electricity to the host engine's spark plugs. Turbine engine's employ a variant: A unit that transposes system voltage to even higher voltage to supply ignitors for light off and any time they're otherwise needed, such as in weather or where possible flame-out is of concern. But they have no moving parts, as does a magneto. A finely tuned magneto can be a joy when an engine's tachometer registers a miserly fifty revolutions per minute drop during an operational check.

Conversely, a magneto can be a source of utter frustration, causing the most knowledgeable mechanic to suspect his personal and professional credibility. Also shaking his self-confidence to the core. It doesn't happen often, but magnetos can and will malfunction or quit completely without warning. The root cause or causes of the problem may be varied. Still, magnetos aren't delicate in a physical or mechanical sense.

In the very early days of aviation two very important features were incorporated in engine development: Two spark plugs were provided for each cylinder and two magnetos, instead of one. The former assures excellent flame propagation across the piston head which enhances overall engine operation. The latter additional safety because, in essence, two magnetos provides two distinctly separate ignition systems. Thus, if one magneto fails, its companion fires its set of spark plugs and engine operation continues albeit not as aggressively.

Most engines have two individually-mounted magnetos, a concept still common in today's piston engines. But engineers astutely decided that if two magnetos were incorporated into one case, such a device would not only meet safety and engine operational requirements but save space as well. On many engine designs space is at a premium on accessory and nose cases. Therefore, double magnetos were the practical solution to limited space.

Double magnetos were used as early as the 1930's on a few Lycoming nine-cylinder radial engine models and later on other larger, double-row engines. They're also used today on flat, horizontally-opposed engines. Wright R-3350's that powered the superbly graceful Lockheed Constellation were equipped with double magnetos. Additionally, they were easy to time to an engine, in spite of their complexity.

But double magnetos truly found favor on Pratt & Whitney's massive R-4360 engines. No less than four were mounted on the nose section to fire the engine's fifty-six spark plugs in their four rows of twenty-eight cylinders, seven cylinders in each row. In truth, dual magnetos are an engineering marvel.

On this night at Honolulu Airport my good friend and boon companion, Clyde Carson, didn't think dual magnetos were any kind of engineering marvel.[22] He was having a confrontation with one on the nose case of a Pratt & Whitney R-4360 mounted on a Boeing Stratocruiser. The longer the encounter wore on the more lucid his comments on the mental integrity of the engineers who designed the hellish — in his words — 'device'.

"Engineers," he decided, "are nothing more than mechanics with their brains knocked out!" That acid comment was one of his more kindly ones as his frustrations mounted; admittedly a callous, hollow attribution since he had some engineering background himself. It made him a better mechanic though, by his admission.

Carson had graduated from one of the most venerated aircraft mechanics schools on the East Coast, Casey Jones, just prior to the start of World War II. Incidentally, it was the same Casey Jones that was Roosevelt Field airport manager and provided a hangar for *The Spirit of St Louis,* while it was being prepared for Lindbergh's flight. That was when written examinations for an Aircraft and Engine [A&E] license demanded that the answers be written, not selected from a short list of possibilities.[23] He held a six-digit license number — one less than mine — and worked out a stint in an Army Air Corps repair depot on the Mainland. By the time he transferred to the repair depot at Hickam Field the shelves in his mental storehouse of maintenance knowledge were well-stocked. He had left the Hickam Field depot after the war to enter commercial aviation.

Out of the depths of his vividly inventive mind he once devised a scheme for stringing an electrical cable by helicopter across the shaggy, verdant depths of one of Oahu's more impressive canyons. He claimed it to be the first in another use for 'choppers'. In another money-making strategy — he hoped — Carson became involved in a venture to haul fish from a small distant Pacific atoll to a canning factory in Honolulu.

He installed auxiliary cabin fuel tanks and ancillary plumbing in a surplus Curtiss C-46 which would be used as a freighter. But the first outbound flight very nearly ended in a water landing instead of a normal one on solid earth, at their destination.

About five-hundred miles outbound from Honolulu, with nothing in sight but the blue Pacific Ocean, the flight crew failed to wake Carson, who was asleep in the cabin on a life raft, in time to transfer fuel from the auxiliary tanks to the main tanks before the engines began to complain of fuel starvation. They were on the cutting edge of ditching before he frantically managed to establish fuel flow from the main tanks to the back-firing, nearly famished engines that were beginning to try to run on fumes.

Some of Carson's visions were dangerously close to practical development. To him, they would not only be earth-shaking, but make an investor instantly and enormously wealthy — him included.

"I sometimes hate to see him come home," his wife, Norine, confided once to me in resignation. "He scares me and someday I expect to be involved in something without my knowledge and wake up in the poorhouse." He was a pioneer without portfolio, but then he wasn't too concerned with carrying one stuffed with credentials.

Carson even caught me up in his enthusiasm, in 1946, soon after I was discharged from service. He persuaded me to join him in a newly formed company that would engage in crop dusting, air charters and flying instructions. It was Pacific Skyways, and the company didn't have much of a market area, but did have an extremely attractive logo.

Pacific Skyways was formed by three ex-Air Force pilots. They pooled what money they'd accumulated and purchased two Piper J-3's, a Stinson L-5 and a Cessna UC-78 from war surplus sales. One J-3 would be the first crop duster, the L-5 a general purpose aircraft while the Cessna (Bamboo Bomber) would fly charter.[24] The second J-3, joined later by another factory new one, would also be used for flight instruction.

Like the real gooney birds at Midway Island that are ill-equipped to get off the ground easily and land gracefully, so it was with Pacific Skyways and the promises of a rosy future it offered. We never sprayed pineapples, had only three students in about six-months and failed to promote a charter business.

Crucial to start-up was to repair a J-3. Carson and Gardiner, the latter a close friend with whom I had worked at Wheeler Field, had converted it to a cropduster. It was hangared in an open shed on the old 47th fighter squadron airstrip at Haleiwa, awaiting an inspection for its civil license. Then it was damaged by an unforeseen natural event.

A tidal wave generated by a shudder in the earth's crust some-where near the Aleutian Islands rolled through the Pacific Ocean and slammed against the North shore of Oahu, spilling over the beach onto the airstrip. The wall of water rolled inexorably over the field and struck the shed, partially collapsing the roof, which fell on the fuselage. We worked virtually around the clock for three days and two nights restoring the J-3 to flight status.[25]

For nearly one year I struggled with Carson and the others to make the operation a viable entity until finally, and reluctantly, I decided that just maybe Pacific Skyway's future was farther over the horizon than anyone realized.

It seemed my wheels were starting to spin. The pittance of twenty-five dollars a week I was paid — sometimes — influenced my decision markedly to return to the Mainland. That and I needed to obtain my A&E license.

The time spent with Pacific Skyways wasn't wasted; I learned much from Carson. Four years later I went back to work in the Islands. First with a crop dusting company at Honolulu, then with Trans-Ocean Airlines. Carson meanwhile had left Pacific Skyways, worked briefly for the ill-fated Matson Airlines, a subsidiary of Matson Navigation, and then joined United Airlines. He had ceased flogging a dead horse.

Carson wasn't prepared for the new problem with this dual magneto. For that matter he always felt unprepared for the malfunction of anything on any aircraft. He figured everything should run in normal fashion until *he* was ready for a breakdown. There was always something else to do on United Airline's out-station without the added burden of repairing something. This magneto had him baffled, and threatened to exhaust his store of corrective options.

The difficulty centered on the No. 3 mag', mounted with its three comrades on the nose case of the enormous Pratt & Whitney. In turn, the engine was mounted at the No. 3 position on the Boeing Strato-cruiser in UAL livery. The squat-looking airplane, simply crouched in the soft Hawaiian night, patiently awaiting succor for its ailing engine.

"I've set the cussed thing twice and it still won't stay in time," he snorted. "I've never seen anything like it."

"Why don't you try another magneto?"

"Because I don't have another magneto, that's why. And there isn't anything wrong with this one — I've already looked into it." His instant indignation at my suggestion to one obvious, possible solution to his problem was somewhat tempered by our friendship. Even so, I got the impression he was hovering on the brink of a pointed suggestion as to what I could do with it. I half-expected him to tell me to get back to Trans-Ocean's maintenance dock, next in line to United's, where I belonged.

His crew hovered nearby, nervously awaiting his next move. We were all ignored while he resumed pacing back and forth, head bowed in thought, dragging hungrily on a cigarette. He probably hoped the smoke would produce a genie that would instantly solve his difficulty. Now and then he would stop and glare up at the recalcitrant magneto, as though willing it, through mental telepathy, to either cure itself or go away.

The stand-off between Carson and the magneto hadn't yet been resolved because he was stymied about how a magneto functions. He hadn't reached his level of maintenance expertise without having his feet held to the fire by a obstinate magneto.

The telephone on the wall of the nose hangar blared insistently. Muttering a temperate blasphemy, Carson jerked the handset off its hook He listened with unconcealed impatience while rubbing the back of his neck with a soiled hand. A faint, rosy flush then began creeping steadily from his open shirt collar toward his hairline. The higher it progressed the deeper its shade.

"How do I know when it'll be ready? All's I can tell you right now is when it's done. And if you don't quit calling, it'll never get done!" He slammed the receiver on the hook and heaved a big sigh. Obviously a nervous dispatcher, watching the pitiless creep of his clock's hands closer and closer to departure time, had inquired into the status of the massive Boeing. The No. 3 engine and its companions on the wing of the Boeing weren't strangers to Carson, nor was the aircraft type.

After he had left Pacific Skyways, while I was on the Mainland, and prior to hiring on with United he had helped maintain Boeing Stratocruisers when Matson Navigation Company used them to start air travel to the Islands. It was an attempt to supplement the company's ocean liner service.

Matson had served the Islands with its passenger and freight ships, it seemed, since Captain Cook discovered the archipelago. But the excursion into air space from sea waves was short-lived and the budding airline collapsed. Never mind though: United thought the idea a good one. It began daily flight service that ultimately evolved into its present far-flung operations throughout the Pacific.

The Pratt & Whitney R-4360's that loomed on the wing of the Boeing were the ultimate in the development of radial engines. But they were the swan song to a design that played such a huge role in aviation's progress.

With four rows of cylinders, seven to a row, their bulk was formidable, almost intimidating. But, because of an extensive accessory section and nose case, their length complimented the massive profile so that, when cowled, they weren't unattractive. They were capable of producing 3,500-horsepower for takeoff, could maintain the aircraft at its service ceiling of 32,000-feet and pull it along at 375-miles per hour at high speed cruise. Or, using only 1,900-horsepower, the 4360's would provide a cruise speed of 340-miles per hour at 25,000-feet.[26]

Considering their design, 4360's were no more or less mechanically troublesome than any other high horsepower radial engine. But they had a unique trait: They were wonderfully capable of external self-lubrication.

Like any radial engine at rest, oil would collect in the bottom cylinders' combustion chambers. In the 4360's, the characteristic was compounded because there were more bottom cylinders than any other design. This was responsible for a extraordinary phenomenon.

On start-up, each engine would belch a great cloud of blue smoke. Then the dense storm of smoke pushed by the propellers' blast would sweep like a fast-moving ground blizzard or fog bank over the airplane's wings, sprinkling them and anything behind with minute specks of oil. If an airplane's four engines could be induced to start in rapid succession, the sight was eerily awe-inspiring: The aft fuselage would become nearly obscured, but for the top one-third of the fin.

To an observer the effect was like a surreal painting: A disembodied fin protruding against a blue sky out of swirls of bluish vapor. In time, as the engines warmed and purged their cylinders the smoke would eventually disappear and the ghost of the remainder of the airplane would leisurely emerge as a real presence. It was like a spray application of sun tan ointment to anyone who happened to be behind the airplane at the time.

As to the airplane itself, the Boeing 377 — otherwise known as 'Stratocruiser' — was the latest word in luxurious air travel. It was stable and comfortable with a commodious interior featuring a spiral staircase between upper and lower decks.[27]

The passengers were well-fed from galleys bursting with an abundance of rich food, one of the primary selling points for air travel to the Islands. Many flights weren't fully loaded and often aircraft arrived at Honolulu with ample quantities of delicious meals crying out to be eaten. Just as often this was at once a cause of temptation to Carson and irritation to Norine. Not one to ignore opportunities, Carson would assign an underling to taxi a Boeing, just arrived from the Mainland, from the terminal to the maintenance hangar — while he appeased his avaricious appetite with tender steaks, ice cream desserts or whatever other morsels struck his fancy. Often, after one of the excursions into a gourmet's fantasy, Carson would drive home in a torpid state, to fall on his bed and become instantly submerged in dreamless sleep.

"I hope the loveable glutton gets heartburn!" Norine would fume.

Having reset the magneto to the engine, with a heavy sigh and an "Aw' right, let's try the blasted thing again," Carson disappeared into the maw of the Boeing's cabin to reappear on the flight deck. His crew hastily pushed the airplane back until the immense four-bladed propeller cleared the hangar's work platform. The crew snapped shut the engine cowl, started the ground power unit and plugged the cable into its receptacle on the belly of the airplane. Now, the Boeing looked exactly as though it had given birth, with the umbilical cord still firmly attached to its offspring.

In the faint, reflected glow of the flight deck's lights we could dimly see Carson making ready for the start. Finally he toggled the starter switch and immediately the power unit bucked while emitting a shower of sparks from its exhaust, protesting the sudden demand on its generator. The engine's starter whined in agonized complaint, but the huge propeller began to rotate like a ponderous windmill in a mild breeze, then a cylinder caught and twenty-seven others followed.

The propeller became a gleaming disc in the hangar's lights while the engine disgorged the usual cloud of bluish-white smoke to violate the soft darkness of the Hawaiian night. Having purged itself, the massive 4360 settled down into a smooth roar, as Carson waited for heat to build in the oil and cylinders and the engine's instruments to stabilize into steady indications.

After what seemed to be an interminable wait, the engine began to snarl with wrathful purpose as Carson advanced the throttle. A solid wall of sound reverberated from the hangar's walls as the tachometer's needle swung towards 1,800 r.p.m.'s. The metallic soprano of the propeller's tips harmonized with the deep, throaty bass of the engine's exhaust.

Then something seemed to make the engine labor. A subtle sluggishness became apparent. The exhaust's flame pattern lacked the normal exuberant snappiness of proper combustion, nor did it have a well-defined pattern. Carson retarded the throttle and slammed the mixture control to 'IDLE CUTOFF'. The 4360's defiant roar died in an apology of clattering crankshaft dampers and the engine stopped. The silence, as they say, was deafening as Carson emerged from the airplane.

"Hell!"

"Which one was it?"

"No. 3," he spat in disgust. "The same blasted one!"

"On both positions or one?" I asked.

"Both sides — the whole cussed thing is dead. The same way it's been acting until I retime it." He turned to his crew. "Get the bloody engine uncovered."

The crew promptly did his bidding, swinging the engine's cowling open, much like the petals of a gigantic flower in bloom. The workstand was wheeled into place and Carson dragged himself up the steps to confront the recalcitrant magneto. With infinite care he removed the hold down nuts and painstakingly lifted it from its mounting pad. Probably as a last resort he stuck one little finger into the end of the magneto drive shaft in the engine's nose case. And then he twisted his finger slightly.

"Well I'll be monkey's uncle," he sputtered in amazement. "Look at this...the miserable drive shaft is sheared!"

It was indeed. As he raised his little finger the stub of the shaft dutifully followed. In the hangar lights his finger seemed to have grown an extension. The shaft had sheared about one-half inch below its spline where the magneto's drive spline mated. The break extended downward slightly, on a shallow angle. It was bright, indicating the break was fresh, not one of progression.

"You know what's been going on, don't you?" and then he answered his own question. "The torque of the lower half would separate the two pieces when the engine was run-up; there's just enough end play on the entire shaft for that. That would throw the magneto completely out of time.

67

"Naturally when the engine wound down, the upper half would re-engage at the break and be in place when I set the engine up to re-time the mag'." He wagged his shaggy head in amazement. "This is about the nuttiest thing I've ever seen."

Much to the disgust of a frustrated dispatcher and the delight of its passengers, the Stratocruiser waited patiently, immobilized at Honolulu, while Carson's frantic call for a new drive spline was answered by his base at San Francisco.

Carson's problem with the magneto on the 4360 was a rare occurrence, not something often seen on the list of common magneto faults. Otherwise, if anyone thoroughly understands their theory of operation and how the internal parts are designed and assembled to achieve the desired results, there should be no riddle installing them on any engine. It's even possible to time two magnetos on the same engine and see a barely discernible difference in r.p.m. drop between the magnetos.

After I left the Islands I knew an airport 'manager' who also sold new and used airplanes. He indulged in considerable bootleg maintenance — he wasn't a certificated mechanic — a not unusual practice in general aviation. He knew enough to be dangerous and somehow got by. However, the man was totally at a loss when it came to magnetos and ignition systems in general. He often called on me to rescue him from a dilemma had and the conversation was nearly always the same. "I've got a magneto that just won't time to the engine," he would say, as though it was the magneto's fault.

"Don't blame the magneto. You've screwed up another one. If you live to be one hundred years old you'll never understand how to time a magneto to an engine," I would retort. "If you weren't so cheap you'd get a full-time mechanic."

"I can't afford to hire one," he'd say, a statement we both knew was patently untrue. I always accommodated him, but never went beyond actually timing the magneto to the engine. You might say I indulged in mechanical extortion when I collected my fee because I felt he should pay some dividend for running an illicit 'shade tree' operation. Reporting him to the FAA would be an empty effort. "We have to observe such activities," I was told. The problem with that statement is inspectors are rarely, if ever there, to observe such activities.

But if magneto maintenance is serious and can cause an inordinate number of headaches there can be a lighter side, as in anything else. I observed a memorable one before going to work for Trans-Ocean Airlines and being Carson's neighbor when he was with United. The incident had to do with the crop duster company I worked for.

The manager's name was Reynolds, and his relationship with his employees was less than agreeable. He was taciturn and sullen, speaking only to his pilots and shop manager — when he spoke at all. I can't remember having any semblance of even a short conversation with him, except during the brief ritual of completing the necessary paperwork when I became an employee.

The company had Stearman's converted to 450-horsepower Pratt & Whitney engines, and Reynolds reserved one for his personal use, a 'two-holer'. It hadn't been converted for crop dusting. The baggage compartment had been re-worked so his Irish setter, an emaciated, gaunt example of the breed, could fly with him. He also cut a hole in the top of the rear cockpit bulkhead and padded it so the dog was able to stick its head and neck into the rear cockpit. I suspected Reynolds looked upon himself as a later day Roscoe Turner, who carried a lion cub with him. Forget any comparison between the two men — or even the animals.

Reynolds was working on the ignition system of the Lycoming R-220 engine on his Stearman, the original engine configuration. From where I was working on the right wheel of a Stearman spray plane, parked adjacent to his, he seemed to be having more than his share of trouble. Since he preferred doing maintenance on the airplane personally, it was no surprise that he didn't ask for help. Why fate dictated that Carson walk into the hangar at that moment will remain a mystery. Perhaps it was to pass the time of day, since he had once done some work for Reynolds. He shouted a greeting to me and stopped by Reynolds.

"What're you doing?" Carson asked in his usual blunt manner.

"I'm installing new ignition cables on the engine," Reynolds replied sourly.

Uninvited, Carson thrust his head into the area of the Lycoming's accessory section. "Are you installing them properly?"

"Of course," Reynolds retorted indignantly. "The magneto's marked to show what ignition cable goes to what cylinder. How can anyone go wrong?" The answer brought an outburst from Carson that made my day. "Reynolds, you dummy!" Carson exploded, following up with a tremendous guffaw. "You're really screwing up: That engine will never run the way you're doing it." By now I was in a deep crouch behind the landing gear leg and wheel of the Stearman I was working on, convulsed with silent laughter. I could visualize Reynolds' mildly florid features beginning to take on the hue of a young rooster's head in the prime of mating season.

"Here...let me show you," Carson generously offered. "Those numbers on the magneto's outlet cap only indicate the sparking sequence of the rotor. What you have to do is match the firing order of the engine to the sequence." I raised and looked over at Reynolds' Stearman. I could see his face through the opened accessory section. Sure enough: It looked like it was blizzard-whacked and a study in humiliation and perplexity. He still didn't understand.

"Look," Carson continued patiently. "You install the No. 1 cylinder's cable in the No. 1 cable receptacle on the magneto. Then you put the cable of the next cylinder to fire in the No. 2 hole in the magneto's cap and so on." All the while he explained the procedure he was grinning with obvious pleasure at the chagrin Reynolds displayed.

Then Carson launched into a brief lecture. "I don't know why you think you're a mechanic," he chided, with his head wagging in amazement. "Any of your mechanics could have told you if you'd asked. Maybe you'd better stay in your office." Carson never stopped grinning at the now infuriated Reynolds. Laughing still, Carson stalked out of the hangar as abruptly as he had come in. I went to the restroom where I could relieve my aching ribs with un-restrained laughter.

Although Reynolds had a less than cordial attitude, in all fairness, he was an efficient manager. There was never a question about money for maintenance. Consequently, we kept the airplanes in top shape.

The work was tedious and dirty at times. Maintenance included not only airframe and engine but, material tanks and systems. There was also the detestable job of crawling into the fuselages to clean tubing of spray material residue. Invariably, it collected mostly on the after surface of the tubing, which made the job doubly difficult in removing the residue. I have no idea when a wonderfully sensible, modification was designed for Stearman ag' aircraft but it eliminated hours of difficult cleaning.

Someone somewhere on the Mainland, a clever maintenance person installed aluminum side panels for the fuselage, which could be easily removed. Thus, instead of twisting and warping a human body around tubing, the tubing could be easily cleaned in a dignified stand-up-and-reach-in mode, from the hangar floor. Spray nozzles and spray booms, of course, had to be cleaned and checked for optimum function. That operation was also easy since the equipment was readily accessible hanging under each lower wing panel.

The Stearmans were strong and durable and once in peak condition, required only routine attention. The only time-consuming task was rigging the wings while installing them on the fuselage. It was more or less repetitious during installation of 'N' struts and the flying and landing wires, constantly re-setting wire tensions in conjunction with dihedral, angle of incidence and wing panel stagger. If one changed a setting on one element, it was necessary to recheck another. Once all work was completed and fine-tuned, however, there was seldom if any need for re-adjustment, until it was necessary to remove and install wings for whatever reason.

Reynolds never thanked Carson for his help and advice on the ignition system wiring. We in the maintenance crew were not character analysts so it couldn't be determined what his state of mind was. Unappreciative? Couldn't be bothered? Angry because of Carson's less than diplomatic comments? Why bother trying.

Shortly after the incident of Reynolds' magneto problem I joined Trans-Ocean as assistant crew chief. The airline had become very busy in the heat of the Korean Airlift and required more help at its Honolulu station. It was a real pleasure to leave that ag' company and move across the airport. I had returned to the genuine world, of air transport.

6

Of Motivation, Futures
And DC-4's....

Dutch was positioned somewhere between being a hardened optimist and a shirt-tail philosopher.

He didn't deliberately or continually press his positive thoughts and homey, philosophical commodities on anyone; they were simply spur-of-the moment utterances, if and when he thought a situation was important enough to warrant a comment. Generally they mostly floated through the air and vanished like the soft, gentle rings of water caused when a pebble is tossed into a quiet lake and travel outward to expend themselves, leaving no trace.

He had one adage that he used often to rationalize diversity, a sudden change in a situation or, to excuse mistakes.

"Everything turns out for the best," he would postulate.

As a rule, though, the phrase applied to life down the road, but was sometimes difficult to reconcile at the moment. I don't know if Dutch ever thought about it, but his well-worn maxim was proverbial if the best and worst of World War II were argued. History has recorded the savagery of that conflict, but it had merit, too: It produced thousands of mechanics and pilots who garnered invaluable experience at their trade, one of several 'bests'. Enduring aircraft designs may be added to that word, too.

While they were being trained and tempered in that crucible of violence, many of those mechanics and pilots put their subconscious minds to work, thinking of the future life-after-war and planning to be ready for it.

They schemed and dreamed while they were flying airplanes or repairing shot-up airplanes, depending on their duties. Meanwhile, most saved money; there was little else they could do with it anyway, being so far away from crass commercialism. The ones who decided to put their hard-won education and money to work were destined to become instrumental in shaping post-war aviation.

After the first euphoria of not having to live life according-to-war and the Air Corps had passed, their dreams began to blossom into full-blown reality. Mechanics didn't have much trouble being picked up by the existing scheduled airlines or, at least, the better career-minded ones didn't. Many pilots returned to continue their professions. Some were 'on loan' to the flying services, others who decided to continue what they'd been doing in the war, pursued their goals in civilian life. The airlines had to regroup and get on with the business of hauling passengers and they needed help.

In the many ex-servicemen there were entrepreneurs who immediately got to work to project their positive expectancies on the world of aviation and they needed help, too. Dutch, that Air Corps buddy of mine and sometime philosopher, would have been pleased that one of his favorite homilies would be an influence on them: 'The doors to opportunities are unbelievably wide open.'

The visionaries would have a tough row to hoe, but they set to work on the basis of their savings, determination and hours of devoted toil, with enthusiasm as their most important commodity. Many immediately challenged the domination of scheduled airlines head-on. There was only a handful operating under the auspices and blessings of the Civil Aeronautics
Board (CAB).

The up-starts were well aware of the opposition they faced, but they also realized the public was turning more and more to air travel. Besides, an airplane was capable of uses other than hauling passengers hither and yon. Cargo, for example. There could be room for new companies in those unknown skies. So the entrepreneurs set to work to decompose traditional air commerce concepts. Some failed. But out of the efforts of the ones who persisted and succeeded, came dramatic changes in post-war aviation.

In this period of 'enlightened' deregulation and operational permissiveness the apparition of the CAB's severe regulations has been relegated to the mists of time and the vapid memories of those who dared confront the system in their attempts to spool-up a new airline.

The CAB's policy was to establish and maintain a strong, viable national air transport system, a commendable goal, to be sure. This was accomplished by controlling and allocating air routes, air fares and the operational conduct of the airlines. They could not afford to be careless even about not meeting arrival and departure times. The CAB even went so far as to see that the scheduled carriers were generously subsidized to insure their stability. But the boat of smug comfort enjoyed by the airlines began to rock.

It may be difficult for people to visualize how passengers in that era were treated as valued customers, in contrast to the present air carrier cattle car atmosphere. There were on-time arrivals and departures, silverware with meals, the captain visited with his passengers and an air of common courtesy prevailed. Air travelers could even buy a ticket without first consulting a list of restrictions, nor did they have to be mathematical wizards to understand fares or schedules. Air travel was orderly, but then, also a mite expensive to the masses.

World War II produced an essential ingredient to help further the dreams of the new wave of entrepreneurs: A supply of good, operational transports. These were suddenly thrust on the open market in 1946 as surplus and at attractive prices. Even if one didn't need a DC-4 the price was irresistible. One couldn't afford not to buy, at approximately fifty-thousand dollars a copy — give or take a few thousand dollars. Lodestars and DC-3's were priced anywhere from ten thousand dollars to twenty-five thousand dollars. It was truly a buyer's market.

Everything was in place for change. Enter the non-scheduled

airlines and the introduction of a new concept in the use of large airplanes: Hauling air cargo exclusively, in most cases.

Seaboard & Western began with DC-4's; Slick Airways used DC-6's. Trans-Ocean, with whom I worked, had DC-4's and one DC-6. However, the DC-6 was lost without a trace or hint of why on an eastbound flight somewhere between Midway Island and Honolulu.

It was mostly the DC-4's that the non-skeds turned to, but scheduled airlines bought them as well. The type was straight-forward, without frills and with flight controls and other systems that were simplicity personified. The hydraulics were artful, exceedingly fundamental and remarkably leak-free. The airframe, structurally, was well-conceived.

Their spacious cabins were graciously accommodating at adapting for a wide variety of uses: Carrying wounded to succor during the war; transporting cargo of all descriptions during and after the war and, of course, passengers.

By today's standards, DC-4's were tortoise-slow: A Cessna 210, with its ability to cruise effortlessly at 180 m.p.h. or more, would embarrass a DC-4. A flight between Honolulu and Oakland, California, consumed about twelve-hours of plodding, boring flight time — depending on winds aloft. The DC-4, however, was very capable of carrying out such long over-water operations.

If there was anything bothersome about Trans-Ocean's DC-4's it was that cabin heaters were often miscreants and engine fire-warning systems frequently cried 'wolf', because of a faulty sensor. But, no matter. If one couldn't see anything unusual at the engines, such as smoke emanating from an engine's cowl, simply flick a switch and shut off the strident clamor of the fire-warning bell. But, there would be considerable personal discomfort if a heater quit, and the cockpit and cabin began to cool.

DC-4's were powered by Pratt & Whitney R-2000 engines of varying dash designations.[28]They were wonderfully reliable, perhaps because they didn't have an impressive compression ratio, as did Wright R-3350's or Pratt & Whitney R-2800's. At Capital Airlines we checked cylinder compression during routine light checks with a peculiar, shop-made tool. It consisted of a brass safety chain the length of the circumference of the engines. A tapered rubber plug was attached to the chain with a short leader, positioned on the chain at each cylinder's front spark plug hole.

With the rear spark plugs in place, the rubber plugs were pushed firmly into the front spark plug holes and the propeller rotated by hand. If the plugs were ejected with a loud, vigorous 'pop' we could assume the cylinder assembly was in good condition. That, of course, includes piston rings and valve seating. When a plug was barely ejected, 'f-o-o-o-f', or not at all, even a casual observer with minimal mechanical sense would realize the cylinder's condition wasn't up to par. Such results cried out for further investigation.

The system worked well, as compared to the usual method of checking cylinder condition: Measuring how many pounds of compressed air one would hold with the piston at top dead center and both valves closed. On the light inspections we were only interested in how well air was compressed at the top of the compression stroke under the 'ramming' effect of the piston. I have seen some cylinders that would barely hold a pitiful five pounds per square inch of compression at best, with compressed air injected into the cylinder, perform fine when running the engine on ground tests or, in flight.

Somewhere in the dusty archives of Trans-Ocean Airlines there may be recorded the total hours accumulated by the tireless R-2000 engines that powered the airline's DC-4's over endless miles from the Mainland U.S. to their ultimate destinations in Korea and the Western Pacific. But, in all those hours, whatever they happened to be, the archives will surely reveal the minimal trouble the engines gave us. I cannot recall an aircraft arriving at Honolulu with an engine shut down.

Once, an eastbound DC-4 lumbered into Honolulu with a horrendous oil leak at a cam follower housing. Inspection revealed the housing completely separated just above its mounting flange. In upscale parlance, a visually-impaired individual wouldn't have had a problem finding it.

When we ran the engine, every time the cam ring rotated and lifted the follower, the broken follower housing would separate slightly at the break and expel a spurt of oil. It was, for all the world, like a miniature oil well. In fact, by the time the airplane landed, the engine's auxiliary oil tank was nearly empty. We corrected the leak by simply removing the rocker arm, push rod, push rod housing and the broken follower housing. The procedure then was reversed, using new gaskets, hoses and a replacement housing.

Eastbound flights from the Western Pacific were required to park at the terminal to clear Customs. This exercise generally consisted of the agents boarding the aircraft to make a cursory inspection for undeclared goods and illicit drugs. In particular, the crew's sugar supply was often given careful scrutiny. Occasionally a box of sugar packets was summarily removed and taken to the Customs office for more detailed examination. But the true reason for these confiscations was obvious: The sugar supply for the Customs office's coffee bar needed to be replenished.

Now and then the Customs officials would cause us immense aggravation by demanding to inspect the tail cone area of an aircraft's fuselages to make sure nothing was being secreted there. This entailed unlocking the access door from the cabin to the tail cone. Invariably this would happen when neither the flight nor ground crew would have a key.

What strange perceptive powers did these people have? In our suspicious minds we harbored the thought that Customs was really accepting gratuities from the scheduled airlines, especially Pan American, to place more obstacles in the path of progress of us, the 'non-skeds'.

The DC-4 with its failed generator dutifully parked at Customs and I met it with my crew; one would taxi the aircraft to the hangar with me, the other would drive back.

After wheeling the boarding steps to the cabin door we retreated and stood under the left wing waiting for the crew to emerge from the airplane. When we met an eastbound flight we always kept at least twenty-feet away from the crew; it was in quarantine until cleared by Customs. Meanwhile, a Customs agent would appear at the office door to make sure we didn't associate with the crew. It was standard procedure.

"The No. 2 generator failed," the captain said and began to walk toward us. "It quit over an hour out." Horrified at his approach the three of us began to back up, meanwhile holding out our arms with palms up, as though fending off an evil presence.

"Don't come any closer — stay there!" I entreated him. "We'll look into it at the hangar." He continued toward us, ignoring my plea.

What the hell's wrong with him, I wondered. He's told us about the problem and the malfunction will be in the flight log anyway. Also, he was a veteran pilot on the Pacific routes and knew our procedures. Now he was under the wing and we were well out in front of it. We were desperately trying to still maintain the rule-of-thumb, twenty-feet separation. Soon we would be on the taxiway if the pilot couldn't be stopped. A Customs official settled the matter.

"Alright, you guys...come into the office," he ordered.

"What for? He didn't get close to us," I protested vigorously. "We kept our distance." Bill Chang, a ground service man standing beside me, began muttering darkly in Chinese, his face suddenly ashen. He had heard — as I had — of what lay in store when someone got too close to incoming international passengers. Our protests were in vain, so we had to follow the agent into the office, all the while glaring balefully at the aircraft's captain, the perpetrator of our impending discomfort.

In the office the doctor on duty briefly examined the crew's medical declarations of required immunization for traveling to the Orient and then turned to us.

"Do you three have your shot records?"

"No, of course not. We don't need to have them with us all the time we're working," I answered with justifiable indignation. "Besides, we tried to keep the crew away from us, and they didn't get near enough to contaminate us."

I may as well have been talking to a deaf person. Without comment the doctor prepared a wicked looking hypodermic needle, into which he sucked a quantity of ominous looking serum.

Reluctantly I unbuckled my belt and, in abject humiliation, suffered him to viciously jab the needle into one cheek of my butt. The process was repeated with fresh needles twice more as my companions surrendered to the doctor's ministrations. It occurred to me that the medic was thoroughly enjoying his work. With just a little guilt, I smiled inwardly as the gleaming, fiendish needle plunged deep into Chang's skinny, startlingly-white ass. The insertion elicited an emotional, heartfelt response in Chinese which I took to be dreadful curses, or several variants of a basic one.

Freshly immunized against yellow fever, cholera and other unknown, despicable viruses, we were excused. The shots guaranteed immunization against an unthinkable fondness for Customs agents, too. We stomped out the office door with hateful, parting glances at the crew, doctor and agents.

We had consumed approximately one-half hour of valuable ground time, not to mention suffering unwarranted personal indignities. Also, we still had a damaged generator to attend to. Probably a Pan American ground crew witnessed the entire episode and rejoiced. There was no love lost between them and us non-scheduled crews, whether aircrew or ground crew. Their aversion to others included the scheduled United Airlines, as well.

If the engines on our DC-4's were consistently dependable and remarkably trouble-free, the airframes themselves were more so. Hydraulic leaks were practically non-existent, and only occasionally we would change a flight instrument or a set of Loran navigation units. They were always matched pairs; if one set malfunctioned, you changed both.

The gasoline cockpit/cabin heaters became balky at times, but their status on the minimum equipment list was plain on cargo flights: Operational or not, they were a 'go' item. Flights were scheduled for two hours ground time eastbound, to compensate for the vagaries of Customs inspections. Westbound, we were allowed one hour. Consequently some crews continued their flights without heat on the flight deck — and with cold feet.

We took pride in rarely having delays, but on one memorable occasion trying to uphold that tradition backfired. There was no question an on-time departure would not be met, but, while attempting to avoid extending the delay further than was absolutely necessary I was inadvertently responsible for a mishap. The result was a flight crew was forced into a period of fasting, much to its collective disgust and outrage — and my ground crew's delight.

The right magneto on the eastbound flight's No. 3 engine responded to its ground check with a sickly r.p.m. drop. In the heat of seeing that the aircraft was fueled and serviced, cleaned and given a visual inspection — besides curing the suffering magneto — ground time was exceeded. Finally, forty-minutes past scheduled departure time, the crew boarded, and took off for the Mainland.

After every departure my mind would sub-consciously review the events and activities that occurred while preparing an aircraft for further fligh.t. It was a personal reassurance that nothing had been overlooked. As we performed our usual post-departure clean-up and reorganization of the hangar a subtle doubt became a nagging certainty that I had neglected something. But what?

While re-timing the magneto to the engine I had used a six-inch steel scale to line up marks on the edge of the magneto case and the flat on the circumference of the points body. That done, while reinstalling the magneto's outlet cap the scale had slipped out of my shirt pocket and fallen into the maze of cylinder, cylinders' fins, baffling and sundry other remote places. At least two pairs of eyes looked for it but with ground time running out we abandoned the search. We determined it would cause no more harm — wherever it was. It was impossible for the scale to enter the engine so some mechanic would doubtless acquire a spare one.

In my mind I ran through what else we had done to, and with, the airplane while it was on the ground. It wasn't the magneto; that had performed beautifully during the ground check after it was attended to. Besides, the flight crew wouldn't have accepted it if it hadn't functioned properly during the pre-takeoff check. That was the only major work we had accomplished. Service and fueling had been accomplished correctly and we didn't find any discrepancies — other than the magneto — during the visual inspection.

An hour and a half had passed since the airplane's takeoff and still I couldn't put the nagging doubt in my mind at rest. By now the DC-4 would be approximately two-hundred and seventy-five miles eastbound over the Pacific — give or take a few. The telephone hung like a mute, black wart on the shop wall's grey expanse. We would have known by now if the DC-4's operations weren't normal.

I happened to walk into the room that served as a shop, dressing room, storage space and office, on some errand, and glanced idly at a clean, medium-size cardboard box on a large, general purpose table.

The tip of a white paper bag stuck up between the box's half-closed lids. It was the type of bag that restaurants generally use to put carry-out food in.   My God! I had neglected to put the crew's lunches aboard the airplane! That was the very last thing to do before closing the cabin door for departure. It was generally the crew chief's responsibility.

The crew would not have dared turn the DC-4 around and return to Honolulu to claim their lunches if the men valued their jobs. That would have been an absolute waste of time and money, in the eyes of Operations. In any case, the crew wouldn't have starved, as there were several cans of soup aboard the airplane and they had the makings for coffee.

Since the 'fat was in the fire' there was only one option for us: I called my crew together and we ate the lunches. The next day I was reprimanded for the foul miscarriage of duty in a message from the Mainland. However, the wording left doubts as to its severity.

If there is ever a 'Hall of Fame', for aircraft designs, the DC-4 has certainly earned an honored niche alongside the DC-3 and others. As the venerated DC-3 opened the skies to the indisputable fact that air travel was not only dependable but practical, so the DC-4's extended the concept. They also opened new vistas in the expanded use of aircraft in the bargain — especially hauling cargo. While they didn't have the speed or capacity of a DC-6, their worth was proven on the the Berlin Airlift and later, the Korean Airlift

DC-6's, in limited numbers, were used as well. They too, were veritable work horses, in spite of their sometimes irritating R-2800 engines. Both DC-4's and DC-6's flew the Korean airlift with loads that were more often than not overgrows. But that didn't seem to be of any consequence to the companies or flight crews. The saying on the Airlift was, "We carry cargo, the Air Force carries gasoline!"

If a flight crew was uneasy about weather forecasts and the dispatcher's fuel load, we were often begged to " ...give us a little pocket fuel." We accommodated the crews by fudging an extra two-hundred gallons or so into the tanks. Mechanics were well aware that the Pacific Ocean was vast and landfalls widely-spaced.

In the final analysis, the Korean Airlift may be seen as a proving ground that substantiated the pioneering efforts of Pan American Airlines and the China Clippers. In all fairness, much credit has to be extended to Pan Am in opening travel by air to the Orient. But it didn't need to think it owned the Western Pacific. Pan Am was never helpful, nor did its people show a spirit of co-operation with other airlines — particularly the non-skeds.[29]

Shortly after the end of World War II and during the Korean Airlift more and more people were traveling to the Islands by air with United's acquisition of a Mainland-Honolulu route. The airline flew Boeing Stratocruisers. Now the public could spend more time in the Islands; it quickly accepted flying in land planes over an ocean. In that time, the death knell of passenger ocean liners as a primary means of transportation was sounded.

Beyond the Islands to the Orient the mechanics, pilots and aircraft involved in early trans-Pacific operations, established the practicality of air travel to the islands and throughout the Western Pacific for all time. DC-4's played a prominent role in the drama — with the help of the new wave of visionaries. Dutch was right: Everything turned out for the best!

7

Sepia Haze
in a Stink Pit....

If there is any individual of the 20th century to be singled out for un-
conditional acclaim and admiration for his dedication and what must
have been countless tiring hours of unselfish toil toward the
betterment of mankind, I would nominate one whose profession is far
removed from aviation.

Because of his persistent efforts and devotion, the world was
largely rid of the scourge of a dreadful disease that relegated thousands of youngsters to life as a cripple or worse: To face an early
death.

He is Dr. Jonas Salk, who developed the vaccine for polio in 1953.

Two years later Dr. Sabine improved on Salk's achievement, not by an enhanced vaccine, but the method of immunization; Sabine produced an oral vaccine. With all due respect to the good physicians, I think I can be forgiven for claiming some credit in helping Dr. Salk in his work, which cleared the way for Sabine. I was economically compelled to sustain Salk's initial research; my heart and mind rebelled at the time, but my wallet urged me on.

Doctor Salk undertook his work, in the interest of his profession and humanity. Never mind extending a small portion of the accolades due Dr. Salk, to me. The awful but pervasive experience in the lean fringes of medical knowledge and my introduction to 'Live Cargo Handling 101' was partial compensation. Additionally, I wasn't compelled to pay tuition.

Both sides in the Korean War had had enough and the political battle began to determine the boundaries of a divided country. An end to hostilities marked the phasing out of the Korean Airlift. Now Trans-Ocean's DC-4 loads began to be more diversified: Service personnel to the U.S. Mainland, mining machinery to Australia, supplies for the Gilbert Islands, goods for Trans-Ocean's far flung stations and commercial ventures in the Western Pacific. The assortment of cargo was infinite. Go anywhere with anything.

An hour before dawn one day a DC-4 landed at Honolulu, destination South Korea. Since no flight discrepancies were logged, the aircraft required only routine servicing and refueling. Its cargo was unknown to us until the airplane taxied to the hangar after it landed. Other cargos to come would be more startling.

A wooden platform had been installed the length of the cabin from the entry door to the forward cabin bulkhead. Space was allowed for a walkway along the port cabin wall. Approximately three-fourths of its length was partitioned off, the open side fitted with wooden rails much like a livestock corral, which it actually was.

Resting comfortably on a thick bed of straw were sixteen milk goats. The remainder of the platform was partitioned off from the goats and held forty white Belgium rabbits in boxes. There were two rabbits to each box. The goats and rabbits were all fine-looking animals, destined to take part in a recovery program for Korean families.

Unexpectedly, the goats didn't smell like goats are supposed to smell. They were clean, with sleek white and black fur glistening under the cabin lights. One pregnant nanny had responded to the dictates of nature by giving birth to a kid somewhere over the Pacific Ocean between Honolulu and Oakland, California. A few goats stirred and stood up to stretch and, being curious like most animals, watched attentively as the service crew began replenishing their drinking water and feed.

Somehow three rabbits had smothered, which were disposed of, However, there was no untoward concern, rabbits being rabbits. The population would far exceed the original forty in due time. But there was more live cargo.

I began a conventional check of the DC-4's cockpit equipment just as the new sun was brightening the Hawaiian skies with a suffused pale rose. Both side windows were fully open, allowing a breath of refreshingly-cool, aromatic air to drift lazily into the cockpit. A typical Hawaiian at-dawn morning.

Flicking the electrical master switch on, I commenced checking instruments and cockpit lights when a faint humming sound began to insinuate itself into my sub-conscious mind. It grew louder and more insistent, gradually distracting my concentration, so I paused to determine the cause.

Had a radio been left on? There was no modern solid state, electronics equipment in the airplane; that was several years into the future. The radios were massive with vacuum tubes and dynamotors. After checking, I found them all switched off. The flight instruments were vacuum operated; with the engines shut down they couldn't be running. I searched and checked switches while the humming became more intense. Suddenly I realized the sound was coming from behind me. I whirled around.

There on the flight deck behind the pilot's and co-pilot's seats were stacked a double-column of small, wooden boxes. Actually they were no more than frames with screen wire for sides, tops and bottoms. They were approximately one-foot square, the stacks reaching to nearly the height of the flight deck bulkhead.

My flashlight beam caused the humming to rise to a crescendo and then I saw bees, literally thousands of bees, a colony in each box. They were awakening with the progressively brightening sky and apparently were becoming frenzied to escape and go about their business of gathering honey. The thought of what could have happened on that flight deck somewhere over the ocean, had even one colony escaped, was chilling.

I wagged my head in amazement and wondered idly what the next cargo would be. Whatever it would be it shouldn't come as a surprise. The non-skeds were in the business of pioneering air freight hauling on a commercial basis. Therefore, any commodity that would fit in the fuselages of the freighters was accepted. It wasn't long until my question was answered. And the answer would mean far more discomfort and work than this load of goats, rabbits and honey bees.

A week later, almost to the day, an eastbound DC-4 trudged in from the Western Pacific. As the airplane with the goats, rabbits and bees did, this one also arrived just in time to meet the first sunbursts of a new day.

The flight originated in the Far East and, of course, needed to clear Customs. Naturally Customs would presume the airplane to be contaminated with a host of vile insects and diseases, not to forget contraband. "The Customs inspectors should have their usual field day," I remarked to Vargas and Chang, as we stood waiting for the engines to shut down. We could see considerable activity on the flight deck; it seemed overly full of men.

"What's the cargo?" I asked Freddie Vargas, the crew chief.

"Monkeys," Vargas replied.

"Monkeys!"

"Yeah, monkeys," he cameback, almost absently. "They're going to Georgia to be used in polio research." He seemed to be enjoying a secret thought.[30]

"How many monkeys?" I asked.

"It's full," he answered with a sardonic grin. Which was no answer at all. I couldn't recall seeing any factory documents spelling out how many monkeys a DC-4 was designed to hold.

My imagination began to run amok at the thought of a DC-4's cabin full of monkeys. Were they herded in like cattle or goats? Maybe they were tied in small, writhing bundles stacked under cargo nets. Or, perhaps, they were strapped comfortably in passenger seats, chattering, scratching and eating peanuts. The captain broke into my vapid fantasies with a plea from the cockpit window.

"Please get that stairway up to the cabin door." His face seemed ashen and drawn. I saw four other men behind him, including the co-pilot. Six grown men crammed into a DC-4's cockpit and tiny crew's quarters?

We quickly wheeled the boarding stairs to the cabin door and retreated to our customary position under the left wing to wait. The Customs inspectors, normally eager to board an eastbound aircraft, were strangely reluctant to approach the DC-4. In fact, they gave us permission to taxi the aircraft away as soon as the crew deplaned. From the doorway of their office!

The cabin door burst open and a rush of vile, warm air streamed out of the cabin, followed by six pilots, hard on each other's heels. There was no breeze and an indescribable odor began to permeate the immediate area outside the cabin door. The crew practically stampeded to the Customs office.

"You taxi it to the hangar," Vargas ordered, and an evil grin creased his thin face.

"I'm not getting in that airplane," I declared heatedly. "It's your turn to taxi anyway." I had visions of becoming deathly ill and knew, for sure I'd vomit if I entered that cabin. Vargas looked at me sternly.

"You either taxi it to the hangar or pack your tools," he insisted grimly. "Take Chang with you." It was an order Chang anticipated. We often relied on Chang to help taxi airplanes. Also, when we needed two more hands to help correct a mechanical discrepancy. He was the best helper we had.

When Vargas issued his order Chang recognized the obvious: If Vargas didn't go with me, he Chang, had to. His normally expressionless face had suddenly assumed deep lines of apprehension. I looked at Vargas hatefully and turned to climb the boarding steps. I was his assistant crew chief and knew he had the power to dismiss me, and probably would have, in spite of our friendship. I did need to work, and discrimination suits were unheard of then.

"All right...but you get the stairs away and the chocks out and don't waste any time," I said. Motioning the reluctant Chang to follow me, we mounted the boarding steps into the cabin. The noisome air hit us like an invisible blow to our faces. Immediately, perspiration began to saturate our shirts from the awful hot air in the cabin.

I involuntarily gagged. Behind me, Chang ripped out a litany of what I took to be choice blasphemy in Chinese. It was somewhat muffled because he had a hand clapped over his mouth and nose, for whatever good that did. He was certainly cursing; no one with a lick of sense would be happy!

Chang slammed the cabin door and latched it. I was shocked to see a male figure strapped in the lone passenger seat just inside the door. I merely nodded as Chang and I hurried forward through a maze of hundreds of tiny, beady, brown eyes set in a sea of lilliputian, wizened furry faces. The monkeys were in cages after all — not on seats!

Early on I had learned that truths in old axioms would surface sooner or later if one lived long enough. When I stepped into the DC-4's cabin the old saw 'You could cut the odor with a knife,' became a reality. But I didn't think this was the time to prove or disprove the saying with my pocket knife. This opportunity to indulge in research would have to be ignored.

The air in the teeming cabin of the DC-4 seemed opaque with a

suffocating vile haze from the feces and urine of hundreds of monkeys. Vargas later said there were approximately twelve-hundred, but we didn't
learn the exact number. I suppose that figure was close to being a reasonable one, since there were two monkeys to a cage.

They were small, probably weighing about seven pounds each. The cages had wooden frames and floors, with stout wire mesh on the sides, ends and tops. Cages lined the cabin's walls to the ceiling from the door to the forward bulkhead. A double row occupied the cabin's center. There was a narrow walkway on each side of the that row.

As I climbed into the captain's seat I wondered, for a fleeting moment, about the man in the cabin. He couldn't be a member of the flight crew. God forbid that one of the elite would suffer the companionship of a cabin full of monkeys, even clean-smelling monkeys if there was such an animal. He probably wasn't a mechanic either, deadheading from somewhere to somewhere else. Mechanics have pride in person and profession, too! It was obvious he was of an entirely different persuasion, removed from aviation except for travel.

As we learned soon enough, he was the monkey tender, an occupational title which may or may not have been official. But we thought it to be entirely appropriate.

We learned his name was Mason, when we introduced each other. He was a pitiful sight, slumped in his seat. He had long straight black hair slicked back and he wore baggy brown trousers. There were seamed, scuffed, tired black shoes on his feet. His thin sweaty shirt, travel-worn and well-soiled, completed his 'ensemble'. The shirt might have been white at one time.

When I glanced at him as I hurried toward the flight deck, large

94

washed-blue eyes stared back at me from an exceedingly pale face. That guy, I thought, needs fresh air desperately. Probably his lungs were frightfully corroded from breathing foul air hour after hour over the vast expanse of the Western Pacific.

Chang was hard on my heels as we hurried for the cockpit and the fresh air at the open cockpit side windows. I regretted my inability to understand the language. Although he had been born in the Islands he spoke Chinese fluently. His emotional, aggressive chattering had to be a continual stream of invectives. If so, I could imagine they would put to shame the legendary profanity of early American mule skinners.

I scrambled into the captain's seat as Chang slammed the cockpit door shut. While he was clambering into the right seat and locking it into position I stuck my head out the side window to gulp in a few breaths of warm, though fresh, air. By now we were sweating profusely from the closeness of the cabin air we had just scurried through. The awful odor, plus the body heat from hundreds of primates back there, seemed to have helped the temperature rise considerably.

"Stay clear!" I shouted at Vargas. He signaled the props clear, all the while with a twisted, triumphant grin.

"You bastard," I muttered and pulled my head back into the cockpit. We busied ourselves getting ready to start the engines.

"Go ahead, Chang, start No. 3."

Sometimes when engines are still hot from running as these were, they will balk. That requires delicate manipulation of throttles and mixture controls to coax them into life. With Chang operating the starter, boost pump and ignition switches I pushed the throttle up to clear the induction system of stale fuel-air mixture. Then I eased it back after several revolutions of the propeller and called for ignition. I moved the mixture control forward gingerly and, wonder of wonders: No. 3 caught and rumbled into life. Now a faint breath of air began drifting through the cockpit.

With oil pressure assured on No. 3, Chang began to crank No. 2. It caught, hesitated and began to die. Too much fuel! Bring the mixture control back full-stop. I was beginning to die, too. Ease the throttle forward to clear the engine. No. 2 caught again, back-fired and I slipped the mixture control forward while carefully retarding the throttle. The engine caught again and settled into a smooth growl. I released the brakes. With two propellers turning and the airplane moving, the flow of fresh air through the cockpit increased wonderfully. As the DC-4 began to creep toward the taxiway, the flow of fresh air, was like balm to our fevered faces and sweaty bodies. If two engines turning two propellers helped that much, I reasoned, two more would be appreciably better.

"Let's start No. 1 and No. 4, Chang," I said. As we turned onto the taxiway we had all four engines running nicely and we began to gather speed. By the time we passed the Pan American complex west of the terminal we were indicating a comfortable forty m.p.h.

We felt as though we were immersed in a container whose atmosphere resembled the air after a passing rain shower. Our flushed faces were anointed with a cool, soothing balm. Unconsciously, I suppose, we were trying to leave the terrible odor of monkeys behind us. I visualized a contrail of monkey stink in our wake. Did the line personnel at the terminal smell us? Like they'd smell an eighteen-wheeler with a load of cattle or hogs passing by?

At the hangar I enjoyed a reprieve from association with the cargo of monkeys. Poor Chang did not. He and the three members of the service crew had to help the monkey tender feed and water the monkeys, so, reluctantly, they set to work. I had a sense it wasn't the work they were hesitant about, it was the monkeys. They simply didn't like the little creatures and their aversion was blatantly apparent. Of course, the stink in the airplane's cabin didn't help their attitudes either.

The monkey tender's name was Mason. As it turned out he was an Englishman whose profession was caring for live cargos such as this one. He and his wife also operated a small animal refuge near London where they treated animals that had become sick or injured on flights he had worked. He had cared for many different species of birds and animals, and a cargo of monkeys was just something to take in stride.

"How do you manage to survive sitting back there hour after hour with those smelly creatures?" I asked. We were standing at the cabin door talking, he on the inside of the cabin, me on the boarding steps outside. I hadn't become acclimated to the cabin's atmosphere and needed the fresh air. He smiled weakly and reached into his seat pocket where magazines are usually carried.

"With this," he replied", and he pulled out a bottle of gin. "A nip now and then helps." He pushed the bottle back into the seat pocket and slouched out of the cabin. He was bleary-eyed and weary, but being terribly 'British'.

I quickly shifted to make room for him on the small landing at the top of the steps, making sure I was up-wind. It was horrifying to see him nonchalantly smooth his already slick, ebony hair back and a long

97

strand fell over one eye. After all, he had been using that same hand to attend to his charges: Handling dirty water containers and disposing of two monkeys that had died during the flight. Mason seemed unconcerned about the loss.

He went on to say that animal odors didn't really bother, him but they did cause some annoyance to others when his flights stopped for re-fueling. In his dry humor he said he would walk into an airport terminal restaurant to eat and bring other diners to near-nausea because of the animal odor emanating from his clothes. A valid reaction, I admitted. Mason didn't have a bag which meant he didn't have a change of clothes, but it would have taken a wardrobe to keep fresh clothes on his back.

"Sometimes the other passengers would look at their shoes, perhaps thinking they inadvertently had stepped in dog poop," he continued, with obvious delight. "Finally I realized the extent of discomfort I was causing and took my meals at the airplane. The restaurants at our regular stops were happy to deliver them."

I wondered if he washed his hands before eating. The only water supply aboard would be for drinking; there wouldn't be enough for washing. In fact, restroom facilities were basic on our freighters. But, on the other hand, that would be academic. He would be eating in an aura of stink anyway, so would clean hands really matter?

In another hour the DC-4 was ready for departure. The crew arrived and clambered aboard with undisguised reluctance. Mason settled his angular frame into his seat, after assuring himself that his bottle of 'tranquilizer' was in place. We latched the door, pulled the wheel chocks and the DC-4 departed on another leg of its steamy odyssey.

Approximately seventeen days later, another eastbound DC-4 landed and taxied to the Customs ramp. Different airplane and crew, more monkeys, and again, Mason. And again, with Chang, I was ordered to taxi the plane to the hangar.

After being mildly chastised by the control tower for our taxi speed we parked at the hangar and shut down the engines. Chang and I scrambled down the boarding stairs into the bright, fresh Hawaiian morning, flinging a greeting at Mason on the way. He followed us and began pacing to and fro, as though undecided how to react to freedom from confinement in the evil, pungent atmosphere of the cabin. Vargas walked out of the hangar.

"We have to off-load the monkeys," he declared. I stared at him in disbelief. He wasn't kidding; usually faint twitches of a building smile would tease the corners of his mouth when he was. This time he was dead-serious.

"We've got to off-load, clean the cabin and feed and water them," he continued. "But first, you and me are going to get the airplane serviced and made ready."

In his voice I detected a hint that our work could be extensive. I gratefully began to do the through check and service, and Vargas issued orders to the ground service crew. Under Mason's directions they set to work at their odious task. They really had no options.

It's doubtful that any DC-4 on a through flight, or any other airplane, for that matter, had ever been given a more exhaustive check than the one Vargas and I bestowed on that DC-4!

We leisurely serviced the oil tanks, checked tires and landing gear struts, examined each engine's exhaust collector rings through the open cowl flaps with unusual attention. The cockpit windows sparkled after we studiously cleaned them —from the outside — and gave the landing and navigation lights' lens the same treatment. We contemplated the condition of wheel wells as a geological researcher would the structure of cliffs and canyon walls.

I opened the 'hell hole', the mid-fuselage belly compartment that contained the heart of the airplane's hydraulic system. My pride knew no bounds in the thoroughness of my inspection of the array of aluminum tubing, couplings, valves and other various and sundry system elements. Normally DC-4's hydraulic systems seldom leaked, but I, nevertheless, refreshed the area with several shop towels until the exposed parts of the hydraulic system glistened.

Our service work and inspection for further flight was so diligent and detailed it was becoming obscene. But, by the time it was becoming apparent we were killing time, the crates of rhesus monkeys were neatly stacked in the sunshine on the ramp. The hubbub of their fright and bewilderment rent the air in a cacophony of howls, screeches and hoots. Our small hangar dog, a mixture of Fox Terrier and something else, didn't help matters. She wandered near the cages, which caused the general uproar to increase in volume as the monkeys cowered with undisguised apprehension at her approach.

The service crew busily began cleaning the DC-4's cabin while Mason bustled about, removing several dead monkeys that had perished during the flight, and cleaning cages. He also fed and watered the animals. The marvel to me was that not one escaped while the cage doors were being opened and closed during his work.[31]

I couldn't escape helping to reload the cargo, an activity that produced a continual, ear-splitting clamor of more screeches and howls! It also created a gradual build-up of the same thick, revolting atmosphere that had saturated the cabin air when the airplane arrived. By the time we finished loading, there didn't seem to be much difference in the production and accumulation of monkey poop and saffron urine from the nervous animals than when they arrived.

Once, a monkey dragged its wet tail, slickened with urine and poop, across Chang's jaws and neck. The monkey had carelessly let it hang through the wire of its cage. While Chang was pre-occupied the monkey raised its tail and retrieved it just as Chang turned to attend to something. I was momentarily struck dumb, first by the disgusting act and then, by the stream of invectives and blasphemy poor Chang screamed in Chinese. I wondered if there was a limit to his vocabulary of strident profanity. It seemed not!

At the end of what seemed an eternity, the cages were all loaded and tied down. With immense relief we re-fueled and prepared for the airplane's departure.

Mason had wisely assured himself of an adequate supply of gin, and again, we had the opportunity to chat before he boarded. He suggested he bring a pair of nightingales from England on his next trip in trade for a pair of mynah birds, so common in the Islands. They're not as handsome as a nightingale and they certainly don't sing. Why he wanted one mynah bird. let alone a pair was beyond me.

I thought introducing mynah birds into the British Isles was only justifiable and poetic justice. Hadn't the Pilgrims introduced English sparrows into North America when they made their voyage to the New World? Where the pests immediately began to proliferate, and thrive to this day. The scheme never materialized; Mason never passed through Honolulu again, at least while I was with Trans-Ocean. I wished him well as he clambered aboard with his bottle of gin, behind another reluctant crew, and we closed the door.

It's probable that the engines were started and the airplane waved away in record time, as though ridding ourselves of a scourge. I'm positively certain the crew checked the magnetos while taxing to the runway, to keep air flowing into the flight deck through the side windows, and asked for an immediate take-off. We silently bid it bon voyage as it lifted off and the sounds of its departure for the Mainland faded away.

It would be several days before the odor of monkeys would dissipate. The very pores of our bodies were permeated with the stench, imbedded stubbornly in spite of frequent, soapy showers. I threw away the clothes I had worked in. It helped to rid myself of the awful smell. But it was expensive, since I threw away two sets of work clothes; that, of course, included pants and shirts. I didn't discard my work shoes since they were comfortable and, also, more costly to replace. Besides, they could be washed and treated.

I've often wondered about the airplanes that hauled monkey cargos. What effect did the contaminated air have on delicate instruments and radios? Did the urine seep into the airplanes' cabin floors and lower fuselages? To begin a process of insidious corrosion? I once saw a rat's nest in the corner of a wing on a Gullwing Stinson. The rat's urine had completely eaten away the aft end of the aluminum butt rib and the trailing edge channel where they joined. The structure had to be rebuilt.

Pan American also carried monkeys now and then in its Stratocruisers. The airline had since retired their Clippers. How did the haughty airline clean the aircraft for passenger service? Surely they were very concerned with carrying passengers in one after it had been flown as a monkey carrier. Probably air freshener played a major role in ridding the Stratocruisers of monkey odor — after intense cleaning.

The thought crossed my mind that perhaps the crew's lunches might absorb monkey odor, especially the sandwich bread. But since they were as far forward in the fuselage as Donald Douglas allowed, presumably air flowing to the tail carried with it all odors, which afforded them relief. But that was questionable. If they had the cockpit windows even slightly opened, and the cockpit door ajar, air would flow effortlessly out the cockpit windows. It's normal direction for air flow in an aircraft in flight.

Nevertheless, did their clothes assimilate the appalling smell? Cigar smoke will penetrate cloth and to me, at least, that monkey stench was just as keen and penetrating. By that I do not mean there is an attractive comparison between cigar smoke and monkey stink. Heaven forbid! Cigar smoke is far more appealing to the nostrils.

During all that time we serviced both aircraft carrying monkeys, we not once had a visitor. Normally, the men who maintained other airlines' aircraft were good neighbors. We helped each other when necessary and visited back and forth during slack periods. Now, we were in a state of severe isolation. Not even our maintenance superintendent visited with us as was his daily routine. Well, we thought, perhaps they're not as good friends as we thought, to ostracize us in the face of adversity and needing some solace, even from a distance.

Looking back on those flights it was fortunate that animal rightists were unheard of. If the special interest society had been at work as it is now, it's reasonable to assume the Honolulu chapter would have picketed us in full force. It would have been interesting though, when one considers how animal rightists would have balanced saving monkeys from experiments versus saving kids from polio. Eventually there came the time when bans on trapping monkeys were put in place at their countries of origin.

In any event, the trials and tribulations we suffered while working the monkey flights were worthwhile — as far as I was concerned — when the implications of our efforts were considered: In time, polio was virtually eradicated, saving untold numbers of kids from sure and lasting misery — or sure death. Possibly the others of my crew who had worked the monkey flights never pondered that.

As for me, I could feel secure in my claim for some credit in helping Dr. Salk develop polio vaccine.

8

Flipping Through
Memory's Files....

There's something about most kids' physical makeups, that allow them to sleep like innocent babes on airplanes. Two of mine, Steve and Karen, were sleeping soundly beside me before one of Trans-Ocean's DC-4's, No. 754, had reached cruising altitude. Steve had just advanced well into the toddling stage; Karen was his senior by a fragile two years — old enough to start issuing orders to him. She was watchful over him and an excellent diminutive nanny.

Earl Jr. and Stuart, their brothers, would follow us with their mother when school closed for the summer. I would re-join Capital Airlines at its Washington, D.C. base.

As Diamond Head fell astern and only reading lights pierced the cabin's darkness, I busied getting Karen and Steve comfortable. We had eaten before boarding so that problem was solved. We had also brought box lunches for later, if needed. Non-skeds seldom, if ever, provided food as is the custom on scheduled airlines.

Both kids had grown quiet, tucked under their blankets, fast asleep.

With Diamond Head's craggy outlines fading in the early night, so ebbed seven years in the Pacific. They passed through my mind in rapid succession and the events in that period of transition from a hill teenager over the threshold of manhood I would never forget.

There was a sense of reluctance but not regret in leaving. Far beyond the nose of No. 754 — in Time and distance — awaited my real future. The kids too. It always bothered me that, in The Islands, they would be absorbed in island life, mannerisms, speaking pidgen English and having no certainty in their future lives.

My little family was formed in the busy years after leaving Pacific Skyways to go to the Mainland for my license and steady work. After getting my license, there was a period of six months of factory work at Fairchild Aircraft. Following that stint of manufacturing airplanes, I joined Capital Airlines and worked part time at nearby Beacon Field on light and medium aircraft.

There was a host of aircraft makes there, many now collectors' items: BT-13's, Stearman's, Taylorcraft, Stinsons and Cessna 'Bamboo Bombers', UC-78s. The factory experience at Fairchild, heavy transport maintenance at Capital; and work on light aircraft at Beacon Field opened new avenues in aviation for me.

Then, at Carson's behest, it was back to the Islands. Now we are leaving the Islands for good. Trans-Ocean's operations have declined, and the maintenance staff has been reduced dramatically.

By the time I finished reading the *Honolulu Star-Bulletin* I brought, the Islands had dropped several hundred miles astern. We were getting closer to the decision distance: The point of no return.

From what I could see of the four engines, their sounds and the feel of the vibrations through my seat cushion, I couldn't think of any reason why the captain would turn the aircraft around and go back to Honolulu.

My eyelids were heavy so I didn't resist. I didn't sleep, but started to slide into a light doze; I was only ever able to sleep soundly on an airplane on one flight.

That was on a Continental Airlines 747 between Honolulu and Auckland, New Zealand. Maybe it was a combination of the hum of the turbines, the stolid bulk of the Boeing and the fact the captain appeared reassuring.

He looked to be close to 60 years old, an oak of a man with white hair. He, I thought, looks like he knows what he's going to do and how to do it. It was a comforting thought, since it's about 4,500-miles from Honolulu to Auckland. Over the Pacific Ocean, except for the tiny specks of Fiji, Samoa and lesser South Pacific islands.

Fighting sleep, my eyelids creaked open like stiff shutters. Karen and Steve were still sleeping — how do they do it? — oblivious to everything in their innocent trust that all was as it should be.

I glanced out the window. That thin streak of oil on the top of No. 3 engine's nacelle hasn't progressed appreciably since I last looked at it. Probably a pushrod housing seal is weeping. There appears to be nothing amiss with the other three engines so my eyelids closed once more, as though pulled shut by an insistent weight. The drone of the four Pratt & Whitneys pulled me back into my half-sleep....

Radials don't clatter like the 65-horsepower, four cylinder Continental engine in this J-3, I thought. Batchelder, my instructor, always said that one should never clear one's ears while gaining altitude in a J-3.

"The sudden torrent of engine noise might scare you," he warned. For that reason he never cleared his ears when he ferried a new J-3 from John Rodgers Airport at Honolulu — now Honolulu International. He was flying it to Pacific Skyways' base on Kauai over seventy-five miles of Pacific Ocean. After take-off from John Rodgers he would begin a gradual climb to about six-thousand feet and level off. By that time, the tiny airplane would be about halfway to Kauai.

He theorized that if the engine quit, at least the airplane could be coaxed to glide the remaining distance to reach, at the very least, a beach for an emergency landing. Or, if that wasn't possible, maybe he could make a water landing and wade ashore!

Once his ears cleared inadvertently and the engine's noise filled him with a frightening dread. It was surely going to pieces! Strapped in the front seat was a case of Scotch a plantation manager asked him in Honolulu to bring home on the flight.

"I thought I was going down, for sure," Batchelder said. "But I made up my mind I'd be drinking Scotch to

ease the pain as I was going down."

"Can't you swim?" I asked.

"Hell no I can't swim," he replied. "Besides, that's only prolong the agony of looking forward to drowning."

That exchange recalled a mechanic friend at Honolulu who had completely re-covered a war surplus J-3. Justifiably proud of his accomplishment he called to say he would fly over to Kauai for a visit and show off the airplane. He never arrived at all, let alone at his appointed time.

A navigational error caused him to fly on a course to Johnson Island — five-hundred miles southwest of Kauai. He ran out of fuel and was forced to ditch the Cub in the ocean. A Navy tug, inbound to Pearl Harbor plucked him and his girl friend from the water but couldn't save the J-3.

I finished my preflight check and taxied onto the runway at Burns Field after checking the approaches for traffic. There shouldn't be any traffic since the balance of Pacific Skyways' fleet was parked at the shop and the CAA field station next door hadn't re-ported any impending arrivals.

I lined the Cub on the centerline and pushed the throttle open. One-hundred yards later the wheels broke ground and I was airborne on my first solo flight.

Almost immediately one of the little mourning doves, common on the airport, managed somehow to miss the blades and fly right through the prop. It hit the Plexiglas windshield. By the time I recovered from the shock of the smack of its body on the windshield and saw there were no discernable cracks, the runway had disappeared behind the Cub and Hanapepe Harbor was under it. I swung the plane around downwind and made a shaky landing back where I started. Is this an omen, I wondered, as we inspected the windshield. Maybe a mechanic shouldn't become a pilot?

Pacific Skyways was off to a shaky start from the beginning. I worked under Carson's guidance as we kept our two Cubs maintained for student instructions. We had four students: A banker from Lihue who hadn't flown since his Royal Canadian Air Force days. The J-3's were a marked improvement over the Sopwith Camel he flew at the end of World War I, he said.

There was a young, attractive woman who was Irish's student. She was developing into a good pilot, he said, but hated to fly alone. A doctor in residence at a nearby sugar plantation gave us his entire shirt when he soloed. He was learning to fly, out of sheer boredom. And then there was me, my instructions paid for under the G.I. Bill.

With the company's income gasping for air in the current of diminishing returns we explored all options available and everyone did what was necessary to try to stay afloat. Our Stinson L-5 and the Bamboo Bomber waited patiently for the transition from war surplus status to licensed civil operations. But somehow the money for necessary work on them never materialized.

I was appointed company typist simply because I was the only one who could type. We tried aerial photography with a surplus Fairchild K-20 camera. The object was to sell the service to plantations to be used in engineering their irrigation ditches' layouts. I was pressed into service as photographer, hanging precariously from a Cub's open door. It was an exercise in futility because the first roll of film developed into a twenty-foot long black ribbon, void of images. "Better get that camera checked," the photo lab' advised.

A general merchandise salesman from Honolulu visited various retail stores on Kauai, peddling his wares. We became his freight forwarders, delivering his orders with a battered 1939 Chevy pickup. The products were flown from Honolulu via DC-3, owned by a newly-formed freight airline. But the loads were sparse and so were the delivery fees.

The salesman attempted to establish a network of pistachio nut vending machines in bars and retail outlets in Hanapepe which we would service. Once he handed me two dollars and fifty-cents.

"Use this to buy pistachio nuts and exhort potential customers to do the same," he instructed. "Of course, you may buy a beer, too." I bought fifty-cents worth of nuts at a bar in Hanapepe and washed them down with two dollars worth of beer. It was a delicious treat, one my lack of money precluded.

Then, one day, Mills arrived in his Cessna Bamboo Bomber from Honolulu on his regular newspaper delivery flight. He reported the salesman was dead.

The salesman had hired a pilot to take him sightseeing over Honolulu Airport (nee John Rodgers Airport) and at two-thousand feet handed the pilot a note, un-latched the door of the Taylorcraft and rolled out. The suicide note indicated the salesman had severe personal problems. With that fatal decision to solve them, another source of income, however meager, for the company also died.

For some reason our leaders decided to build an airstrip near Kipapa, on Kauai's northeastern shore. I was assigned to bulldoze the land to level it.

There were a series of huge potholes to backfill and bushes to clear away. I had to learn how to operate a bulldozer immediately and managed to get it stuck halfway down the sides of a pothole. Another came and helped extricate me. Finally, the project was abandoned. I wondered why Pacific Skyways should spend money it didn't have.

As the months wore on I learned much from Carson, but could see that the future of Pacific Skyways looked bleak indeed. It darkened further when one of the J-3's landed on a very short, doglegged 'landing strip' on Kauai's Na Pali coast and rolled into a pile of rocks. We never did get the L-5 and twin-engined Cessna operational. To coin an understatement, money *was tight.*

There were days when a can of sardines and saltine crackers sufficed for lunch. Ringneck pheasants were plentiful and served us well — baked, fried, boiled, or stewed. I shot them with an ancient single-barrel shotgun borrowed from the game warden.

He never asked me if I had a hunting license or what I was going to do with the gun. Spam was a staple, baked with a covering of tomato sauce. Twenty-five dollars a week didn't go far.

There's always a fundamental appreciation of reality in everyone and mine urged me to face it. The Mainland and its opportunities beckoned and I answered by leaving Pacific Sky-ways to its struggles for survival. I had my own problems to face, orchestrating a future....

Somewhere in its system the auto-pilot hiccuped and the DC-4 responded by porpoising mildly. The sudden, though docile, pressure of the seat cushion against my rear jerked me out of my reveries. A quick glance around the cabin and through the cabin windows was reassuring.

The passengers were quiet; the oil leak from No. 3 engine hadn't grown on the nacelle, from what I could see in the dim light of the cabin. The vibrations in the fuselage hadn't changed. I re-arranged the blankets around Steve and Karen, still sleeping soundly, against the slight chill in the cabin, then lit a cigarette. The wisp of smoke formed a thin opaque vapor across the window as though forming a curtain to my thoughts.

The airplane's right wing tip, oscillating ever so gently against a backdrop of far-off, star-lit cumulus formations, seemed dreamily detached through my thought-clouded eyes....

We were flying higher than a DC-4 because the Lockheed Constellation was pressurized. Its left wing tip light was a delicate vermillion glow against the hordes of crystalline stars on the black velvet of night. Now and then it would rise two or three stars from the urge of a gentle air current, and then settle back. We would land at Honolulu in early morning. A non-scheduled airline operated the airplane.

I visited with the engineer in the cockpit and noted that the No. 3 engine's torque indicating instrument was zeroed. All the other instruments were indicating normal operation. The dead instrument was the BMEP (brake mean effective pressure) and took its reading from the engine's nose.

"I don't know why they put them in," the engineer said. "They're worthless."

Which was true. A lagging engine could be readily determined from reading the usual, essential engine instruments. BMEP gages indicated power output in terms of amount of torque. Still, the engine instruments provided operatonal factors. Brake mean effective power indications were merely a redundancy thereby questioning its usefullness in diaognostics.

"We're delighted to see you back," Carson said in greeting. "That airplane (gesturing toward the Connie) is faster than the DC-4 you left on." Now he was with United, having given up on Pacific Skyways several months after I did. "When you get settled I have some work for you."

"I have a job, as you know," I replied.

"I know, but you can help me in your spare time. I have an airplane to recover."

Carson, it seemed, hadn't lost his drive to keep busy and earn extra money to meet Island prices, for survival.

The hangar that housed the crop dusting company I hired on with from the Mainland was surprisingly clean and well-equipped.

There were four of us to maintain eight Stearmans and one Hiller 'chopper. Barney overhauled the Pratt & Whitney R-985's powering the sprayers and dusters; Harry was shop foreman and mechanic. Cheng and I did the general maintenance, modifications, fabric covering and airframe overhauls. He was very good and thorough at what he did.

Two part-time welders came in when we needed them and that was often. Santos welded in the Navy shops at Pearl Harbor and was remarkedly adept with his huge torch. His stainless steel and steel welds were without peer. Lee, a young Island-born Chinese, could produce aluminum welds with such finesse they ap-

115

peared to be painted with an artist's brush. He was equally adept at welding steel tubing.

Together, we designed and built an over-wing exhaust stack for one of the Stearmans that would be used to dust sulphur.

Sulphur dust is highly volatile, so we designed the stack to exhaust over the upper wing panel, well clear and removed from the dust hopper outlet on the bottom of the fuselage. The system and Lee's welds worked well, but the exhaust noise sounded like that produced by a Cummings-powered long haul truck without mufflers.

We had an all-around helper, Cliff, a strapping Hawaiian lad. He often imbedded discarded 8-32 elastic stop nuts in small chunks of bread from his sandwiches and tossed them to a gaunt Irish Setter, owned by Reynolds, the manager. The dog simply gulped them down.

We often wondered if his owner ever noticed the nuts when the dog defecated in the yard at home.

Cliff disliked Reynolds more than the rest of us did and we supposed that was his way of retaliating for the manager's cold, oafish relationship with his employees. The dog never suffered physically, though, and Reynolds attitude never changed.

There was a Howard DGA in the fleet we modified with a spray system and a primitive vapor sensor. The aircraft was rented to the University of Hawaii for cloud research. How could I know I'd be involved in later, more sophisticated efforts to determine what events occurred in clouds and how man could control them? Barnes would sometimes fly a Stearman through clouds, spraying their interiors with sea water from the spray material tank, the object being to make rain fall. Silver iodide wasn't in vogue then.

"What do you see when you do that?" I asked him.

"Nothing. When I look back, it's hard to say. It seems different. The cloud appears to be somewhat lighter behind the airplane. But I don't know if that's because of the salt water I release, or just that the airplane disturbs the cloud," he said. Years later l would ask a cloud physicist a similar question about atmospheric research and its worth.

"We go where the money is!" he replied.

We experienced a near-disaster in the hangar one day. A sheet of aluminum stood behind the rudder of a Stearman at an angle just right for reflecting the direct rays of a mid-afternoon sun through the open doors, directly on the rudder. It was like a hot sun through a magnifying glass focused on paper. The fabric started to burn.

We extinguished it quickly and recovered the rudder. Nitrate dope burns readily and violently when it gets a good start. Butyrate dope burns much more slowly. I had learned that as a kid building model airplanes.

117

A *Stearman came in for unscheduled repairs to its right lower wing panel leading edge. The pilot hit his flagman at the end of a pass while spraying pineapples. The accident resulted in a head-sized dent in the wing panel; the poor flagman was rendered hors de combat.*

"Oh well, he was only a Chinaman," our Hawaiian handyman observed. We repaired the wing and re-placed the flagman.

One night, one of the pilots — McCarthey — showed a date, one of the more enterprising ladies from Honolulu, around the hangar. She told him she had never had sex in an airplane and he obliged her in a Stinson L-5, parked in the hangar.

The airplane was owned by a pineapple planta-tion manager on Lanai. He had engaged Cheng and myself to recover it. Never mind the masked-off trim stripe along the fuselage which we had painstakingly laid out and would paint the next day. McCarthey simply cut the masking tape, opened the door and the pair climbed in where her desires were satisfied — presumably.

We didn't discuss how the feat was accomplished in the meager confines of the L-5's cabin. Only the rework it cost Cheng and myself.

Honolulu Airport bears no resemblance whatso-ever, after it was expanded, to old John Rodgers Air-port. Its appearance then was far removed from today's Honolulu International Airport.

Although the airport was very active then with the flights of United and Pan Am; the arrivals and departures of lines flying the Korean Airlift; the inter-island flights of Hawaiian Airlines and Inter-Island Airlines (now Aloha), it was a community of close association. Everyone knew or had a good idea of what everyone else was doing. The grapevine worked well.

However much we disliked our manager we couldn't fault him for neglecting the Stearmans. They came in from their stations on the other islands on a regular basis for inspections. We always had a spare, mechanically and aesthetically clean, ready and waiting to be flown back so spraying operations wouldn't be delayed while the other was in-shop.

Agriculture chemicals can cause considerable stress on fuselage tubing, spray nozzles and booms and controls. It was hard, dirty work crawling into a fuselage to remove accumulations of dried chemicals, residues of dusting materials and stubborn stains, from structural members.

There was plenty of engine and fabric work, maintaining material pumps and systems, keeping hoppers and gates working at top efficiency. And there was a modicum of engineering and design (the exhaust stack was one example), especially when a standard Stearman was converted to a spraying or dusting airplane.

Meanwhile, Carson kept me busy moonlighting; the extra money was always welcomed. Once we disassembled a Taylorcraft and crated it for shipment to the Philippine Islands. The two-hundred dollars I received for my share of the project was a godsend.

Carson tells me Trans-Ocean is looking for an assistant crew chief and urges me to apply for the position. My license and heavy aircraft experience I acquired on the Mainland influence Collins, the station maintenance chief, to sign me on. I suspect Carson wielded some influence, too. I'm glad to be back into heavy aircraft maintenance with better pay....

Karen and Steve stirred and opened sleepy eyes and I attended to their needs. There was no meal service on non-scheduled airlines; we had to eat from the box lunches I bought before boarding at Honolulu. There was milk for kids and coffee for adults aboard, though. We had flown into a new day.

My kids finished eating and began to amuse themselves with a battered, dog-eared magazine. The clouds were getting thicker, an indication we were getting closer to land. We also started to encounter some mild turbulence.

I lit another cigarette and sat smoking, contemplating the grey clouds through the window. The airplane rose gently, but settled when the auto-pilot calmed its upward surge....

Trans-Ocean and the night Vargas and I nearly flew a DC-4. We taxied it from Hickam Field, where it had been off-loaded, onto the long connecting runway that was built when John Rodgers was expanded to

120

become Honolulu Airport. We rumble on in the dark, Vargas in the left seat, all four engines running.

A nice firm wind on our nose; the airspeed indicator needle quivering between fifty and sixty-miles per hour. The slight bumps of the wheels on the runway's surface become weaker and we can feel a subtle lightness in the airplane. I glance over at Vargas who is looking at me.

Hurriedly scanning the flight deck and controls I move the flap lever to full 'UP' from its one-quarter extended position. Vargas pulling the throttles back; the airplane settling down and compressing the landing gear's oleo struts.

Trans-Ocean and the monkey flights and those unscheduled yellow fever shots. The nights we work late and sleep in the hangar to meet an early morning flight.

Seeing the frightful glare in the night as a Navy PV-2 flies into a peak in the Waianaie Mountains after a long, over-ocean flight from Guadalcanal. The irony of the crew flying such a long way to die.

Wondering why the fuel didn't ignite when a DC-6's wing tank over-flowed and I fell on the wet wing while scrambling to shut off the fuel hose's nozzle. Vargas believing the hangar's loft is haunted, but doesn't know why or what type of haunt.

The arrivals and departures of Seaboard & Western's, Slick Airways' and Flying Tiger's flights on the

Korean Airlift.

The airlift gradually slowing and talk of layoffs. The tight aviation community in the Islands and few, if any, vacancies for long-time employment.

The decision to return once more to the Mainland where there's work to be had and broader horizons for the kids. Island life is confined to shores with little opportunity to expand young minds.

Beyond an island's beaches, the sea horizon is barren of any future. If there were no positions available, one had to wait until someone vacated one for any reason; and then one had to move fast to apply for a vacancy.

For kids graduating from high school, there wasn't a wealth of opportunities for immediate employment or a viable future. There is only so much to go around.

There was also, for my kids, the matter of having the solid base of grandparents and family to reley on in the event of future, potential problems.

We gradually descended deeper into roiling clouds encountering more severe turbulence, shaking me out of my thoughts.

I checked the kids' seat belts and Karen, suddenly and without warning, vomits, but mostly on the tray she's using as a drawing board. Thankfully, her dress remains unsoiled. By the time we cleaned up she is settled. No. 754 has broken out of the clouds.

San Francisco Bay is under us; the Golden Gate Bridge and an inbound freighter pass below our wings.

I wondered if my tool box is on it. It's a wooden, Air Force issue box that I found in a corner of an empty hangar at John Rodgers Airport, before it became Honolulu Airport. It was well-made and serves me very well, still.

The kids' eyes were huge with astonishment at the spectacle spread out below us: The ships and docks, the vastness of the bay and the tall buildings of San Francisco poking up into the low-hanging clag of broken clouds.

Although the flight from Honolulu was lengthy and monotonous (about twelve hours), the kids seemed not to mind. And why not? They slept practically the entire flight.

They were all eyes now, peering out the window while I give them a brief lecture, pointing out various objects below. Karen's stomach seemed to have settled since she didn't react to the maneuvers of the airplane as the captain guided it onto final approach.

Privately I admitted that the scene was vastly different than Honolulu Airport. Back there on Oahu the sun was probably just peeking over the Koolau Mountains through early morning showers. Island weather makes it a good place to work: A person will always be warm, never to work in freezing rain or falling snow. The only snow in The Islands falls on Mauna Kea on the Big Island.

In honesty, although there were many advantages in living in the benign climate we had just left. I found myself looking forward to the change of seasons. There is much to be said about diversity, even to weather.

No. 754's tires scruff the runway at Oakland in baritone protests of sudden acceleration.

We collected our baggage and arranged for a taxi to take us across the bay to San Francisco Airport to catch a United flight east. There would be an overnight stay in Chicago and on to Washington, D.C., the following morning. The United DC6 is much faster than Trans Oceans DC4.

Thirty-five years would pass until I saw the Islands once more — Carson never.

Book II

My Left Mag' is Out

9

Snow is For Skiers,
Ice For Cocktails....

The postal creed forswears faint hearted mail carriers who cannot keep their appointed rounds. Sleet, wind, rain, hail, snow, thunderstorms and snapping dogs must be taken in stride. As the play must go on, so must the mail be delivered.

Environmental conditions, but not the dogs, are shared by aircraft mechanics with mailmen, especially those working in line maintenance. The difference is, mechanics work forever under the watchful and unforgiving eye of the clock. Mail carriers need only to trudge over routes designed for completion within an eight-hour period. Mail carriers rarely work overtime, but mechanics often do. Paying overtime is eluded by the simple expedient of hiring temporary mail handlers. Mechanic temporaries are unknown.

When departure time is drawing near and there's still much to be done or a heavy inspection is scheduled for completion on a given date, maintenance personnel must bite the bullet. Very often, weather has a direct influence on whether the baleful stare of the clock is to be satisfied or not.

There are any number of reasons why an airplane isn't rolled into a cozy, warm hangar if it's necessary to clear up a flight-reported discrepancy or do routine servicing. Hangar space may not be available, for one thing. For another, a 'squawk' could be corrected in the time required to open doors, put the airplane in, work off the squawk and roll the airplane out. Or, the nature of the squawk might require testing and adjustment in a clear area.[33]

It would be unthinkable to run an engine in a hangar, although turbine engines may be 'spooled' up for a number of reasons. Combustion, of course isn't initiated. I don't know of an instance where a turbine engine, whether pure jet or turbo-prop when combustion has been mistakenly initiated, but I'm sure that has happened somewhere. But piston engines have inadvertently been started many times. These incidents are not planned but occur due to inexperience, inattention, or mis-communication. When they happen, such events are impressive, to say the least. Engines are simply not run in hangars; it just isn't the thing to do. It's dangerous to personnel, shop equipment and propellers, Also, prop wash blows things around, totally disrupting shop layout and routines.

A good acquaintance who owned a maintenance facility on old Harbor Field, at Baltimore, Maryland, came very close to not only losing his portly stomach, but other body parts and his life, too. The engine on a Howard DGA was accidently started with 'Turdy' standing in front of it with his back literally to the wall. A whirling propeller has no mercy for anything or anybody that chances to be in its path.

He froze in abject terror in position, desperately sucking his gut in with the prop's tips slicing the air within inches of his shins and knees. He said afterwards: "I could see my reflection in the prop spinner but it was a solid blur, like a blotch of dirt would make as the spinner rotated." He survived the ordeal but the brush with death lingered for a time.

My experience wasn't quite as dramatic but I can live it again and again, in my memory, and in some respects, it had some humor to it.

Four of my crew, myself included, was completing an engine change on a 749 Constellation that the day shift had started. All that remained was clearing up loose ends: Control checks, electrical system checks, cleaning and checking cowling. There was an inspection to do on the fuel injection system for leaks. Meanwhile, the balance of the crew was doing an airframe inspection. The airplane was scheduled for an early morning departure.

I climbed up on the outboard side of the newly-overhauled No. 2 engine, to begin checking the fuel lines and nozzles on the top cylinders. My feet were on a cowl support frame, my left hand holding onto another higher on the engine. I was literally draped over the R-3350 Wright, with a flashlight in my right hand. We needed to turn the engine through with fuel pressure in the injection system. The spark plugs had been installed, their ignition leads were attached.

Rodgers cleared the prop and guarded the area immediately in front of it. Borden stood on a work stand in the nacelle at the rear of the engine with his head and shoulders in the accessory section, to inspect the fuel system there. Cummings was at the engineer's station in the cockpit to operate the necessary engine controls. I heard the boost pump come on and the order to start turning the engine. It was relayed to Cummings by the leadman, Rasher, standing at the stairs to the cockpit.

The starter dogs engaged with the usual thump, the big prop began turning. Instead of turning smoothly, though, the engine hesitated several times through two full revolutions of the prop and I began wondering why and then found out. It was trying to start — and did! All eighteen cylinders burst into life, the prop almost instantly became a gleaming disc of whirling metal. Almost just as instantly I dropped my flashlight where it rattled down amongst the top cylinders and grabbed the upper cowl support with the empty hand.

There was no where to go; my only recourse was to keep a desperate grip on the cowl support. And I swear, the support's flanges were threatened with being deformed because of my death grip. The blast of the prop wash seemed to be trying to take me with it over the wing. I was draped over a growling mass of parts moving at high speed and an awful thought flashed through my mind: What if a cylinder head separated from a cylinder barrel? I would be propelled against the No. 1 engine with the head firmly imbedded in my chest.

There's no experience in the world like that unless it's being shot at with a 75-millimeter gun. Thinking about it afterwards, visualizing those pistons lunging up and down in the cylinders with practically your entire body laying on them, made me tremble. The possibility, however remote, was there that a hail of shrapnel from broken cylinder heads would reduce me to shreds. I have seen instances of a separated cylinder head blasted through heavy cowling when metal failure occurred, leaving an enormous, jagged, gaping hole.

It seemed the engine roared for minutes, the sound amplified horrendously within the confines of the closed hangar. But it was actually only seconds. Cummings alertly slammed the mixture control into idle-cutoff and flipped the boost pump switch off when he saw the tachometer jump to life and heard the engine start. Later, he said the tachometer needle climbed to 1,700 r.p.m's. The throttle had been advanced to assure positive fuel flow and pressure to the fuel lines and nozzle connections.

The gale of the prop wash swept the area clean behind the wing. Shop towels, several empty cardboard boxes and some articles of personal clothing were blown against the hangar's back wall. A small cloud of dust and fine debris from the hangar floor accentuated the general scene of flying objects. Coulter, who was visually inspecting the belly of the fuselage, later said: "When I heard the engine start I started running to the tail. When that blast of air hit me in the back I just let it push me along!"

There was no damage or injuries. I climbed down from my hazardous perch while the cause of the engine start was sorted out.

The night foreman, understandably upset, to coin an understatement, demanded to know "What the hell happened?" and, expectedly, read us the riot act. The leadman, of course, suffered the brunt of his tirade.

The answer to the foreman's question was that the day shift had failed to tell us the ignition system disconnect plug at the firewall was still disconnected when we assumed completion of the engine change. Deprived of its grounding circuit through the wiring to the ignition switch in the cockpit, the double magneto was actually alive when we started cranking the engine.

From that time on, a turn-over form was required to be completed by the crew leaving the job, detailing what had been accomplished and, especially, where the previous crew had stopped work. There was also a brief verbal exchange of details between the former crew's lead man and the new crew's lead man.

Hangar space and the economics of opening huge doors to admit an airplane are contributing factors which help dictate where line maintenance is to be accomplished. It's one thing to maneuver several Boeing 737's in and out of a hangar, if a dimensionally compatible hangar is available; it's another to shift twin-engine commuter types or even smaller general aviation aircraft.

In any case, opening hangar doors of any size imposes stress to various degrees on a company's operating budget, never mind labor costs involved. And so, line maintenance mechanics look on working in severe weather conditions as a way of life. They become, more or less, seasoned to the whims of the outdoors, although they may not always like it.

Nevertheless, it was not unusual to ignore crass economics by opening hangar doors, close down heat and push an airliner into the hangar to load passengers, after having snow brushed off of its surfaces. It accommodated the passengers from boarding in a snowfall and allowed the airplane to remain relatively cool to prevent snow from sticking on the skin. Thus, the loaded airplane could be taxied with minimum time to the take off position. What snow accumulated on the skin, from hangar to takeoff, would be disposed of during the initial takeoff run.

The same method was used in our corporate operation frequently. Although hangar heat was turned down when the operation closed for the night, the airplane would be much warmer than outside air in the morning. And so the hangar doors were opened completely with hangar heat shut off. This afforded the airplane's skin to cool even more. The passengers were loaded, the airplane pushed out, engines started and immediate taxi to takeoff occurred. We sacrificed spending money to reheat the hangar in the interest of safety.

I knew a Boeing 707 mechanic who was unique in his attitude toward inclement weather, especially cold weather. He thrived on winter weather and always had such an optimistic, cheery outlook he tended to be disgusting. His normally friendly, outgoing nature would surge to such unbelievable heights of euphoria in cold weather his companions tended to look at him askance.

Their remarks indicated serious doubts as to whether 'his biscuits were done'. He constantly encouraged them to persevere and enjoy what he perceived as invigorating. But they all rejected being brainwashed into believing the good life lay in frigid winds and temperatures, ice, snow and slush. The mechanic was of Norwegian extraction, so his compatibility with cold weather extremes was reluctantly understood — although pitied.

Almost without exception general aviation and corporate aviation mechanics work in heated, well-lighted hangars simply because of the nature of those fields.[34] The former are providing a service to customers, much as an automobile garage would, and to do so on a ramp wouldn't be conducive to a fixed base operator's success.

Many private aircraft owners take a dim view of not hangaring their beloved aircraft while work is in progress. And rightfully so. If an engine is opened outside there's a chance of dust and grit drifting into its internal cavities, or components being damaged by wind or rain. Also, it's expensive for a mechanic to walk back and forth to get parts or hardware or tools. That's time-consuming.

Corporate aircraft are very expensive, highly sophisticated and customized; they're normally kept in secure, privately-owned hangars. It would be unthinkable to not work on them there. At any rate, both groups of mechanics enjoy more comfortable working conditions than their counterparts in the air carrier field, in line maintenance.

Working conditions in winter at Washington National Airport were the worst I've ever experienced. Although outside air temperatures seldom dropped below fifteen-degrees, the air seemed colder; a raw, penetrating, bone-racking chill that saturated our bodies to the very core. We attributed the always high humidity to be the leading contributing factor to our discomfort. The well-insulated 'jump' suits mechanics — and others who work outside — wear on winter ramps now, were unknown then.

We had to change cylinders often, not so much on the Pratt & Whitney R-2000's on the DC-4's or the Wright R-1820's on the DC-3's. It was the Wright R-3350's on the Constellations that demanded the most attention.

Frequently, the reason was the 3350's valve seats had a propensity for 'floating'. Changing one of those cylinders ran the course from burn to freeze. Invariably, a cylinder change occurred on the ramp and they chose to fail in cold weather. It was bare-handed work entirely.

By the time the rocker arm covers and rocker arms were re-moved, the cylinder hold-down nuts un-safetied and all the necessary baffling removed, the engine had cooled considerably. We could cope with the initial heat well enough, but when the cylinder was lifted off, the distress began.

An overhauled cylinder had to be set over the link rod — the piston would already be in the cylinder — and the piston pin slid through the piston and link rod. Then the cylinder hold-down nuts would be installed torqued and safetied. Next followed the easy part, and that word is used somewhat loosely. Baffling, push rod housings and the balance of the installation, the rocker arms and covers and, ignition leads.

The very worst operation was forcing hands and wrists between the new cylinder and its neighbors to safety-wire the hold-down nuts. On a physical basis the result was angry red scrapes and scratches on the backs of hands and wrists from wearing on the edge of a cylinder barrel's baffles. Whatever the medical explanation for very cold skin being more susceptible to that abuse, as opposed to very warm skin, is left to the good physicians. We only knew it required a couple of days for our hands to recover. Cracks in the ends of our fingers longer.

Most of us wore 'long johns', warm trousers and shirts. Hooded, lightweight cotton shirts were popular, worn under a warm but not bulky jacket; gloves of course, when you could wear them. Bouts with bursitis were common. The frequency and intensity of the miserable attacks of aching joints fluctuated in direct proportion to the rise and fall of temperatures. We welcomed working off flight discrepancies on hot engines and the one night every week on an aircraft in the heavy inspection dock in the warmth of the hangar.

The wet snow that fell — and doubtless still does — didn't help the movement of aircraft from the terminal to the hangar ramp, and vice versa. The state-of-the-art snow removal wasn't as advanced as we know it today. Consequently, much difficulty was experienced in shifting aircraft.[35]

There were occasions when we had to use a combination of tow tractor and engine power to budge an aircraft when its tires froze to the ramp. Taxiing could be hazardous because of deep, frozen ruts and great chunks of ice on the ramps. Nose wheel tires especially suffered from cuts; brakes and throttles had to be used delicately, as steering aides.

One night Coulter returned to the hangar visibly shaken. He had towed a Lockheed Constellation to the terminal, rather than taxiing it because of the frozen, rutted pavement.

"You wouldn't believe what I almost did," he said.

"Try me...I'd believe anything you did or almost did," I retorted.

"I'm serious...I almost ran over a drunken soldier," he explained. "He was passed out on the ramp. I just barely got the 'Connie' stopped in time to miss him. Simmons was riding the airplane's brakes, but he couldn't see the guy and I couldn't turn to yell at him or wave my flashlight for him to start braking.

"When I turned the wheel and started braking the tug, it started sliding and went a little sideways. I got stopped at an angle to the guy. If I hadn't been able to stop, the nose wheel of the Connie or the tug would have squashed him."

The airport police happened to see the incident and took the drunken soldier away. We never found out how he came to pass out on the ramp or how long he'd been there. If the tug or the Constellation hadn't run over him he undoubtedly would have frozen to death.

The super DC-3's in the fleet were characteristically tricky to taxi, even on dry pavement. Snow-covered or icy ramps and taxiways compounded the trait.

Super DC-3's were derivatives of the DC-3, with stretched fuselages and wheel well doors, and were re-engined with higher horsepower Wright 1820 engines. As a result, they were faster than their parent and pleasing to the eye. Their squared-off wing tips, fins and rudders and ventral fins, contributed to the esthetics of their overall appearance.

The engine installations made them a delight to service and maintain. The engine mounts were extended to maintain center of gravity integrity when the airplane was loaded. Doing so, resulted in accessory sections being spacious beyond a mechanic's wildest dreams. A small mechanic could clamber into the accessory section and comfortably change a starter or generator or correct some other problem. A larger man easily could insert his head and shoulders and still have ample room to maneuver his arms and hands.

But that lengthening of the mounts could cause alarm and embarrassment when taxiing the airplane. Empty, it was extremely tail-light; consequently, a sudden application of the brakes could present a hair-raising panorama of the ramp when the nose suddenly descended from the normal, nose-high attitude. We learned very quickly to manipulate the brakes with uncommon delicacy, as though eggs were between the soles of our shoes and the brake pedals. Especially on ice or snow.[36]

Probably there's a medical explanation why skin cracks and

135

becomes raw more readily in cold weather. But crack and abrade it does, especially on fingertips and knuckles. These conditions are irritating, painful and take a long time to heal.

Constantly using hands and fingers to do the hundred and one things mechanics must do in a day's work means constant flexing of skin, which retards the healing process. It's difficult, if not almost impossible, while wearing gloves to start a 10-32 nut, or attach a ring terminal to a circuit breaker. Tractor mechanics who habitually wield massive wrenches on easily accessible — and huge — nuts and bolts can and probably should wear gloves.

On aircraft and engines the order of the day is nooks and crannies. There are recesses where the object of attention is often out of sight. A mechanic, therefore, is hard put to insert two cold, stiff fingers into a crevice, stretched to the limit, while trying to manipulate a wrench. Or even recesses that are fairly open. That's when a mechanic has to have fingertips as sensitive as a safe cracker's. These predicaments are more common than uncommon.

Since working with cut, chapped and aching hands also increases the ever-present possibility of a wrench slithering into the depths of corners, clusters of wiring, groups of instruments, or fearful restrictions of engine installations an intangible presents itself: As far as I know, there are no statistics addressing the amount of lost time fumbling and trying to work with club-like hands, or searching for dropped tools. I venture to say, though, it is probably substantial.

Maintaining aircraft in bitter cold makes for a huge proving ground for hand lotions advertised to contend with chapped hands cross-hatched with cuts and cracks. I've tried several concoctions, and I can't speak for men I've worked with. But, in spite of the protestations of advertisements, most didn't measure up to the propaganda. However, I wasn't a fisherman in the North Atlantic either. Pure lanolin, I discovered, has the best healing properties. I used it often, but wore a surgeon's gloves after applying it, to preserve it against wipe-off and keep it where it would be the most effective.

Mechanics have prevailed in adverse working conditions since the beginning of aviation, using common sense, desperate measures and ingenuity to accomplish what they had to do. Tales by contemporaries who worked in Alaska only reinforced my total revulsion for working in climates colder than the 'temperate' latitudes.

I have a friend who was in Army aviation, based in Alaska. He revealed a simple method of warming equipment for a new day of flight operations.

"Many times, we actually built a small fire under the ground power units to get them warm, " he said. Whatever is necessary....!

Another thing: Draining oil from engines at the end of the day for overnight storage in a warm area, as a routine activity, didn't strike me as reasonable either. It's difficult enough doing that now and then without making a habit of it. Also, continually thawing frosted spark plugs in lower, above zero climates, — never mind doing it in sub-zero conditions — doesn't need to be on anyone's agenda.

Once I refused a — questionable — generous offer by the owner of a fleet of bush planes while I was on a hunting trip to Alaska. He mostly operated from a narrow landing strip about twenty-miles from Fairbanks. There were no hangars on the strip so he tied his air-planes down along the highway that lay between his house and the airstrip.

"I'll pay you twenty-three dollars an hour to start," he declared.

"I can't find anyone with experience, and I have several major jobs to do."

Instantly, several thoughts raced through my mind. I would spend long hours in a cold shop and on a colder flight line. There would be little if any help and parts procurement would be difficult and nerve-wracking. Given the well-known propensities of characters in bush aviation to disregard the niceties of proper maintenance, also caused considerable concern too. In the final analysis, it was the prospect of working in bitter, permeating cold in glacial-like conditions that swayed me. If one has to work, his environment should be reasonably amiable.

From all indications his operation bordered on the cutting edge of an exercise in minimum maintenance versus maximum utility of his fleet, a scenario completely understandable to him, but just as unacceptable to me. When I told him I held an Inspection Authorization endorsement, he positively drooled and began making plans for me.

If the wrong operator has the right captive I.A., he'll exert pressure on the I.A. to keep his aircraft in license, and that will be accomplished. That's called 'Parker 51' maintenance. Conversely, if the wrong operator has the wrong I.A., the association could be very brief. In any event, those types of operations are always available if any I.A. or mechanic is attracted to one. At least one's neck could be stretched in comparatively warmer conditions, if a mechanic chooses to exposes his or her neck in such an exercise.

Without hesitation or any qualms whatsoever I politely declined his offer. The appealing fringe benefits of enjoying Alaska's wonderfully alluring hunting, fishing and overall enchanting environment, if time allowed, would have to be sacrificed. Besides, considering the more expensive facet of living in Alaska where practically everything needed to be shipped in, the wage he offered me would have been academic.

Circumstances often arise that dictate major work must be done away from home base: An engine failure, airframe damage, or perhaps heavy repairs or maintenance. The airplane simply cannot be moved, let alone fly, and reconditioning must be done in place. Such incidents aren't uncommon, and often the work is accomplished in adverse weather conditions. It's is then that common sense and ingenuity prevail. The work scope and personnel must be protected from the elements. Some un-informed observers may wonder about the methods used.

When one of our Viscounts slid off an icy runway into a snowbank, the No. 2 prop and engine were damaged. The airport lacked the most basic — even primitive — of hangars. The weather was an intriguing combination of brisk wind and near-zero conditions; the wind-chill factor, of course, was alarming.

That left two options: The airplane could become a memorial until the weather moderated, or a shelter built in which to change the engine and prop. Understandably, the latter alternative was chosen. Airplanes need to fly to be productive.

Local carpenters built a simple, very basic wooden frame around the engine area, complete with a peaked roof, and covered the entire structure with canvas. Portable ground heaters provided a liveable environment for the mechanics, although they suffered somewhat when the end was opened for the hoist to remove and replace the engine and prop. But overall, they were able to work in relative comfort and the airplane was ferried home within four days for detailed completion.

At another airline I worked for, one of the Boeing 707's developed a crack in a fuel pump mount in one wing's fuel compartment. Such failures can be expected in aging aircraft. Since hangar space was occupied by another 707 in heavy check — and it was the only hangar — the repair had to be done outside. Doing it in the bone-cracking chill of a Denver January gave pause for much concern. Intensive measures had to be taken not only for the mechanics' protection but to provide a suitable environment to conduct the repair, and allow the tank sealant to cure properly.

An enormous tarpaulin was rigged that encompassed the working area. It stretched over the wing from the leading to the trailing edges with both ends touching the ramp and weighted. To complete the enclosure, 'drapes' of canvas were secured to the underside of the wing, both inboard and outboard. The corners were clamped shut, except for one with a flap for access.

Under the circumstances the tarp's edges were remarkably well-sealed against the frigid temperatures and wind. A large ground heater positioned outside provided ample heat through a duct exiting in the 'tent' flap. By the time the mechanics had assembled their tools and other equipment necessary for the repair, the tent was warm enough to shed jackets and cold suits.

Before long the work space assumed a comfy atmosphere complete with a radio and the mechanics' work progressed smoothly. I suspected they were downright ecstatic to work in the tent away from the constant scrutiny of their foreman and leadman. They quickly developed resentment at anyone not a member of their exclusive 'club' entering their cozy habitat. I was in the engineering department and needed to visit them for consultation from time to time. They accepted me, but I always kept my visits as brief as possible.

Between the time they started work removing and replacing the faulted fuel pump mount, the wing's lower skin and interior were nicely warmed; consequently, the tank sealant cured under near-ideal conditions. There were no fuel leaks when the tank was serviced for tests.

I've often marveled at how ground crews and some pilots who were mechanics in their own right, long before my beginnings in aviation, managed to repair and service aircraft with cold weather ground equipment that was the crudest of the crude by today's standards.

How did the early flying explorers and their crews — Byrd for example — cope with seemingly insurmountable below zero weather conditions? Surely the oil was drained from engines and kept warm overnight, maybe even in sleeping bags. Did they have little tents pre-made to drape over engines and heat the frigid, cold-soaked metal with petite gasoline burning stoves?

How much fumbling was done with gloved hands when maintenance was necessary and the danger of warm hands sticking to cold metal was always present? We all know they found a way. The distasteful alternative of being marooned on a polar ice cap is a powerful incentive to inventiveness. Aviation's chronicles give short shrift to behind the scenes maintenance in cold weather conditions more suitable for furry animals.

Today's mechanics may think it unbelievable that wages after World War II ranged anywhere from three-hundred fifty dollars a month to six-hundred dollars a month, depending on where one worked and for whom in the 1950's. That was below modern poverty levels. But the dollar went much farther then, a dubious consolation indeed. It was still expensive to buy warm clothes for outside working conditions during winter, though.

Because an extra dollar or so was welcomed, many mechanics were 'moonlighters' of opportunity, working where an extra hand was needed, free-lancing or part-time. I contracted (verbally) with a businessman who owned a Lockheed Lodestar. The carburetor on the left engine needed to be overhauled. In spite of my abhorrence for cold weather I agreed to do the change. The leading attraction was the extra money — I didn't need the experience.

He owned a small manufacturing company and bought the airplane for demonstration tours of his equipment and products. An idea that never got off the ground.

The airplane was always parked outside because no hangar was available and he was obviously reluctant to build one. As to the carburetor, from all indications it had failed its mission because its internal diaphragms had hardened with age and idleness. The airplane had not flown for nearly one year before the man bought it.

I removed the carburetor for overhaul one December day when the temperature would have been approximately twenty-degrees, if a fifteen m.p.h. wind hadn't been blowing. My perch was on top of the engine where I could get full benefit from the freezing wind. What should have been an elapsed time required to remove the carburetor of one and one-half hours, nearly tripled because I frequently paused to warm my cold-soaked body and hands.

It was virtually impossible to work with gloves. The fear of dropping a washer or nut into the depths of the engine compartment or worse, the diffuser section, was always present, even with bare hands. That would have meant removing the engine, and the prospect forced me to work in slow motion. Numb fingers tend to feel and move like Chinese chopsticks and one works within a performance anxiety spectrum. In other words, one tends to become as nervous as a hummingbird and the prospect of becoming the patron saint of fuck-ups is horribly prominent in one's thoughts!

I removed the carburetor without mishap and sent it away for overhaul. In January I re-installed it, again without mishap, but again, in similar weather conditions. The one-hundred seventy-five dollars I charged was questionable compensation, all things considered. I spent it prudently; the money represented a surge of hard-earned, almost elegant opulence.

In retrospect, the development of airplanes through the 1930's and after World War II was accompanied with the development of ground support equipment: ground power units and particularly, heating and de-icing equipment. Time was when passengers had to suffer miserably until engines were started to provide cabin heat. Those circumstances had to be addressed and the development of gasoline fueled cabin heaters resulted. They were accompanied by efficient ground heaters that provided forced, warm air into fuselages.

But, in spite of those accomplishments to control — or, at the least cope — with the vagaries of brutal winter weather during ground operations, it would be impossible for mechanics to conduct maintenance outside, in any other mode than one-on-one with whatever weather has to offer. And accept it.

Philosophically, I like to think there is more to a mechanic's acceptance to working in grievous conditions other than the need to earn a wage. If he or she is, indeed, a professional mechanic. From my perspective it has been an inherent, indefinable dedication to aircraft that has provided impetus. If that opinion lacks credence to the reader, consider this illustration of passionate dedication.

During support operations of scientific research programs in the Antarctic, a Navy LC-130 Lockheed Hercules crashed on an ice dome, at 10,548-feet in January 1975. Extensive damage required that the center and starboard outer wing sections be replaced. Two engines also had to be replaced. It goes without saying that other repairs needed to be addressed when a crash of that magnitude is considered.

After viewing the report of the salvage operation I cannot help but admire that Lockheed/Navy group for their perserverence and commitment. Reportedly, average temperatures were 22-degrees below zero, not to forget working in bulky clothes and gloves — on solid ice and snow. The Hercules was flown off the ice in 45-days, 30-days ahead of schedule.

In the later years of my career I moved inside to rewrite Boeing maintenance manuals for a start-up airline. After that program was completed, I was assigned to structural engineering. Sometimes the position required that I go outside — but briefly!

I shamelessly found comfort in this thought: I wouldn't have to work out in miserable, wintry weather as a matter of course. That wasn't likely to happen, if at all preventable — and it was!

BOEING P-26 - The last of Boeing's fighter line, a total of 136 were produced for the Army Air Corps. The 18the Fighter Group was equipped with the picturesque fighters at Wheeler Field. Although P-26s did not participate in the Battle off Hickam Field and Pearl Harbor, some saw combat in the Philippine Islands. Unfortunately, they were outclassed in the face of more advanced Japanese aircraft.   Photo' Courtesy The Boeing Company Archives.

CURTIS P-40 - Succeeding the P-36 as the Air Corps' front line fighter, it first saw action in the Battle of Hickman Field and Pearl Harbor. This example, a B Model, reputedly took part in the battles. It is displayed at the main gate at Wheeler Field, Oahu. The number of kills indicated could be called into question since information is sketchy at best about the number of Japanese aircraft shot down during the battles, or how many U.S...... fighters were airborne. Photo' by the Author

10

Turbines and
Transition....

I suppose we were all in a mild state of shock as we walked
around the airplane. The differences in its overall form and
bulk contrasted with the airplanes we had been working with
before this one arrived. It had the usual wings, empennage and
landing gear any decent airplane would have, but still, dissimilarities
were apparent. The airplane was parked in front of Capital Airline's
main maintenance hangar at Washington National Airport when my

crew and I came on duty. It seemed to be almost meekly awaiting approval of our critical appraisal.

The airplane's fuselage appeared to be more round than a DC-4's; the nose section was more aerodynamically attractive. Aft, there was no delicate taper to the tail cone. The blend to the termination of the fuselage was almost abrupt, rather businesslike. The horizontal stabilizers had pronounced dihedral. All-in-all the fuselage was relatively clean and it had tri-cycle landing gear. But it was the four engines and propellers that were the focal points of our attention.

The intimate configurations of radial engine installations and three-bladed propellers were absent. Absent also was the solid, round bulk of nacelles and cowlings wrapped around a radius studded with cylinders and there were no oil stains trailing toward the aft end of the nacelles. Instead, there were four slender aluminum tubes, their diameters barely exceeding the thickness of the wings' airfoils. They resembled massive, shiny cigars with the tapered end culminating at the propellers. The nacelles were so clean and graceful it seemed indecent to believe they housed engines. Modestly proportioned shiny metal plates on each nacelle with the letters RR in black finish, aristocratically proclaimed the engines to be made by Rolls Royce. The Vickers Viscounts had finally started to arrive. We had heard rumors they were coming and one day, the first — the substance of our concentration — appeared quietly, without fanfare. This airplane simply materialized, it seemed.

Most of us had heard and read about ram jets and the turbine-powered aircraft the Air Force was acquiring. But, at least as far as I was concerned and I'm sure there were many others, exposure to a turbine engine in the flesh wasn't a part of our mechanical experience.

The Viscounts had Rolls Royce Darts — turboprops.

Sir Frank Whittle pioneered the development of the turbine engine which, like rockets, operates on the same principal: Cancellation of pressure at one point of a pressurized vessel. An inflated balloon operates on the same principal, when the neck is released to allow air to escape. The vessel moves because there's still force exerted on the remainder of the containment's internal surfaces. Whittle applied the theory in his new aircraft engine.[43]

We may have the Chinese to thank for early research on the principle of rocket thrust: They are attributed to developing rockets centuries ago. But like many innovations and new ideas history has chronicled, the practical application of the cancellation of pressure theory required some time to develop. Perhaps it's possible the Chinese who fired the first rocket didn't even think about why it soared into the skies when the fuse was lit. Maybe that person made a firecracker and one end wasn't closed tightly and that started a thought. But shooting off rockets had to have some practicality: Amusement perhaps?

As we stood there on the ramp there was little comment. Our thoughts were private as we gazed with a mixture of awe, perhaps apprehension and certainly wonder. Especially, studying the sleek cylinders of gleaming aluminum nacelles housing the engines. We could only speculate what the engines looked like. We knew they were a propulsion system of new dimensions but old concepts. But a feeling of familiarity reigned in the huge, four-bladed Dowty-Rotol propellers mounted on the noses of those mysterious engines. After all, the time-honored radial engines were so equipped.

There was something else embodied in this aircraft: It made us privy to another event in aviation's continuing evolution. Although it never entered our minds at the time, at least it surely didn't mine, Rolls Royce was in transition. England's respected engine builder was crossing a frontier into a new age. No longer would its assembly lines produce engines that had figured largely in the effectiveness of Allied combat aircraft used in World War II. The epoch of high-powered, liquid-cooled piston engines was rapidly drawing to a close.

I likened the Darts to thoroughbreds as compared to the ponderous workhorse radial engines. Mostly, we had theoretical knowledge of how turbine engines developed power. Several of us were designated to immediately begin in-house training, not only on the Darts but the Viscounts, as well.

With the arrival of the Viscounts we had stepped over the threshold of a new age in air transportation. Being mechanics and not prophets we gave little if any thought to the realization that piston engines, as a means of powering transport and military aircraft, were also on a threshold. It was the beginning of the phase-out of radial engines and the Viscount could be held largely responsible.

The type wasn't the world's first turbine-powered transport. That was the Tudor 8 — which never flew![44]

Vickers' Viscount made the world's first turbine-powered commercial air service flight from London to Paris's Le Bourget Field in only fifty-seven minutes. The twenty-six passengers had to be enthralled with the quiet, vibrationless flight. Vickers' scheme of one eye on the drawing board and the other to aviation's needs was justified.

This product of British engineering made it possible for commercial air travelers to not only fly higher than they were accustomed to, in the venerable DC-3's, DC-4's and their British counterparts, but

148

they could do it more comfortably and faster. Insofar as competing with our DC-6's, DC-7's and Constellations, the Viscounts' attributes, lack of vibration and hushed flight, were their leading attraction. As the Viscounts heralded dramatic changes in the world of flight, the changes in our mechanical world were no less striking.[45]

As our introduction to the trim, slim turbine engines progressed so did our thinking. Our technical vocabularies were being added to with strange words and phrases, too. It would be fuel controls now, not carburetors. Burner cans replaced cylinders; igniters would start fuel burning, not spark plugs and magnetos.

Air would still be used for combustion, of course, but a different regime for cooling was employed. Oil coolers were a familiar component, but we'd never seen it used internally. Cooling air was mostly crucial to main shaft bearings and the burner cans themselves. Air was delivered through an intricate maze of passages throughout the engines. We also found that the engines consumed immense quantities of air to be compressed and charged with fuel. When the mixture was ignited, the burn reached pinnacles of heat comparable to Dante's inferno, necessary for ultimate thrust and turbine rotation.

It boggled our minds that revolutions per minute were counted in five figures, instead of the plodding four figures of the radials. And now, throttles were replaced with power levers. Phrases like 'ground fine' and 'beta range' were novel, for us, in propeller operation. For the engines 'high pressure turbine', 'P-3' and 'compressor bleed valves' confronted us.

We were all delighted to note the absence of oil leaks, a hallmark of radial engines. Now we didn't have to contend with streaks and puddles of heavy, black oil that, no matter how precisely and carefully an engine was assembled, somehow managed to find freedom from within the radials. This became more evident in the improved condition of our hands, work clothes, tools and dispositions.

These new turbo-prop engines and their operating concepts were indeed refreshing. They reflected promises of relief from many of the diverse, continuous functions necessary to maintaining reciprocating engines. But more than those attributes, the changes we saw in a different airframe with its systems were interesting, to say the least.

No doubt about it: The Viscounts opened an entirely new world for us. We had become a part of aviation when it entered the golden age of sophisticated aircraft propulsion. Rocketry, too, was part of it. Although at a distance from our profession that science was making impressive progress, too. The research and development was interminable, and flight trials were faithfully reported, although marked by occasional, spectacular failures.

Incidents at Cape Canaveral raised questions among us about the apparent fumbling in the haste to put reliable rockets on the launch pads. Those occurred in the 'into the Banana River' days, a snide reference to the loss of several rockets at the Cape. They would initiate grand lift-offs from the Cape Canaveral launch pad, only to end an erratic, uncontrolled brief flight by plunging willy-nilly into Florida's nearby Banana River. Rocketry excited the national imagination, though, in spite of mishaps. I was aroused too and decided to enter this new field.

My first rocket was fashioned from a three-quarter inch diameter piece of aluminum tubing; one end was closed by hand-working it into a streamlined nose cone. The nozzle was designed by 'educated guess', which had to take into account the length and shape of its exit orifice.

The nozzle, of course, plugged the opposite end of the rocket body after the rocket was filled with a mixture of black powder and aluminum powder. The aluminum powder was meant to slow the burning of the black powder. My formula for arriving at the proportion of aluminum powder to black powder is lost in the mists of time. In fact, I don't remember where I got the idea to use aluminum powder to slow the fuel's burning rate. Stabilizing fins were, of course, provided. That was elementary.

The first rocket exploded on my crude launch pad with a magnificent roar, obviously a problem in the nozzle's design. A second rocket with a redesigned nozzle replaced the first prototype.

Ignition was acquired and with awe-inspiring determination it lifted straight off the launch pad but leveled off gracefully about four-feet above the ground instead of going up. In horizontal flight it zoomed arrow-straight with astonishing speed over the ground. Then, to the horror of my audience, it exploded with an ear-splitting blast behind the rudder of a vintage Waco biplane parked about ninety-feet away.

Ignoring the snide remarks and tactless urging of my 'advisers' to abandon the experiments, I built a third rocket with improved fins. A redesigned nozzle also was installed and minute adjustments made to the ratio of aluminum to black powder. Achieving ignition and burn, the rocket lifted heroically off the launch pad. With pleasing, ever increasing acceleration it streaked skyward in a giddying climb. Its solid fuel motor roared nobly, pushing it ever upward in a delicate, handsome arc about three-degrees off the vertical. Evidently a stabilizing fin had become slightly disarranged during liftoff.

At approximately one thousand-feet, its fuel became exhausted and the rocket pitched over. With a faint wisp of smoke trailing from the now-empty motor's nozzle it toppled back to earth. It was a glorious flight and I accepted the well-earned accolades of my audience with proper grace. That was my only excursion into rocket powered flight. Understandably, I prided myself on, at least, having a batting average equal to the professional rocketeers at Cape Canaveral.

There was no doubt in our mechanical minds that the turbines made life easier for us in line maintenance. Prior to the arrival of the Viscounts a major part of our time was spent working off 'squawks' on the radial engines after a flight. Now, the time spent on attention to the turbines was relatively minimal in comparison. Cowlings were rarely streaked with oil and there were no flight generated complaints of running rough because of fouled spark plugs or errant magnetos, no cracks in exhaust systems or cylinder heads.

Personally, I found myself strangely at a loss, at first, not to work on an engine on a through trip or turn-around inspection. Even oil changes were simplified clean tasks, the oil itself a far cry from the heavy, sixty weight oils the radials demanded. The turbines didn't require as much as the radials, nor was there any comparison between the unused appearance of turbine oil after many hours of engine operation and the ugly, black composite that flowed sluggishly from the drain holes of the radials', at an oil change, with comparable operational times.[46]

But if those turbo-props were a maintenance delight the transition to pure jets, for me, in later years, meant completely discarding some old career patterns. Now another component was eliminated that eased the maintenance burden: propellers. Otherwise, everything else was essentially the same in the core engine as in the turbo-props, except a gear box drove generators and other accessories. In both examples, there was no requirement for separate elements to provide cabin pressurization and cabin heat. The engines' compressors supplied ample quantities of both.

Simply put, jet engines suck in gargantuan quantities of air, compress it, add fuel and ignite and burn the mixture. The climax of the series of events is a holocaust of heated, pressurized air, translated into pounds of thrust, exiting the exhaust nozzle. The engines epitomize the theory of canceling internal pressure of a chamber at one point, producing thrust which pushes the chamber and, therefore, the airplane to which it's attached. Turbo-prop engines also produce thrust from their exhaust tailpipes, but it's residual and minuscule as compared to that of pure turbine engines.

Those days in the transition from piston engines to turbines began a massive learning curve for individual mechanics, as well as the aviation industry in general.

At the outset, especially in overhaul, t was another ball game. Turbine and compressor wheels must be finely balanced in order to prevent self-destruction at unheard of r.p.ms. A deformed compressor or turbine blade could drastically alter the performance of an engine, as far as producing thrust was concerned. Losing a blade or blades would do the same, only self destruction was virtually assured. Turbine wheels became a matter of major concern because of the hellish environment they operated in. Now faithfully detailed records must be kept of their lives as well as other components. Fuel controls were a major field unto themselves.

Some aspects of the learning curve were slow to perceive, but there was one that was readily apparent: Turbine and compressors could not and would not countenance an infusion of anything other than clean air. Foreign object damage — FOD — was added to our vocabulary. FOD was common at the outset, especially in pure turbines, until intensive education began to influence maintenance personnel. A cloth shop towel, a flashlight, a wrench, left in or very close proximity to an engine's air inlet, could almost certainly assure disastrous consequences on an engine's life. A wrench or bird or flashlight being sucked into an engine was certain to create havoc on compressor and turbine blades, in effect destroying the engine, is an implicit certainty.

Unfortunately, a few mechanics have become victims of the awesome suction the larger turbines are capable of. They have suffered hideous deaths, pinned against inlet guide vanes by the air's dreadful velocity, their lives literally sucked out of their bodies.

Like the wheel that has been developed to the point where further improvement to the basic design isn't likely, it seems to me that turbine engines have very nearly reached the ultimate limits of the concept. Some other, highly sophisticated form of propulsion will be imperative.

Perhaps it will be a sublime derivative of rocket power over the relatively crude engines currently used to initiate space flight. Or it may be that a source of high density, intensely concentrated light waves in the tradition of Buck Rogers and UFOs will be the answer. In any event, our ponderous propulsion schemes have nearly achieved practical limits. The answers are somewhere in the future and until they're found, humankind cannot escape self-destruction on a planet that's being tortured and dying a slow death.

For now, turbine or jet engines — your choice of nomenclature — are to the point where bigger is not necessarily better. Over the history of their development, engineers have continually sought the Holy Grail of more thrust, less weight and miserly fuel consumption. On balance, though, it appears their search becomes more and more arduous.

Because of turbine engines I was privileged to look down on the tops of several thunderstorms over eastern Texas, instead of suffering the distress of flying through them. It was a night flight and an unforgettable sight to me. Lightning in the storm clouds' interiors caused their tops to suddenly glow in beautiful, diffused light, like soft sudden glows of fleeting sunsets, often and quickly repeated.

The engines were comfortable in that element of rarefied air at forty-one thousand feet. I marveled that the dizzying spin of their compressors and turbine wheels could effortlessly sustain flight. And that is one of the jet engine's uncontestable contributions to air travel, among others. It elevated passengers above the middle altitudes of the Constellations, DC-6's and DC-7's to heights where turbulence and weather were spurned. Confident passengers could drink a cup of coffee, reasonably assured it wouldn't slop over the rim and stain their clothes.

As far as I was concerned, in my mechanical relationship with the turbo-props and pure jets, there was always a tiny feeling of strangeness in that association. Something seemed to be missing. Maybe it was the long years of work on the radials and the familiarity that had been generated in ferreting out and correcting their complaints. While they have their unquestionable attributes of power and less maintenance they somehow seemed to be an intangible element. One had to

155

have a high degree of intimacy with piston engines so that seven or nine or fourteen or eighteen cylinders and the collection of assorted parts that made up a complete engine were maintained to maximum efficiency.

After a cylinder change, or rehabilitating a sickly magneto, or analyzing and correcting a wheezy induction system, my self-worth soared. I always had an almost sinful feeling of pride and certainly satisfaction after a successful ground run. It was a delight to see the cowling remain rock solid and the instruments indicating all was well once more. It was really something to realize you had been triumphant over such a mass of often irascible machinery.

That accrued ingrained feeling for the radials didn't affect my attitude toward maintaining turbine engines. But being an entirely different departure from round engines required intensive learning concentration. It was almost like the transition to learning the metric system of measuring.

Once, the visit by a CAA (then) agent during an inspection activities review session with me, digressed into 'shop' talk. The subject turned to more efficient flight, and he offered an incredible observation. "What we need," he said, "is a means that would suck the air from in front of an airplane so that it would move forward into the vacuum." I'm not making that up. I say incredible because turbine-type engines had been proven for some years. Even as we spoke, Boeing was designing the venerable 707 which would have four pure jets on its wings.

I didn't have the heart to remind him of that, nor that Sir Frank Whittle's efforts had initiated serious development on a somewhat similar concept years ago. Only sucking air from in front of the airplane was a function of developing thrust that would push the airplane. Privately I wondered what he'd been doing to keep abreast of aviation's progress, and concluded, apparently not much. But it wouldn't have mattered anyway, at least for him. Shortly thereafter he retired.

Turbines have relentlessly pushed radials into the files of history, at least as powering large, transport aircraft is concerned. There are still a fairly representative number flying, though, and wherever they fly heads turn in admiration and respect — with a feeling of nostalgia. From my perspective it seems turbine engines operate in the abstract; they seem to lack a personal inter-connection between mechanics' — and pilots' — technical instincts and gut feelings. This is manifested in a comparison of starting radial versus turbine engines.

A mechanic standing on the ground will hear the clash of a starter dog engaging and the first, hesitant cough of combustion in one cylinder. Following in rapid secession the remainder of the cylinders belch out evidence that power is being produced. Then he sees the engine settle into a smooth muttering readiness, its propeller a gleaming solid disc. The cowling is rock-solid. In the cockpit a subtle, steady resonance and mild insipid vibration has seeped through the aircraft's structure. It physically binds the crew with the engine's dynamics. The engine gauges vigilantly authenticate that an event has occurred: That mass on the wing or nose has created life.

But with a turbine engine there is only the clash of the starter engaging, the rapid-fire snap of the ignitor and the anguished moan of the compressor beginning to rotate. Gradually there's a change to higher and higher decibels of sound until, finally, after fuel is introduced, the ear-splitting shriek of madly revolving compressor and turbine wheels in combination with the blare of furious combustion. The exit of high pressure, heated air compounds the bedlam. There is little if any transmittal of accomplishment through the airframe. The engine is disassociated with the cockpit except for the umbilical cords that offer some measure of rapport through gauges and the stingy array of controls. The crew knows the engine is running because it has prodded the gauges into action. On the ground, the mechanic knows it, too: The engine's whine and the roar of released combustion pressure tells him, filtering softly through his noise-suppressing ear muffs. If wing-mounted a nacelle simply hangs there immobile on its pylon, a mute motionless article. If an engine is buried as in a B-727, a mechanic can surmise something happened when smoke issues from the tailpipe.

Turbo-prop engines are a little more revealing when started. There is the usual whine of compressor and turbine wheel beginning to turn, but they're somewhat more subdued than those in a pure jet. The propeller is a dead giveaway, though, because it begins to revolve when enough power is developed through a gear box to drive it. Beyond the propeller rotating there is no other discernable action to indicate the engine is, in fact, running.

In applying myself in the practical sense there was little problem in the transition from piston engines to turbines. It was only a matter of becoming educated to the latter's totally different mechanical approach to producing power. Psychologically though, I had to become accustomed to the comparative change in routine maintenance.

There were very few hoses or flex tubing, being replaced with hard lines because turbines are a true 'heat' engine. Electrical wiring was also minimal; what little existed was of the highest quality undisturbed by vibrations such as radial engines were capable of. Even engine controls were reduced: two for turbo-props, one for pure jets. On the whole, routine inspections and occasional corrections of flight discrepancies were noticeable by their relative simplicity.

Airframes and systems were, on the other hand, more complicated. There was a host of differences in hydraulic systems, flight controls, steering, pressurization and cooling, and a multitude of other considerations. Even battery maintenance was more complex. The new airframes and their electrical systems were worlds apart from piston engine-powered transports. These electrical schemes commanded profound concentration to master. It was a totally new maintenance environment, demanding a turn-about in approach, both physically and mentally.

In retrospect, the development of turbine engines was fore-ordained. By 1939, jet-powered aircraft had flown in Germany. With conditions and necessities caused by World War II, Frank Whittle's first jet engine needed to be further developed; General Electric was selected due to its long history in the field dating back to 1903.

Conventional piston engines continued to offer considerable advantages in fuel economy and in engine power-to-weight ratios over early jet engines and efforts to make jet propulsion more practical were accelerated. The floodgates were opened, overwhelming the tried and true piston engines.

I accompanied a Beechcraft King Air to Airwork's overhaul facility in New Jersey. The engines were due for a hot section inspection. Airwork had overhauled radial engines and accessories for years. Now it was phasing out its piston engine overhaul and transitioning into turbine engine overhauls and service.

159

As I stepped into the overhaul shop to confer with the shop foreman I stopped short. A Pratt & Whitney R-2800 engine stood on a teardown stand amidst an array of new tooling for turbine engine work.

A lone mechanic was disassembling the enormous engine. His coveralls were splotched, his hands and tools grimy with black, ropey oil and dirt. The air was heavy with the acrid smell of the products of combustion escaping from the tainted oil. No other odor compares with it.

There was a drip pan littered with deteriorated exhaust and intake gaskets, seals, worn nuts and pieces of safety wire and bent cotter pins. The debris was firmly imbedded in the sour oil that dripped from open rocker arm boxes to form a pool on the drip pan. The skin on the mechanic's hands and knuckles was wrinkled with lines like chintz threads. I noticed an angry wound on the top of his left hand.

For a moment I stood silently, absorbing the scene, and years past flashed through my mind. Then, with a nod to the mechanic, I turned away and a silent question tinted with wonder surfaced in my mind.

Did I actually do that, too?

11

Working Relationships, Creative Thinking....

Whature a comparison is made between the number of flight-related accident statistics and those attributed to maintenance errors, remember: There's a broad disparity between the time available to a flight crew to correct, or attempt to correct, a dis-integrating flight situation and that of a maintenance crew eliminating a mechanical problem.

Time favors maintenance personnel simply because the airplane will remain on the ground and won't fly until it's made whole again. Unless, of course, the broken or inoperative component is on the Minimum Equipment List, if the airplane is required to operate under one. Or the pilot-owner of a general aviation aircraft decides maintenance can wait. And not a few of them do just that. Often with unsavory results.

In an example of how some owners stretch their fortunes to the limit, and this is by no means a rarity, three men departed on a supposedly 'must' trip in a Cessna 210.

The cabin door was inoperable: It wouldn't unlatch to gain entry. Several of us watched as the men tried to coax the door open, but it wouldn't budge. Instead of taking the time to have a mechanic determine the reason and correct the problem, they boarded the airplane through a cabin window. The window happened to be designated and placarded as an emergency escape exit.

They encountered instrument landing conditions at their destination airport that far exceeded the pilot's capabilities. Instead of returning to their original airport — there was enough fuel to allow that — the pilot decided to attempt a landing.

Two men died in the crash that followed and the third barely survived. The jammed cabin door did not, of course, have an impact on the cause of the accident, excepting rescue personnel may have been able to save another, or perhaps all of them, if the door latching mechanism had functioned as it should have. Probably a mechanic could have repaired the faulty latch in thirty-minutes. In that time it's quite possible the foul weather could have cleared at the destination airport, as well.

The fact that time is on the side of maintenance personnel, as compared to air crews, could partially explain why maintenance crews enjoy a somewhat relaxed work atmosphere. This is not to say their work is fun and games. It's simply that more time is spent together with the same individuals, and a small family relationship, if you will, is formed. Everyone learns each other's traits through constant association, their habits and idiosyncrasies. This tends to generate an unusual rapport.

The results can be good-natured insults, harassment, some arguments, practical jokes or unusual or amusing situations. If rationalization is necessary to forgive those actions it could be there's an intrinsic value in relieving the stress of knowing that safe flight depends on a mechanic's personal work ethic and responsibility to proper maintenance. But when it comes down to the nut-cutting, they know the airplane's welfare is paramount.

There were times when I was compelled to worry whether a few mechanics I associated with had a full load of bricks, and I'm sure some worried about me at times. In one example, it was apparent that an uncontrollable, sudden torrent of exuberance caused a display of startling behavior.

It was Bosner, when an impulsive urge to imitate Tarzan overcame his common sense and left those who saw it utterly dumbfounded. But then, he was the type who never stood out as an accomplished technician. Only doing what he had to do and taking a long time to do it.

The Air Corps C-54 was hunched in the main hangar-shop of the Hawaiian Air Depot, patiently awaiting various maintenance projected for it: Engine changes, airframe repairs and some incidental work. The cabin was cleared of the usual equipment, bench seats, stretcher hangers and other components necessary for hauling cargo or personnel.

Inside the cabin, the fuselage's ribs were bared; there were no amenities such as cabin wall liners or insulation. Here and there an aluminum container was attached to fuselage frames. Those were used to carry such items as first aid kits, life vests or flares and charts. One was attached to the main cabin door frame. It was a lidless box that held a ditching rope. One end of the rope was usually fastened to the frame with a heavy metal snap. If it was necessary to use the rope you simply threw it out the cabin door and slid down. Escape chutes were a long way into the future.

The overdose of irresistible exuberance must have struck Bosner about the same time he had to leave the front of the C-54's cabin for a part or tool — no one ever knew. He trotted madly down the cabin and grabbed the tag end of the ditching rope; they always hung loose to be readily available.

Uttering a mighty Tarzan yodel Bosner jumped out the door — and collided with the concrete floor of the hangar with a resounding thump. It might not have been faster to use the stairs we used to go up in and down from the cabin, but by virtue of using the rope with the resulting sudden stop, was very painful.

Apparently someone had neglected to re-secure the anchor end of the ditching rope to the fuselage frame after inspection. But Bosner was essentially none the worse for wear and tear, except for some impressive bruises.

Years later one of my foreman duplicated the feat without the benefit of any type of descending device.

We were having a problem with the No. 3 engine on one of Capital Airline's DC-4's. The foreman, Herkemeir, was in the cockpit observing the engine run-up. As usual, he was in a fretful, worried state of mind. I never saw him smile and doubt anyone else ever did.

The consensus was, judging from his permanent, dark-red face and prominent veins, there was a very real potential for him becoming a guest in a hospital intensive care unit. Everyone agreed that was highly conceivable: The man was a walking symbol of the definition of stress.

A mechanic trotted out of the hangar, across the ramp and thumped on the fuselage to get our attention. Mike Frazer stuck his head out of the open door behind the cockpit.

"Tell 'Herk' he's wanted on the telephone. They said it's urgent."

Mike turned and relayed the message to Herkemeir. He was leaning across the back of the co-pilot's seat watching No. 3's engine instruments. Without a word, Herkemeir wheeled, took two steps and simply walked out the open door — and fell about eight-feet to the ramp.

Without even a momentary hesitation, as though it was ordinary behavior, he picked himself up and ran across the ramp, through the hangar to the office to answer the call. We noticed, to our astonishment, he had only a slight limp. It was the most awe-inspiring display of absent mindness I have ever seen.

The truly frightening aspect of the episode was he landed about four feet in front of the still-running No.3 engine. If he had turned the wrong way, in possible confusion, the horrible result need not be mentioned.

His precipitous detachment from reality was the result of significant stress, more self-induced than imposed. We did, in fact, feel sorry for him. But his actions always aroused much speculation among us as to when he would be hospitalized for a rest — or worse. After I left Capital Airlines I did learn, over the grapevine, he was the victim of a massive heart attack and died.

In comparison, another foreman, when called to the telephone, always did so at a slow walk. Operations always knew when Smoott was on duty, by the number of times the telephone rang before he answered it. It wasn't unusual for it to ring twelve or fourteen times.

He was like Satchel Paige, the famous baseball pitcher. When he was called to the pitcher's mound in relief he always sauntered out at a turtle-like shuffle. It's been said that when someone asked him why he walked so leisurely to the mound, Paige would reply: "They ain't no sense hurrin' into trouble."

But if Herkemeir and Smoott were at opposite ends of the stress column, another foreman, Williams, guarded the center. He invited practical jokes from our crew because he seemed to be always undecided whether to descend completely into the stress pit, or hover in pitiful uncertainty on the brink. He was one of those people who are naturally vulnerable as a target for inoffensive pranks.

More than once when an airplane was scheduled for an early departure and required an oil change, in addition to other attention, we could see a change in him. Especially when time was getting particularly critical. Williams would become more attentive and edgy, to the point of being unbearable. His fear that the aircraft wouldn't be ready to meet its flight commitment bordered on paranoia at times.

One of our favorite deceptions he never seemed to catch on to,

166

was when we would cut a piece of steel safety wire or a small cotter pin into tiny pieces. After the magnetic sump plug was removed and inspected for debris, we allowed the plug's magnet to draw the chips to its irresistible attraction. We never used but a few pieces.

Sometimes we would suck metal filings from near a bench vise. The idea was to simulate interior engine metal, insinuating an impending engine failure. When we showed him the contaminated sump plug he would tear his cap off and throw it on the hangar floor in horrified disgust and frustration.

"Why does this happen to me?" he would wail. "What am I going to tell operations?"

When he looked closer at the sump plug he would see the nature of the chips and stamp away, muttering what we thought were obscenities.

Not being psychiatrists we never questioned his hyper-sensitivity. But we would admonish him from time to time to 'take it easy'. His emotions were often responsible for a gaffe.

One night he rushed from his office after answering the telephone and, in his best authoritative voice, shouted: "Moose (an alias of one of the crew), you and Wilson start 514 (a DC-3) and taxi it to the terminal. Just use two engines!"

Moose and I looked at each other in disbelief. Finally Moose turned to him and said: "But Williams, 514 has *only* two engines."

We stared at his back, grinning, as he turned in pitiful, red-faced retreat to his office. We never brought the incident up later, but an opportunity surfaced in several weeks to show we hadn't forgotten his momentary mental block. We were actually fond of Williams and never harassed him out of disdain.

It was Mitcher who found the dead rat in the mechanic's break room. It had succumbed to the deadly campaign of a professional exterminator. We contemplated the rodent's carcass for a night or two. Brian suggested a use for it. We would tie it securely out of sight under William's desk chair. There it would decompose at its leisure. That deed was quickly accomplished with the utmost secrecy.

We quietly awaited results with cheerful anticipation. There is nothing to compare with the smell of a dead rat or mouse, or other rodent, in various stages of decomposition. Not even monkeys!

Several days and nights passed until, finally, decomposition and putrefaction became unrelenting in the rat's corpse. It became more conspicuous by a gradually increasing volume of abominable, reechy pungency. As the terrible, purulent aroma continued to gain strength we, more and more, obtained directions or ask questions of Williams outside his office.

After about two weeks the news came over our 'grapevine', that Williams had at last located the source of the suffocating stench. It was removed by a janitor and for several days afterwards, his office environment had the essence of a thick pine forest. Williams seemed to mellow after the incident and we congratulated each other on our remarkable achievement.

For quite some time afterwards, the phrase, 'Oh rats!' was commonly used in our crew to express frustration.[42]

Within the various maintenance crews I was a part of there were always good-natured barbs and mild insults flung back and forth at one another. These did no harm; instead, they were indications of the popularity of an individual. Consequently, opportunities for innocent gags were always available.

The thoroughly likeable, mild-mannered Street was a typical example.

Of average height, Street was slightly on the rotund side. He was like an over-the-hill bowling ball looking for an alley. This characteristic was re-enforced by his enthusiastic anticipation for the arrival of lunch time. On the stroke of the appointed hour he would stride determinedly toward his lunch box, usually resting on a wooden bench, and grab the handle.

Without pausing in his haste he would hurry on to a pre-selected spot to enjoy the contents. He reminded me of a hawk swooping down to snatch a field mouse, then fly off to a tree limb to consume it. Street's routine offered wonderful potential for a diversion and one night we took advantage of it.

Coulter and I slipped into the small room where we did light shop work. We carefully removed Street's lunch items from his lunchbox and nailed it to the wooden bench with two roofing nails. Then we just as carefully returned his lunch to the box. We shut and latched the lid. Meanwhile five of us in the crew, who had been alerted, managed to precede Street into the room by a bare minute and busied ourselves with a pretext of getting ready to eat.

The door burst open and Street, in his usual rolling gait, approached his lunch bucket, as usual on the low wooden bench. As usual, without slowing, he clutched the handle. The lunch bucket never budged, straining the handle's attachments to their limits, so great was the resistance to the momentum of Street's arm and body. Remarkably, even the box's lid catches held.

Street's body jerked to a complete stop, causing his right arm

169

to stretch full length while his left leg flew up in stride. The wonder of it was he didn't topple over on his back. It was immediately obvious to him someone had fastened his lunch box to the wooden bench!

"Now who would have done that?" he wondered aloud. Then, with some good-natured remarks about the group's collective mental processes, he sat down beside his lunch box and proceeded to devour its contents. Two of us helped him remove the nails afterwards while vehemently denying any part in the prank.

Ground electrical power units weren't as sophisticated then as now. Realistically there was no requirement for high ampere output. Consequently, at Capital Airlines we used battery carts as mainstays for ground electrical power, including starting the DC-3 and DC-4 engines. But we did have two engine driven units used mostly for starting the R-3350 engines on the Constellations, and later, the Rolls-Royce Darts on the Viscounts. It would be extremely risky to attempt a turbine engine start with a battery cart.

On the other hand, if a piston engine fails to start while battery power is deteriorating, one simply stops cranking. But still, the possibility of disastrous consequences is always present if an engine is over-primed and a fire should start in the exhaust system.

Hopefully, the battery cart would have sufficient reserve power to continue cranking the engine until it would clear itself to allow ignition and start. Thus blowing out the fire.

With the advent of turbine engines, which includes turbo-prop types, ground power units developed apace, to answer the demand of hungry starters, following the law of development begets additional development in support of the initial advancement.

Thus powerful piston- engine driven electrical power units were developed which produced 1,500 amperes or more. These were modified to a 'soft start' feature which supplied all the starter required initially. Then, when the turbine began to spool up and the starter didn't need the power unit's initial output, its generator would reduce amperage proportionately. These types, of course, are in common use now.

At Trans-Ocean Airlines we had a valiant, thoroughly reliable shop-built power unit. It was pure simplicity: It had a generator, a twenty-four volt aircraft unit driven by a small four-cylinder gasoline engine of unknown ancestry.

No sophisticated relays, controls, or limiters. Start the engine, plug the umbilical cord into the airplane and throw a switch by hand. It was pure delight to watch its unparalleled determination and tenacity when we started the big Pratt & Whitney R-2800 engines on DC-6's.

The instant a starter switch was toggled for engine start the power unit's diminutive engine's happy purr would change to a throaty, aggressive growl as the airplane's starter demanded electrical power. That, in turn became the power unit generator's responsibility; passing the buck stopped at the engine.

Answering the call, the little engine would literally rock on its coil spring shock mounts under a sudden burden of torque. Then grey combustion gases would spurt from its exhaust and every so often the engine would backfire. It was quite a production! But the unit never failed to meet the demands of an engine's starter.

At Capital Airlines we used heavy duty battery carts for ground power, six of them, in fact, in addition to two engine-driven power units.

Therefore, it was necessary to maintain those batteries on a regular basis — aircraft batteries, as well. It was a full-time job. Battery shop duties was handled by an elderly man named Bernie. We knew very little about him. He was reserved and quiet; there was never a close association with him since he kept mostly to himself.

Although he did his job well, Bernie had an overly protective attitude toward his charges, the battery carts. In fact, he would often become absolutely contentious about us using them. In present up-scale parlance he would probably be called an over-achiever. To us, Bernie was often a blatant irritation. In time he came to be referred to as 'The Old Goat'.

Bernie was lean and mean; his arms looked like they'd been squeezed from tubes. He wore a perpetual frown on his craggy face, as though he was in constant pain or intense thought; we could never figure which.

He patrolled the ramp and hangars like a security guard at Fort Knox, on the lookout for one or more of his battery carts. If we unplugged a battery cart from an airplane, rather than leave it unattended while there was a brief pause in our maintenance activities, perhaps to go for coffee or some other reason, chances were when we returned to the airplane the battery cart had disappeared.

This required a long walk to the battery shop to retrieve it, or look for one not being used. But ninety percent of the time we could be safe in going directly to the battery shop where we were sure it had been spirited away to, and placed in protective custody.

172

More than once we caught him in the act of making off with a cart we were using. The usual result was a protracted, heated discussion about his role in life on the ramp and our need for electrical support. These incidents, of course, did little to mend the gap between us.

Bernie's vinegar-tainted attitude and outright possessiveness were generally addressed in pointed, lucid terms during the debates. The battery carts, we insisted, were the property of Capital Airlines and at the disposal of maintenance for the good of the cause.

These emotional confrontations had no effect on Bernie; he never changed his modus operandi. Clearly, it was evident that revenge was not only justified but overdue. A scheme was concocted by a delegation formed from volunteers.

Virtually without fail Bernie would park his 1948 Oldsmobile in the same spot, a choice one adjacent to the door we used to enter and leave our maintenance hangar. It was accessible to a street that paralleled the short row of hangars and a small parking lot across the street.

Bernie's car, being so close to the door, was a fortuitous arrangement: It was very convenient to carry the necessary equipment from the hangar by the perpetrators of the exercise. Their identity was well hidden for the time I was at Capital Airlines. I don't know to this day who they were. But the grapevine was a-buzz with news that an 'event' would take place soon. One morning, before quitting time we received an alert.

On the fateful morning Bernie, as usual, hurried to his car in anticipation of home and sleep. As he emerged from the hangar door an eager audience of mechanics quietly crowded at the few windows that opened on the street. There was considerable whispering with almost breathless expectation at the promise of Bernie's discomfort-to-come.

In the soft glow of the street light we saw him get in and start the engine. The headlights came on and we could faintly see his arm as it moved to engage the transmission.

The engine revved up slightly, but the car didn't move. A little more r.p.m. might do it and we heard the engine respond to increased pressure on the accelerator. Still the Olds' lingered, as though the wheels were glued to the pavement.

Try the parking brake, Bernie, maybe it's stuck. We could faintly see movements apparently designed to make sure it wasn't. Back to the engine and gear shift lever, Bernie. The Olds' refused to budge, in spite of the engine's response, goosed by Bernie's building frustration. Obviously his fuse was getting shorter.

Ah-h-h...now. The door opens and Bernie emerges and looks at the car, totally baffled. He walks around it as though to see if all the wheels were attached and peers carefully at the tires. They're all in place and properly inflated.

Finally he got down on his knees ahead of the left front wheel and peered under the car, perhaps to see if there was a possible problem with the drive train, or perhaps the transmission was lying on the pavement. Satisfied everything was as it should be he repeated his inspection by looking under the rear of the Olds'. Then he straightened with a litany of sizzling curses that caused us to cringe.

He never stopped cursing all the while we watched as he opened the car's trunk, removed the jack and proceeded to raise the back of the car, one side at a time.

As Bernie removed concrete blocks and odd pieces of wood he would hurl them away in nearly uncontrollable rage. Someone had placed them under the rear axle housing with delicate precision. The rear tires barely cleared the pavement. The blocks were placed as closely as possible to the wheels to conceal them. Probably, the clearance between tires and pavement was no more than twenty thousandths of an inch. Personally, I thought it was an engineering feat worthy of the highest praise.

There was a startling change for the better — but not excessive — in Old Goat's attitude thereafter; he never protested when someone needed to take one of his battery carts to the line. He seldom spoke at all, but would glare in stony silence at the person who took one. In a way he was missed when he resigned two weeks after the incident. He had taken a challenge of sorts with him.

It's unfortunate that the general public, most especially the segment that fly, knows very little about an aircraft mechanic's professional life. People only see the up-front personnel: The pilots, flight attendants, station agents and ticket clerks and, at a distance, ramp staff. How many look behind those people to maintenance people, and the mechanical care of aircraft? It would seem very few.

Any perception seems to stop at the aircraft parked at a gate much like groceries on shelves in a store. Maintenance and mechanics, food production and farmers, are submerged in a grey area. This is a real pity because the public is deprived of first-hand observation of craftsmen with alert, knowledgeable minds at work.

Trained minds that react quickly to various circumstances. Some mechanics I've worked with had minds like a steel trap. Mitcher was an example.

He and I were assigned to complete a cabin supercharger change on a Constellation. The superchargers were in the No. 1 and No. 4 engine nacelles. They were mounted aft of the firewall and driven by a shaft routed from the accessory section of the engines through sealed cut-outs in the firewalls. Access was gained to the superchargers and accessory sections through a door in the bottom of each nacelle large enough for an average man's shoulders. For two men to enter the nacelles, some planning and maneuvering was required.

We placed our work stand under the No. 4 nacelle and Mitcher went first. He inserted his upper body after raising his arms and wiggling his shoulders through the access hole's frame. He weighed about two hundred-thirty pounds, much larger than my one hundred-seventy pounds.

I wriggled up past his lower legs and stood facing him with the drive shaft between our chests. It was not an uncomfortable work position except the nacelle's interior temperature was about ninety-five degrees. There was little chance for air circulation because our lower legs nearly blocked the access opening.

Our work progressed smoothly. We chatted and gossiped, thankful that neither of us had eaten onions or garlic and that we bathed regularly. Tainted breath or bodies in combination with the nacelle's oven-like atmosphere would have been abrasive. And then, just when we started safety-wiring the drive shaft flange attach bolts at the accessory drive and supercharger, Mitcher, in basic language, farted. It was one of those long, drawn out wind passages that begin with an authoritative, hoarse resonance and babbles over the air waves for seconds, ending in a high-pitched whine.

Its volume and duration were enhanced by the size of Mitcher's intestinal tract, obviously larger than mine because of the difference in the size of our bodies. If a flatus has to be admired this one was unsurpassed in volume and a shockingly lurid, redolent pungency. Like something had crawled up inside him and died. The clamor of its emergence was amplified by the aluminum walls of the nacelle, as though we were in a barrel.

The flatus before it expired, changed our work atmosphere from just bearable to totally appalling — for me, not Mitcher. It's mortifying, foul stench instantly ballooned into stomach- wrenching proportions, enhanced by the hot air in the nacelle.

"You dirty bastard," I moaned. "How could you do that?"

"Nothing to it," Mitcher said, laughing uproarishly.

I immediately sank and began to struggle to escape the awful, noisome stench. The air in the nacelle was so thick now it seemed to dampen my asepses. But as I began to bend my knees to wiggle down past his legs, Mitcher bent his — and I was trapped!

The only relief available was to crouch under the drive shaft with my head as close as possible to the access opening. I stayed there desperately sucking in meager breaths of outside air. The fumes from the fart, I reasoned, would drift upwards like hot air does; I would, therefore, be moderately free of them, although not completely. All the while Mitcher quivered with convulsions of laughter. It bounced from the walls of the nacelle like a demon gone berserk, further amplified by my distress.

"If you think I'm gonna help you finish up you can go to hell," I raged. "I'm going to stay here until you're done, so don't be all night." He must have taken some pity on me because in less than ten minutes he finished the safety wiring and straightened his legs. Without hesitation I wiggled down past them into the sweet freshness of the summer night. As I walked around beneath the nacelle regaining my composure I had to silently admit Mitcher's mind was indeed alert in trapping me, although misdirected.

One of the most ancient of practical jokes in aviation was sending some neophyte mechanic or helper for a bucket of prop wash. Of course, that worked only if propeller driven airplanes were involved.

The plan involved directing a new mechanic to a specific person who would send him to another and on and on. The victim's mental alertness was generally scored on how soon he caught on to the scheme. I don't know of any who never did. Some have been finally told to 'get back to work' by an irate supervisor.

It's important in the overall scheme of things in maintenance that members of a crew get along with one another. This is not to say there should be a sense of total togetherness, cloning if you will.

Never, throughout my career, have I seen any examples of dereliction of duty to their work, resulting from light hearted banter between members of a maintenance staff.

We kept to our limits like dogs peeing their boundaries in order!

12

Flexibility is Good,
A Familiar Niche is Better....

Throughout my career in general and corporate aviation, as well as scheduled and non-scheduled airlines, I've been flight steward, flight mechanic, 'baggage smasher', cleaner, co-pilot, freight forwarder, structural engineer, clerk, and aerial photographer. There was also a time when I had to be a psychologist of sorts. The latter persuasion was used to correct a supposedly rough engine.

We had been struggling through heavy weather for nearly forty-five minutes over the last land barrier to the Los Angeles basin and our destination, Burbank, California. The airplane was a Lockheed

Lodestar, a heavy twin-engine type that was quite capable of handling the weather. We were at fifteen thousand feet, give or take a few because of the turbulence and non pressurized   cabin. We were in solid instrument conditions.

The scenario   seemed to be fraying the pilot's nerves; he was starting to yell at his co-pilot, who wasn't having an easy time of it either. Besides navigating and operating the radios, monitoring the instrument panel and the pilot's activities, Los Angeles Center had re-quested he relay messages to an aircraft that was having communications problems. Finally it was my turn to be yelled at.

"Wilson!" In my seat just aft of the cockpit bulkhead I jerked fully awake from my fitful dozing. As I said before, I never was able to sleep soundly in an airplane. It was the only seat in the small compartment between the cockpit bulkhead and the cabin bulkhead. The seat was on the left side of the compartment and a small galley was built-in on the right side. A carry-through spar transversed the compartment. It was padded and leather covered to hide the structure. The seat was comfortable: I could stretch my legs over the spar and, being within the center-of-gravity envelope, you didn't feel the turbulence as much as you would back in the cabin.

"The right engine is running rough!" he yelled. I unbuckled my seat belt and stuck my head and shoulders into the cockpit. "Look at it!" he demanded.

I looked out the cockpit's side window past the co-pilot's weary face. A wreath of heavy vapor hovered around the steadily turning propeller. It streamed back into a shallow, opaque cylinder. Profiled against the dirty-grey backdrop of heavy, rain-soaked clouds, the engine's power section and accessory cowling appeared as it always did. The power section cowl was relatively short, extending aft of the exhaust collector ring. That was enough to cover it and overlay the accessory section cowling. The engine was only a single row radial. A Wright R-1820.205.

There were no cowl flaps. A gap between the accessory section's cowling allowed cooling air to exit from the power section back over the collector ring. The trailing edge of the power section's cowling quivered mildly, but then it always did. There simply were no provisions for supporting it. But, in all reality, there didn't need to be.

Stepping back into the galley area I peered through a side window. Through it I could see almost all of the inboard section of the exhaust collector ring under the aft edge of the power section cowling. Since the collector ring was bolted to the engine's nine cylinders, if it shook that could be a good indication of whether the engine was running rough. Cowling is generally shock-mounted, so you don't depend on it for a clue.

But it wasn't. Its heat-stained circumference seemed to be welded in place, it was that steady. After watching the engine for a couple of minutes or so, I was satisfied that nothing unusual was happening. Turning away I poked my head back into the cockpit.

The twin needles of the tachometer indicator were locked on 2,250 r.p.m.'s; the tiny wheel in the center of the instrument was quivering indecisively. If it spun to the right, the right prop would be turning faster than the left prop. If it spun to the left, the opposite would be true. But both props were in synchronization as indicated by the wheel's gentle uncertainty. The beat of both props was steady, too.

The magneto switches on the lower center of the engines' controls console were pointed to the 'BOTH' position. When the pilots frequently checked magnetos and spark plugs in flight, a practice I never agreed with, now and then, they inadvertently did not return the switches to 'BOTH'. On Lodestars, the positions 'LEFT', 'RIGHT', 'BOTH' were difficult to see unless you leaned back and craned your neck like a rooster looking down a bottle's neck with one beady eye.[37]

Oil pressures, fuel pressures, temperatures, both oil and cylinder head, were normal. Carburetor inlet temperatures indicated above freezing with the help of carburetor heat. I could see nothing amiss with the operation of either engine, let alone the right one. I said so and stepped back into the galley area.

Without asking either pilot whether they wanted any, I then unstrapped a portable oxygen bottle from its hanger on the aft face of the cockpit bulkhead and handed the mask to the pilot. He took it without a word and clamped the mask to his face. After sucking oxygen for five minutes he silently handed the mask to his co-pilot.

It was amazing how quickly both men calmed down. The pilot quit yelling, and the engines' 'roughness' disappeared. Gradually, chatter on the radios subsided markedly and even the dense, dismal clouds began to change to slightly broken.

In a short time Los Angeles Center started us into a descent and the final leg of our flight to Burbank and Lockheed Air Terminal was uneventful, although we were still on instruments in light rain. I, meanwhile, had returned to my fitful dozing. I briefly contemplated the addition of 'psychologist' to my resume but then decided not to. Leave the science of mind and personal behavior to experts of the unknown.

In the final analysis, if there had been a mechanical problem there was little, if anything, I could have done about it anyway.

The title of Flight Mechanic is misleading in both definition and duties. There's very little maintenance a mechanic can do on airplanes in flight, especially on engines.

In-flight duties related more to those of a 'ball bearing' flight attendant's, rather than a mechanic's. If a flight produced discrepancies, the flight mechanic fulfilled his obligations at the trip's destination or an alternate, if the problem demanded immediate attention. And so the title is really academic. Anyway a few corporate and charter operations used both title and man, particularly on long flights.

An acquaintance I met at Grumman Aircraft on Long Island while we were both attending school on the Grumman Gulfstream I, was classed as Flight Mechanic. He regularly flew with the DC-3, a major oil company in eastern Canada owned. The airplane was used extensively on long flights to the company's holdings in the western part of the country. His presence aboard gave the pilots a sense of well-being and confidence in the aircraft, he supposed. Also, he could serve coffee and doughnuts to the corporate passengers — and pilots — in flight.

His name was Ronald. He had an admitted, unabashed love of doughnuts. "I don't know why, but I just can't resist the damn things," he said.

Both pilots knew about Ron's addiction and one day the co-pilot devised a scheme that, he thought, would induce Ron to lessen his desires for the pastry to more acceptable levels. If the plan were successful, the co-pilot thought future supplies of doughnuts could be shared more equitably. The pilots liked doughnuts almost as well as Ron did. The co-pilot's plan was based on a trap, a mechanical one, not a ruse.

Prior to the flight on which the plan was put in motion, the co-pilot cocked and artfully concealed a rat trap in the bag of doughnuts. The kind commonly used in a multitude of houses, warehouses and anywhere else the rodents frequented. As anyone knows, these things are not toys. Soon after the DC-3 was airborne and settled into the long flight, but with no passengers aboard, Ron opened the doughnut bag, his mouth watering in anticipation.

"I don't know to this day why I looked in the doughnut bag," he recalled, "but I did. Generally I just reach in and grab. And I see this big rat trap all cocked and primed for me. I couldn't believe it!"

"At first I started to get mad. Those damn things can injure a person, maybe break fingers. So I decided I'd get back at the co-pilot, as I was pretty certain he was behind the miserable trick."

Ron smeared his right hand with a liberal splotch of catsup from the galley's cabinet. Then he wrapped it neatly with a cloth table napkin. After he was prepared for his act of retribution, he took a table knife and carefully reached into the bag and tripped the trap.

The mighty 'thwack!' of the heavy trap's wire jaw hitting the wooden base of the trap reverberated faintly to the pilots over the engines' drone. They studiously avoided looking around into the galley, although Ron swore he thought he heard the co-pilot snicker at the sound.

Well into the flight the co-pilot was forced to leave his seat to visit the lavatory. But Ron suspected that curiosity was a contributing factor to Nature's call. He found Ron reclining in his seat, cradling his 'injured' hand across his chest.

"What happened to you?" the co-pilot, Dan, asked.

184

"Someone put a rat trap in the doughnuts and I got my hand caught."

"Who would do a thing like that? Is it broken?" Dan was beginning

to show some concern. "Looks like it's bleeding. Are you alright?" His face seemed to reflect a growing doubt that maybe he shouldn't have taken part in so drastic a practical joke.

"It broke the skin on my fingers, but I think it's stopped bleeding. I'll look at it in a little while," was Ron's weak reply. "But I think my fingers are getting numb and they hurt when I try to move them."

"Well you take it easy," Dan counseled solemnly, and then he returned to his seat, lines of guilt by now plainly scrawled on his face. Ron could see the two pilots discussing something quietly. Now and then one or the other would look back at him. After waiting for what he thought should be a reasonable time for blood to congeal, Ron secretly disposed of the catsup stained napkin and wrapped his hand with a fresh, clean one.

For the balance of the flight through Canada's wintry skies Ron lolled in his seat, reading and napping. He was totally at ease with the situation, secure in the knowledge he was going to come out of this one a winner. And he did!

At their remote destination 'airport' in western Canada, actually a gravel and groat airstrip in the bush, Ron was urged to stay in the warmth of the line shack, where he sipped coffee and watched through the frosty window while Dan attended to putting the DC-3 to 'bed'. In the morning he enjoyed the same luxury while Dan, apparently still suffering from a sense of guilt, volunteered to service and pre-flight the aircraft in preparation for the return trip.

It was indeed a pleasure flight for Ron, who said it threatened to become boring. Normally he would have relieved one of the pilots to give them a chance to stretch their legs. By the time they landed at their home base Ron's hand had recovered remarkedly, to the relief of both pilots. They never knew he had been successful in pulling off a counter-deception. It was additionally gratifying to Ron because he wasn't harassed about his love for doughnuts after that.

Early on I learned what airlines had known long before: The mechanic/pilot classification so prevalent in many corporate aviation operations then was nothing more than a stopgap measure. Dressing a mechanic in a business suit and placing him in the right seat not only imposes stress on the mechanic, the pilot and the operation of the flight, but the overall operation of a flight department.

People in either profession have the obligation of staying current with regulations, coping with the physical and mental aspects of maintenance or flying, and otherwise constantly keeping abreast of the state-of-the-art of their respective professions. It's enough to keep up with one without the additional responsibilities of another.

I cannot speak for others who experienced the Jekyll-Hyde syndrome; no doubt for some, it worked well. And there's no way of knowing how many mechanic/pilots switched professions and became full-time pilots. For me the dual role was uncomfortable. When I was offered a co-pilot's position I chose to remain in maintenance. Although I liked to fly and had a commercial pilot's license, I based that decision on my experiences in the dual role of mechanic/pilot and my perceptions of the two professions.

I flew for several years in a corporate operation as a fill-in for the co-pilot during vacation or when other circumstances precluded his presence for a trip. There were three of us: Pilot and flight operations manager, co-pilot and myself. I was the mechanic, parts buyer, cleaner, inspector and general hangar handyman. The corporate aircraft was a Lockheed 18-56, a Lodestar.

I had a private pilot's license with a single-engine land rating. Later on, using the last segment of my G.I. Bill, I trained for and acquired a commercial pilot's rating with a blue seal. That unique endorsement meant that if I inadvertently flew into clouds or weather, I could — in theory — get me and the airplane back into visual flight conditions.

It was not a formal instrument rating. The blue seal's more practical application was to hold the license overhead against the sky. If the sky matched the blue seal, conditions were favorable for flight. If not, the flight should be scrubbed. I obtained the commercial rating because training was available and having it might advance my career.

The very first flight on which I was pressed into service as co-pilot was one hour and fifty-minutes of flight in solid instrument conditions.

It was a shocking introduction to computing times to the next omni with a hand-held computer, communications with air traffic control and the multitude of other in-flight activities. Besides serving coffee and doughnuts to the passengers. Distance measuring equipment, radar, transponders and other navigational aids were to come later. Manipulating the hand-operated computer was the primary tool for figuring distance, time-to-station, estimating time to the next station and a host of other computations.

In time I became more proficient in the duties of a co-pilot with sporadic (at best) in-flight instructions. Eventually I could hold course, altitude and attitude in instrument conditions with considerable dependency.

The intensity of my in-flight training depended on with whom I flew, not that it was all that intense. But I was never to fly an instrument approach or, for that matter, trained to land the airplane entirely on my own. In those years of flying I was supervised on a grand total of five landings — no take-offs.

A professional pilot who might read this account might be of the opinion the chief pilot, or his regular co-pilot-turned-captain, had nothing to work with. I would, of course, disagree.

If I had attained a level of proficiency high enough to navigate and relieve the pilot at the controls while he went to the head or had a cup of coffee, then I should have been considered for further training. I would have accepted the bare minimum of getting the Lockheed on a runway without undue loss of dignity, pride, equipment or life, not necessarily in that order, if the pilot became incapacitated. Perhaps the pilots reasoned they were inexorable and would never become ill in flight. Or maybe the status quo was working well and need not be disturbed; whatever fit the scope of management of the operation.

Was it possible the pilots didn't have the self-confidence to instruct properly, although they were thoroughly experienced and proven pilots? For certain, the chief pilot seemed not to have an operational policy to include looking to the future, except one he publicly stated: "If I'm on the airplane, I'll do the flying."

I still recall vivid memories of a flight from Burbank, California, to our base in West Virginia.

We were dead-heading home in the Lockheed after some extensive modifications on the airplane at Qualitron Aero at the Lockheed Air Terminal in Burbank. We droned across the Mohave Desert into a furnace-like morning sun in fine, calm, clear skies.

Ultimately, the varied hues of Arizona's landscape rolled under us like we were flying over an oil painting of an artist's perspective, while I stared across the brassy skies with little to do. Finally, over New Mexico's spectacular exhibition of evolution's labors through millennia, I was permitted to bestir myself and fly the airplane. The pilot dozed off.

I checked the instruments and noted the time. Now I was doing something other than being the RSR — right seat robot. That's doing nothing more than talking to bodiless voices and twirling radio knobs.

But the radios were silent, the omni needles were pointing to where they were supposed to point and the instruments were indicating all was well with the two Wright engines. Occasionally I made delicate, minute adjustments to the elevators' trim; we lacked the luxury of an auto-pilot. Otherwise the flight continued uneventfully.

It was an enjoyable period for me. The airplane was virtually flying itself but it proved to be a very brief interval of escaping boredom. I chanced to glance over at the pilot and looked into his bleary eyes.

"I'll take it," he announced, and took hold of the control wheel. I felt his feet jar the rudder pedals and pulled mine back. I glanced at the clock. A total of fifteen-minutes had elapsed during my tenure at the controls. There would be no more flying time for me for the balance of the eleven-hour flight.

That attitude and policy, or lack thereof, on the part of the chief pilot caused undue personal anxiety and stress to the regular co-pilot simply because he too was deprived of intensive, on-going training.

He had preceded me in maintenance and was pressed into service as co-pilot, when the previous co-pilot resigned. He had acquired a commercial pilot's license with instrument rating and had a course in weather from United Airlines. Then the time arrived when another command pilot was required. Consequently, the co-pilot was subjected to a 'crash' course in instrument approaches, air work and landings in the Lockheed in order to be rated in type.

He passed his flight check and received his type rating. It was a huge tribute to his perseverance and tenacity. However, the instantaneous, accelerated preparation for the transition and subsequent flight examination told on him. It was an unreasonable demand and totally unnecessary, had he been permitted to share flight legs, approaches and landings. I flew with him for many hours as RSR and found him reliable — a solid, though not a finesse pilot — and would be sure to get the job done.

Meanwhile, even flying with him, the instructions in getting the aircraft safely to earth if I had to, escaped me.

The lack of training tormented me constantly. I often wondered about the end results if I were suddenly forced into a situation where the balance of the flight depended on my inadequacies. Other than being unnecessary it was altogether unfair to myself and any passengers to be subjected to a potentially disastrous situation.

There were numerous discussions between the chief pilot and myself concerning a pittance of training for me, if only to direct the aircraft to a reasonably successful arrival on a runway, but with no satisfaction at all. Once, while returning from New York on an early night flight, I offered to forego a well-deserved raise in pay as a trade-off for training. The offer was neither refused nor accepted and the status quo remained in effect, except for the raise. I did receive that, which wasn't really the point. But, considering the state of things, I didn't object!

Finally, to my vast relief, another pilot was needed in the expanding operation and I was offered the opportunity to move up into being a full-time pilot. I thought instantly of the countless hours of sitting like an automaton in the right seat. The times of manipulating radio knobs, the plotter, talking to traffic control centers, approach controls and towers and enduring the frustrations of trying to answer the tiny, nagging question: "What will you do if...?" a question I couldn't answer.

There was no reason to expect more than the position of RSR in the near future if I accepted the offer. I settled the matter for all time by immediately rejecting it and shook 'the monkey' off my back.

If there was any value to it, the chief pilot's remark: "I'd rather you stay in maintenance anyway," could be interpreted favorably. Nevertheless, I've never forgotten that period of unwarranted, extreme stalling to train me. The saving graces in being confronted with an emergency were: The pilots kept their health; those wonderfully dependable Wright engines performed admirably as did the Lockheed, and there were no in-flight close encounters that could have been disastrous.

It would require considerable research to learn how many mechanics performed in the dual role of co-pilot/mechanic. Suffice to say, from personal knowledge, there were more than a few. Also, the number of Help Wanted ads in trade publications searching for bodies to fill that position would tend to reinforce that perception.

191

Undoubtedly there were, and still are, many who made the
transition from maintenance to piloting. But, on balance, the practice
seemed in most cases to be nothing more than a design to reduce
operational expenses while playing Russian roulette with chance
every time a flight was scheduled.

It is difficult enough to maintain an aircraft properly. There are
constant changes in equipment, new and better methods and materials, keeping records and staying current with regulations and
paperwork. Changing hats from one whole profession to another
evokes considerable mental and physical transition. Pilotage and
maintenance are equally demanding in their own right. To flip back
and forth between them is like ignoring little problems to create
holocausts.[38]

There is another aspect to the transfiguration from mechanic to
pilot: It seems to relegate the former forever, to a cut below the salt.

I cannot speak for airline flying, how many first officers are
former mechanics or flight engineers. But in corporate aviation then,
erstwhile mechanics who elected to become full-time pilots couldn't
quite be included in the 'pilot club'. That was readily apparent when
corporate air crews sat in spaces provided for them at various FBO's,
awaiting the return of company executives from whatever business
they had flown to their destinations to conduct, and then show up to
return home.

During those bull sessions pilots-in-command would dominate the
discussions.

These could include every subject from weather encountered and
the nuances of air traffic control to the attributes of their skill or the
aircraft they flew. Invariably, co-pilots who attempted to join the

conversations were largely ignored. although they had never turned a wrench. But the co-pilots who were known to have been mechanics seemed to bear a stigma. One got the feeling that, in the eyes of the command pilots, they were akin to being untouchables and, therefore, to be somewhat ostracized.

It was remarkable, on the other hand, that if a mechanic was present but not acting in the dual role of co-pilot/mechanic he was treated well, almost with respect. He was allowed to associate with the group and even permitted to contribute some dialogue where appropriate. Thus the class separation was maintained without threat to either. I found that concept true, as most any serviceman has, in the Air Corps. Often I conversed, as other enlisted men did, with officers on some subject.

However, there was an awareness that an invisible line was not to be crossed.

In retrospect it seemed to me that using a co-pilot who held a private pilot's license, as I did at the beginning of my tenure as a spare co-pilot, was on the brink of illegality. But apparently the FAA held the view that a corporate aircraft was, in fact, a privately-owned aircraft — which they are. Therefore, the crew wasn't obliged to strictly meet the criteria of those flying in commercial operations.

That's what I was led to believe, but I didn't directly question an FAA agent on the subject. On the other hand, a pilot-in-command of an aircraft in the class of the Lockheed was required to be rated in type.

Fortunately, corporate aviation has advanced dramatically in employing qualified aircrews. Further, pilots exchange flight legs assuring that co-pilots remain current in flying the aircraft. It is the rule, rather than the exception now.

All in all, there was a plus in my experience of flying as co-pilot, in spite of my concerns. I learned quite a lot about pilotage, handling the airplane, navigation and the idiosyncrasies of the air traffic control system, in addition to weather. At the same time, I could observe and feel how the engines ran and the airplane operated. Since I maintained the Lockheed, I was privy to the sounds, the vibrations that carried a subtle message, how the controls responded to commands and other perceptions.

Those insights were not available with the aircraft sitting on the ground, except for running the engines. Even so, in flight is where engines can truly be assessed while they're running steadily, hour after hour. There is something to be said about being strapped to an airplane in flight to get a feel for what you've accomplished to get it there.

It wasn't that I didn't like to fly. I did (and do) but the primary reason I abhorred my dual role was the training, or lack of it, placing me in an untenable position. Admittedly, I thought it a consummate waste of time to fly someone somewhere, and spending boring hours waiting for the passengers to appear for the return flight home. I have never been one to watch wallpaper dry. There is always something to do that is productive and occupying and, at least, being self-satisfying Not necessarily compensating in the sense of personal monetary gain.

Nor did I feel swindled by the fact that I was filling a higher-paying position on mechanic's wages, although that would have its limits over a long period of time. The fact remains, however, I was trained in, and established a career in maintenance, feeling no compulsion to change careers in midstream. In that sense, flying complemented my maintenance talents; maintenance did not complement my flying.

One night in Chicago an observation was directed to me that more than reinforced , and bared, the truth that I was in the right church but the wrong pew when it was necessary to perform as RSR.

We flew a delegation of executives to Chicago for an overnight trip. They were marketing and sales types and were conducting a seminar for regional dealers. It was a full-blown affair with all the whistles and bells designed to exhort the dealers into more activity — meaning sell more! The flight crew, both of us, were invited to attend.

After an excellent dinner we felt comfortable enough to observe the meeting and the talks. It was the least we could do. When business ended the attendees were invited to partake in free libations at the open bar. It goes without saying the invitation was accepted with gusto by the dealers.

I chanced to be seated at a table with three dealers and got into a conversation with one, apropos of nothing. Finally he asked me what my role with the company was.

"I'm on the flight crew, as co-pilot," I said.

"You don't look like a pilot," he said. "You look more like someone who likes to fish!" It was an off-hand remark without any sense of personal insult or with a demeaning insinuation. I assured him that I, in fact, did like to fish for sport, but wouldn't consider doing so to make a living. But his comment aroused a host of thoughts and questions in my mind.

What are pilots supposed to look like? Is there a generic model that dictates the appearance? I was dressed neatly in a business suit; my hands were clean; my fingernails, while not manicured, were unbroken and trimmed. For a complete stranger to make such a statement seemed as though some unknown power of perception was at work. It emerged as an encouraging omen, rather than an offensive confrontation.

In any event, the situation was resolved in a matter of weeks after that trip to Chicago, with the addition of aa full-time pilot in the operation to relieve me. The wonder of the entire situation was: Why did it take so long to realize another pilot was needed? The regular co-pilot — who quit when I joined the operation — was subject to the same concept of playing RSR. It was repeated when the mechanic moved up(?) to RSR and I succeeded him in maintenance!

I returned to my world of maintenance and ground operations where I belonged, and my life functioned smoothly again. From then on I flew for personal pleasure in light aircraft and gliders or to test an airplane — within the parameters of my license — after doing maintenance on it!

13

Murphy's Law
And Trying Times....

One Sunday, before joining the Army Air Corps, I drove by the Fairchild aircraft factory north of Hagerstown, Maryland. It was also building fabric-covered airplanes then. The smell of aircraft dope hung over the buildings and permeated the entire neighborhood around the buildings with an invisible pungent aura. It would have gladdened the heart of a teen age dope-sniffer. I could relate to it because of building models.

Approximately eight-months after acquiring my license I approached the factory to apply for work; the odor had long since vanished. Instead of fabric-covered airplanes the ones parked on the flight test ramp were sheathed in gleaming aluminum.[39]

They were busy building Packets for an Air Force contract and needed help. My newly acquired Aircraft & Engine mechanic's license smoothed the way for being immediately hired.

I opted for the flight line, but there were no openings. Those positions were normally filled with veteran employees; I'm sure that's the usual operating agenda for most factories. Instead, I was assigned to help build outer wing panels, that part of the wing from a production break at the engine nacelles, outboard. More specifically, the crew I became a member of assembled the section's skeletal framework: Ribs to spars, stringers to ribs and sundry small, intermediate members.

We also drilled rivet holes in spar caps for the wing skin's attachment. We were building C-82's dubbed 'Packets', an acronym relative to their design. They were a new twin engine cargo aircraft with short field capabilities.[40]

For a time, at the outset of the six months I was there it was interesting work. Actually, it was a valuable introduction to working with sheet metal assembly methods. Prior to this, my experience had been accumulated by working with dope and fabric and tubing, as far as aircraft structure was concerned. There had been some few small repairs to cowling and other minor sheet metal components, but nothing compared to this. It was not only a very constructive experience, but it also was an opportunity to gain insight into how an aircraft factory operated. During lunch hour I'd wander through the main assembly area like a tourist, observing the steps a multitude of components went through to be assembled into a whole airplane.

Factory engineering provided templates to lay out and drill rivet holes in the wing spars' flanges. When we had completed the skeleton of the wing panel it would move to another jig where the wing skins were attached. The templates were about three feet long and spanned several wing stations. They were patterned with precisely laid out holes to guide a drill bit. The holes were bushed for a close-tolerance fit. The templates were made of steel and as wide as the spar caps. They were about three-eights of an inch thick and approximately five-inches wide. Information was stamped on them for proper positioning on the wing spars.

There was one template I'd always had trouble with. For some reason, or reasons, known only to engineering or some other section or person, each end was a confusion of stamped numbers, arrows and other hieroglyphics. There were pilot holes in the template that matched pilot holes in the spar caps used to attach the template with cleco fasteners. The trouble was, although the pilot holes were aligned, the template still could be installed improperly, if the stamped instructions were interpreted incorrectly.

"Why is this template so confusing?" I asked Fraley, the lead man on the wing jig. "There's no problem with the others when they're pinned to the spar caps." The first time I'd used it he had helped me install it, but also had cautioned me to be careful and install it correctly. But I noticed he was somewhat confused, too, reading the lettering and numbering on the template's ends while he was instructing me.

"You've asked me that before and I've told you I don't know," he said. "I've warned the foreman, but no one's done anything about it, as you can see."

At the time of this graphic illustration of how Murphy's Law is always present, the skeleton of another wing panel had been assembled on the jig by the previous crew. Its ribs were attached to the spars and some intermediate structural members were attached.

There remained only for the wing skin attach rivet holes to be drilled and a few other steps accomplished. Then the panel would be moved for riveting the skins to the skeleton. I pinned the riveting templates to the spars' upper caps and began to drill. The drill bit I started with was nice and sharp and my work progressed nicely until I started drilling the first hole in the questionable template.

As the drill bit ate its way into the spar cap a satisfying, shiny curl of aluminum began emerging from its flutes. There was no need to exert other than a smidgen of pressure on the drill motor. A sharp drill will easily cut its way through metal without excessive pressure. If a mechanic wants to punch a hole he should use a punch press. But this, the very first hole guided by the template seemed to take more time than necessary, based on previous holes, hundreds of them, that had been drilled in other spar caps. Maybe my drill bit wasn't as sharp as I thought. Perhaps the flutes were becoming clogged.

I withdrew the bit entirely to clear away that possibility, reinserted it and continued drilling. Finally I felt the bit penetrate completely. But I had an uneasy feeling about that hole; a tiny inner voice said something was wrong.

I leaned over the spar and looked at the reverse of the spar cap and shuddered. The drill bit had emerged at the radius of the spar cap flange and the web. The hole was slightly off dead center of the radius. I found Fraley.

"You'd better come take a look at something," I said. He followed me to the template. "Take a look at the other end of this hole." I pointed to it. There was a protracted silence while he stuck his head between two ribs and studied the exit point of the drill bit.

Finally he straightened and turned to me. "Well, I guess we'd better pack our tools," he said calmly. "Take the template off and go on drilling on the next template until I get back."

He took the template and disappeared leaving me in a mental quandry, laced with a dab of worry. Was he serious about a potential termination of employment or not?

Fifteen-minutes later three engineers and the foreman had a high-level conference on the wing jig at the rivet hole. An Air Force representative — I assumed he was an engineer too — attended the meeting. I couldn't hear what they were saying because of the noise of my drill motor. Finally they disappeared in the direction of the engineering section across the assembly floor. Fraley reappeared about an hour later.

"I guess we're safe for now," he said. "They (meaning the engineers) want us to polish the hole at the radius to remove all sharp edges. 'It'll be all right', they said."

We never saw that template again. Instead, just before quitting time that day, an engineer brought a new one to the wing jig. Five sets of distinct directions were plainly stamped in the clean metal with no other confusing, irrelevant symbols. There was 'Inb'd' and 'Outb'd' at the appropriate ends; 'Top-Main Spar', and 'Sta... to Sta...'. (I don't remember the station numbers.) Engineering was also thoughtful in stamping "Aft" with a nice large arrow. Additionally there was a drawing number for the wing series and template. Nothing more!

Dutch, that wise, self-styled purveyor of aphorisms, would have delighted in the incident. It served to reiterate the truth in his favorite expression: 'Everything turns out for the best.' In this instance the wing jig crew got a new template and a problem was eliminated. But the affair was a striking example of what can transpire when Murphy's Law inadvertently influences a technical activity.

I wasn't aware of it at the time, but there was another adventure in pushing that law to the limit close by. It occurred directly across from Fairchild Aircraft's flight line and the building where I worked. I learned about it from a co-mechanic when I joined Capital Airlines later.

His name was Joe Grening. One night we began to compare notes about where we had worked when he mentioned he had worked at an FBO at the Hagerstown airport. The shop was located almost directly north, and across the east-west runway from Fairchild.

His experience involved an Ercoupe, a two-place, low-wing tricycle gear creation with only one flight control: A control wheel on a shaft that emerged from the instrument panel. It operated the ailerons and rudders when it was turned and the elevators when it was pushed or pulled. There were no rudder pedals. The idea of the design was to make the airplane easy to fly. I flew one once and had to land in a crosswind. That was an enlightening experience! It was my first and only flight in an Ercoupe.

Joe had done some work on the Ercoupe's engine and parked it on the FBO's flight line to ground check it. As it happened, the airplane was headed toward Fairchild's flight line, approximately one-thousand feet or so away. He didn't tie it down, a contributing factor to the successful application of Murphy's Law. Then Joe cracked the throttle open, turned on the ignition and swung the prop. There was no one holding the brake on in the cockpit nor were there chocks at the wheels. Everything he did was against the laws of reasoning.

The engine started on the first swing of the prop and the airplane obediently began to move. By the time Joe got out of the way and tried to reach the cockpit the airplane was trundling across the grass toward the runway and Fairchild. Although he tried desperately to catch up with the Ercoupe he couldn't match its approximately twenty-five m.p.h speed!

The airplane crossed the runway on a course straight as an arrow for the open doors of Fairchild's flight line hangar.. Had it succeeded in reaching the flight line and open doors the results would have been horrifying. But fortunately, there was a picket fence along the opposite side of the runway and the Ercoupe hit the fence, the prop chewing up pickets and throwing splinters everywhere. That's where it stopped, impaled on a broken fence post that pierced its underbelly just aft of the firewall.

I didn't know why Joe needed to confess to such a flagrant disdain for invoking Murphy's Law. He seemed to be a sensible, responsible person. But, since confession, they say, is good for the soul, it probably made him feel better. On the other hand, he may have been indulging in self-deprecation, still disgusted with himself. Which would have been understandable; he violated every rule in the book concerning ground-running engines.

Undoubtedly there are untold numbers of mechanics who have experienced, sometime in their careers, situations when the mysterious Murphy has evoked his law. And there are times without number when a routine task has begun that's led to a vicious series of distressing events. A litany of happenings that would make an omelet out of a simple plan. That occurred in what I think of as my 'Enchilada Encounter' . Although Murphy's Law wasn't directly applicable I seemed to sense 'his' presence hovering nearby.

That was when I believe I came as close to dying as I did in World War II. But this wouldn't be a swift, clean death like a steel jacketed bullet would inflict. It would be drawn out and terribly agonizing when it came. I blamed my old friend Ken Burnham for instigating the awful suffering and unusual attempt to make a silk purse from a sow's ear, or several, for that matter.

"Ken Leech needs some help," he informed me. Leech owned and operated a crop spraying and dusting service, one-hundred and fifty miles down state. "He has two Pawnees that need to be relicensed and there's an engine to be overhauled. His mechanic can't handle the work."

"Why don't you go?" I wondered aloud.

"Nothing doing," he declared firmly. "I wouldn't touch that for all the tea in China." The remark didn't make sense, since I never saw him drink tea. He preferred Ancient Age, which resembles tea — in color. I couldn't help but be suspicious. "I told Leech to call you since you're not doing anything. Besides, I'm busy."

I had to concede that was true, having recently returned from spending the summer in Montana on a weather research operation. And Burnham did have a Pratt & Whitney R-985 radial engine disassembled that he was overhauling.

"It doesn't make any difference if I'm working or not," I countered. "You're not telling me everything. I think you're trying to get me into deep trouble."

But, in spite of my suspicions the idea started me thinking. Why not? I would be well-paid, and besides, I could fish the headwaters of the Rio Grande River in the lovely mountains west of the airport. I casually mentioned that possibility, knowing how Burnham would react. He couldn't cope with anyone, especially me, fishing if he couldn't.

"Now listen," Burnham growled, "you're supposed to go down there to work, not fish. That means nights if you have to get that outfit out of the bind it's in, in time for when the spraying season starts."

I reminded Burnham that he wasn't my agent and I'd likely do what was necessary to get the job done. Also, I didn't foresee having to work nights and weekends to do it. Burnham was genuinely disturbed with realizing that good trout fishing would be easily available to me and I would be doing that, not him. Leech called me the next day.

"I suppose you've heard by now I need some help," he said. "I was told that you're available."

I admitted I wasn't doing much or, at the least, anything that could not wait. We discussed what needed to be done to get his Piper Pawnees ready for the spraying season rapidly approaching.

We haggled briefly about pay and expenses and I convinced him what I was asking was truly in our mutual interests. After all, I pointed out, he wasn't dealing with a runny nosed youngster just out of school. Besides, he had had all winter to prepare for the crop spraying season, which would start in two months, and pressure was worth something. Also, there was my overall responsibility to consider.

We finally agreed to a sensible, as I perceived it, arrangement.

I left Burnham in his snug little engine overhaul shop, loaded my tools in my pickup truck and went south.

Leech's Flying Service was housed in a large, concrete block hangar with a corrugated tin roof and sides. Outside, two wrecked Pawnees huddled forlornly against the north side next to a cluster of fifty-five gallon steel barrels. These leaned in tired disarray against each other in rigid, intimate angles.

Along the east wall there was an interesting assortment of boards, metal tubes and odds and ends of sheet metal. There was a small, battered tank truck and some wooden crates. Some tumbleweeds were lodged between the crates and the truck. Obviously the motto here was 'Save a little and have a lot.'

Inside the hangar were two Pawnees that appeared to be in the middle of half-hearted inspections and repairs. Conditions were better than outside, but not by much. I could see the hangar held possibilities if it were cleaned and organized and the several large windows washed to admit more light. I couldn't ever understand why general aviation maintenance hangars, for the most part, are allowed to become filthy, in a state of general disorder. It seemed to be the rule, rather than the exception, in many I've seen. It must be there's another unwritten law that dictates that the accumulation of clutter is in direct proportion to the availability of open space and flat surfaces.

The offices, restrooms and shop occupied an addition built on the length of the hangar's west wall. The south end of the hangar created a vortex when a west wind was blowing, which was often. That created tiny wavelets of fine, gritty dirt along the hangar doors with enough of it sifting under the doors to develop a diminutive ridge of the same material.

To his credit, Leech had an incredible variety of tools, supplies and parts in the shop and, wonder of wonders, a barely-used magnaflux machine.

In spite of those assets though, I was seriously questioning my wisdom in accepting the assignment.

Burnham had told me Leech's mechanic had a severe drinking problem. When I met him, his appearance and breath confirmed that intelligence. He briefed me on the status of the engine overhaul which was simply stated: "The engine is totally disassembled and I've measured the cylinders' bores and installed new valve guides. They're ready," he declared.

He went into the hangar to continue work on the stricken Pawnees and I began to arrange the engine's parts, hardware and components into some semblance of order. Everything was scattered helter-skelter on a long work bench. I always had a problem with accepting someone's word that 'everything was in order', especially a stranger's, when taking over in the middle of a project. After cleaning the work bench and re-arranging the engine parts I began inspecting them for condition, fits and clearances. I started with the cylinders.

They had been cleaned, but the bores were out of limits; the new valve guides appeared to have been reamed with a drill bit. That was, in fact, what had been done. The mechanic admitted to it when I questioned him. He had taken them to a local automotive machine shop to install and ream the valve guides.

Spiraled hashmarks resembling the lands and grooves in a rifle's bore scored the gleaming brass-alloy tubes of the guides. When I inserted the valve stems as a quick check, they wobbled wickedly. The cylinders' walls appeared to be resurfaced with a huge burr.

After informing Leech the cylinders would need to be overhauled and certified I dispatched them by courier Pawnee to a cylinder overhaul shop. Leech dispatched the mechanic to early retirement even before I could ask him where all the engine parts were, and what had been ordered. He was asked to terminate his employment that fast.

While the engine work was on hold I inspected the first Pawnee and was appalled at the results. The list of discrepancies read like a prediction of impending disaster.

Numerous holes in fabric; corrosion on fuselage tubes; a terribly frayed aileron control cable; the throttle control-to-carburetor attach bolt hole in the air valve arm worn nearly through. It chilled me to visualize the consequences if it had broken when the pilot needed more power to pull up over wires or trees at the end of a spray run.

The discrepancy list was long. But, with the help of Byron, Leech's son-in-law, we managed to get the Pawnee airworthy in four long days. He was not only conscientious, but a natural with tools and had a good head on his shoulders.

I inspected the second Pawnee, put Byron to work on it and turned to the engine. It was a Lycoming 0-540 model, one of Lycoming's truly dependable engines. The cylinders had returned from the overhaul shop with approval tags and the balance of the overhaul should go well if I could get the parts together.

But then I became deathly sick!

I had been alternating my meals between two dingy cafes in the little farming village near the airport. One was operated by a stout fellow of German descent, the other by an individual of questionable ancestry. Otherwise the only other option was to drive to a good restaurant in a larger town south of the village. That would require a forty-mile round trip and have an impact on what time I went to bed. I was working twelve to thirteen hours a day.

I've always made a habit of ordering meals at small cafes where, I thought, a cook couldn't wreak on the food. Also I avoid ordering Mexican food if the cook isn't American-Mexican, or, of Mexican ancestry. Violating the latter rule was my misfortune. Did Murphy also operate in the restaurant business?

I ordered two beef enchiladas which, surprisingly, were served within five-minutes. That alone should have alerted me to order something else. They were smothered in a thin sauce that had a peculiar metallic sheen but I passed that off, blaming the dim lighting. I ate one and a part of the second one. After eating I returned to my room in the only hotel in the village, a nondescript two story building, but the bed and room were clean. It was then the first pangs of awful misery began.

By dawn I had not only spent a virtually sleepless night, but came to understand better the meaning of the phrase, 'She looked like she'd swallowed a watermelon.' My aching stomach was horribly distended and diarrhea raged in my intestines.

I struggled through the morning on a cup of coffee for breakfast and a bottle of cold Dr. Pepper for lunch. Between times my path to the rest room became well-worn. The alert Byron silently watched my never-ending trips and could stand it no longer. He had to ask.

"Are you sick?"

"I guess I am, but I don't know why except for the food I ate last night." I had been thinking about that all morning and reached that conclusion. Byron cruelly confirmed my worst fears.

"Where did you eat?"

"At Joe's Cafe," I said.

Byron wagged his head sadly. "You poor devil. Those enchiladas were probably half rotten. That cafe isn't known for being clean and serving good food." His remark made my misery more acute while deep despair infused my soul. I had become an unwilling victim of the law of unintended consequences.

I struggled through the balance of the day somehow and even managed to get some work done, but that night was a repetition of the previous one, with breakfast the next morning no better than before. But at noon I was delivered of the evil in my stomach in a driving dust storm.

The wind started blowing about 11:30 from the west; by the time I left the hangar to try to eat some lunch — I couldn't imagine what — it had risen to approximately fifty-knots. On its brawling lunge across the wide, flat valley it picked up tons of topsoil from the fields surrounding the airport, creating a dust blizzard.

It was the type of wind that blows fine grit in your eyes and hair, and between your teeth, and still roars in your ears after you've gone inside. Visibility deteriorated to about a mere ten-feet or so in front of my truck's radiator so I pulled off the highway and stopped to wait it out. And then my stomach began churning with violent spasms. I was barely able to get out of the truck before the vomiting began.

It was there in the howling, choking dust and wind, that I leaned weakly against the truck and let my distressed stomach rid itself of the devil in it. A natural process I should have encouraged sooner.

I began to improve almost immediately. The wind slackened as

210

I continued to a nearby store and bought a can of mixed fruit. It and the coffee stayed in place that afternoon, while my spirits and health improved dramatically. That evening I ate another can of fruit and a small pastry with coffee — very cautiously. Even the night was restful.

The next morning with some trepidation, I ate a bowl of oatmeal at the German's cafe and had a productive morning at work. There was another lunch of canned fruit and pastry, and by quitting time I was ravenous. In spite of quitting late, I drove the forty-mile round trip to a good restaurant down the highway and ate a steak dinner. My sleep that night was dreamless and exceedingly refreshing.

I worked Saturdays, but not on Sundays. Sundays I spent along the beautiful reaches of the Rio Grande where the fishing was rewarding and the scenery alluring.

In six weeks the two Pawnees were ready for service and the engine installed in the third and prepared for flight. I packed my tools and, with my pay and Leech's heartfelt thanks, returned home.[41]

Burnham's distress was delightfully satisfying when I gave him my report on fishing, but his expressed sympathy for my terrible food-poisoning experience didn't seem sincere. Probably he couldn't empathize with my misfortune because of the wonderful fishing I'd had and he had not. I left him with the admonition to never again find something for me to occupy my time with.

Anybody who reads this can attest to the ever-ominous presence of the obscure Murphy, a character who is never seen, but whose influence can be brought to bear wherever mechanics work.

Some people seem to be especially vulnerable to Murphy's Law, whether by an over-riding fear they could do something wrong or simply being of that nature. A comparison would be in the example 'He seems to be accident prone.' I knew one mechanic who fit that syndrome exactly, which unfortunate attribute only paves the way for the application of Murphy's Law. But unforeseen, unexpected mechanical mis-adventures happen, also, to the most careful, experienced mechanics!

There is one unwritten law I've found that has a decided impact on possible Murphy's Law application: Do not ever close an area where work has been done, without one final thorough inspection before closing. If you're still not sure, look again! The ever-present and alert Murphy will probably take advantage of any deviation from it. Further, the victim of Murphy's Law would be undoubted charged with criminal intent, given the mind set in present times.
Both Murphy and his dupe would then become the victims of unintended consequences.

Fortunately, there have been few disastrous results when Murphy's Law has influenced maintenance activities — or, at least, reported. In general, such miscues have been found and corrected before flight or, they have not directly affected flight operations of an aircraft.

Murphy's Law causes the victim either acute embarrassment or, a severe critique of the victim's common sense, brain power and thinking dexterity and, even ancestry. Or a combination of all.

One episode I've remembered vividly over the years, that had real potential for Murphy's application of his principle, occurred one night when we were reinstalling a Lockheed Constellation's left landing gear, particularly fitting the trunions of the main gear leg to their bearings. They were needle bearings which, as most are aware, normally aren't caged as ball bearings are. They were housed in their races that were, in turn, pressed into heavy forgings attached to structure within the nacelle.

By mechanical necessity the fit was very close between the bearing surface of the trunion and the needle bearings. Whether we had the trunion misaligned, or its edge caught on the end of one or more bearings, we were suddenly showered by a rain of needle bearings. They fell to the hangar floor amidst a layer of oil-absorbent granules — 'chicken feed' was the common acronym. The material lay thick and forbidding on the hangar floor. We were faced with the ancient saying, "Like looking for a needle in a haystack." Only it wasn't hay. We had that to be thankful for.

We stared at the broad accumulation of chicken feed on the floor in dead silence. It was as though we felt the bearings had been absorbed by the material, as it did oil and hydraulic fluid. The air seemed to be saturated with deepest despair.

Since it was virtually impossible to obtain bearings that late at night from a supplier — even from Lockheed — and borrowing a set from a competitor was out of the question because competion was fierce. Why should any airline — and we were competing with larger ones than us — stoop to help another. In fact, if another could hinder — rather than help, it wouldn't hesitate. There was only one option: We had to find them.

We got our magnets — it was night and already had our flash-lights — and set to work.

While the night foreman hovered anxiously over us, we sifted through the chicken feed on our hands and knees with magnets, and

213

recovered every one of them. If my memory serves me, there were six-hundred and twenty four needles.

We knew that because the aircraft's overhaul and maintenance documents said so. Needless to say, there was intense concentration and care installing the bearings and landing gear assembly. Which was accomplished successfully. Murphy's Law was not pertinent to us that night.

We escaped the law's awful ramifications and the wrath of our night foreman, operations, dispatch and any other person or department directly involved with getting that airplane to meet its flight schedule.

God is great!

BOEING 367-80 In lines of this aircraft the parallel to the Boeing 707 is obvious, and rightly so. The 357-80 served in the prototype role for the 707 and the KC-35. The B-707 can be credited with launching the public into fast, long-ranged air travel. Many remain in service today.   Photo' Courtesy The Boeing Company Archives

USS Macon, last of the rigid airships. USS Akron and USS Macon were intended for patrol as was the USS Shenandoah. The Akron and Macon carried Sparrow hawks for protection. The tiny fighters could be launched and retrieved in flight. Sadly, both were lost in storms within two years, ending the era of rigid airships. The Shenandoah had also crashed. Over 700-feet long, gross weight 400,000-pounds, typical of all three airships. The Graf Zeppelin was designed to carry international passengers in the ultimate of comfort approximately 60 m.p.h.   Photo' Courtesy Goodyear Tire & Rubber Company

14

Research Missionaries
and Rainmakers...

Anthropologists long ago determined that the human brain is an intriguing special instrument. In the first year after birth it is said to grow three times its original size and ultimately, achieves proportions double that of a gorilla's brain.

Therefore, natural birth would be virtually impossible if the brain and skull grew with the embryo in the womb.

That observation makes us unique, which is one reason humanity has progressed so rapidly. Added to that is our consummate curiosity. We are constantly urged on by that peculiar trait, trying — and largely being successful — to find out why, why not, or otherwise improving on something. We've also been inventing and developing busily. An inventory too extensive to attempt to cover.

Eventually, these attributes were employed within the definition of 'research.' The spectrum then developed into a means to not only learn but provided lucrative employment!

Depending on individual assessments there have been real advantages as the result of creative thinking; on the other hand, much distress has resulted. There's good and bad in everything. And sour frustration has been experienced in research when scientists have delved into changing natural events to what man thinks they should be and do.

After being involved in crude attempts to make rain — the mysteries of weather have intense attention from researchers — with a high-flying Howard DGA in the Islands, it would be many years later when I would experience research once more. But at the time I wasn't aware of it.[47]

We had removed the rear seats in the Howard and replaced them with a tank and an external spray boom. The tank held approximately one-hundred fifty gallons of ocean water. A cloud-sniffing probe was also installed under a wing with a device that collected cloud mois-ture. When the research technician decided the collection vial had gathered a sufficient quantity of moisture he pulled it into the cabin via a track mounted on a wing strut, emptied it and ran the vial out again with a cable leader to repeat the process.

The information that was collected from those flights are probably submerged deep in the files of the University of Hawaii.

My eyes were truly opened to the field of cloud research and the intensity with which it's pursued, two decades later on the Mainland. That's when I signed on with the National Center for Atmospheric

Research (NCAR) to maintain a Sweitzer, Model 2-32 sailplane. It was to be used in a project on the high plains of northeast Colorado. From the first day I reported to work until the end of summer and the project, the realm in which cloud physicists and their technicians dwelled was a continual revelation. Not only in their dedication and enthusiasm but the associated economics.

One morning soon after I started work at NCAR, I chanced upon some activity near the door of the section to which I was assigned. I paused and watched with amazement and some consternation while two research technicians sawed and hacked at the rear roof of a late model van. They were removing a section just ahead of the van's rear doors.

"What are you doing to a perfectly good roof?" I asked, consumed with curiosity.

"We need to have an opening in it."

"Why?"

"So hail can fall into the van," was the terse, miserly reply. Obviously he wasn't going to waste further explanation on a Mr. Mentally Inappropriate. I let it go at that and continued to my work area in the building. Then I raised the subject of their odd behavior to the technician in charge of our laboratory. In the elevated strata of the sciences one doesn't refer to his or her physical work area as a workshop. Laboratory is the proper word.

"Dee...what are those two guys doing to that nice van in the parking lot?" I asked. "They're cutting a big hole in its roof."

"I know," he replied. "They're going to fit a door over the hole and a wide bench inside the van under the hole. The bench will be covered with a thick pad and a camera installed to focus on the area under the hole and on the pad.

"The concept is to drive under a thunderstorm so when hail begins to fall, some of it will fall through the hole. The hailstones will be photographed as they fall into the van and hit the padded bench. Then they'll record the size of the dents the hail makes in the pad." He walked to the window and stared down at the van.

"I think that project is getting out of control," he sighed in disgust.

I applied my energies to the real world of aircraft maintenance and gave the glider a thorough inspection. Some minor repairs were needed and a new, improved nose skid needed to be installed, which wasn't a complicated operation. Then I helped a research technician install a peculiar scientific unit in the rear cockpit, now an equipment bay.

The element was designed by NCAR's scientists and made in its massive machine shop. The shop in itself was overwhelming, with just about every machine tool in existence. But the unusual product of machining and brains would, I was haughtily informed by the technician, take samples from clouds captured with external air scoops mounted in the glider's rear canopy.

The cloud vapors would exit the scoops via connecting tubes inserted in small vials mounted on the perimeter of a revolving deck on the device. After receiving cloud vapor the vials were sealed by a capping mechanism and frozen with dry ice in the vapor receiver. Ostensibly, the vapor would remain in a frozen state until the vials were rushed to a laboratory for analysis.

In my utilitarian mind I wondered what residue of cloud formation alchemy could possibly be present to analyze. I knew moisture would be present, but beyond that I had no idea. For years I always thought clouds were the result of the collision and interaction of warm and cold air masses — with a little electricity thrown in. But I'm not a cloud physicist!

Since the glider operated in the heady upper latitudes of towering cumulus build-ups, from twenty-thousand feet or higher, there was never any problem with cooling the vials. But the trouble was, the glider would return to earth, very often, with either the air scoops clogged with ice or the vapor receiver operating mechanism frozen, which rendered it inoperable. This posed a serious quandary: If they heated the vapor receiver to prevent it from icing: Likely the vials wouldn't freeze. Besides, the glider had only a small battery as an electrical source for a radio and flight instruments.

But that vapor receiver was an object to be admired, simply because of the commendable craftsmanship in metal it displayed. Those machinists in that stunningly-equipped machine shop were artists! It was impossible for me to guess how much the machine shop or the vapor receiver cost America's ever-suffering taxpayers.

The barograph, a mechanically rudimentary unit, always worked, though. The stylus and drum were operated by a spartan mechanical system of gears that defied altitude, frost, ice and anything else the elements had to offer. The arrangement was driven by a spring like a clock's that was hand-wound before every flight. It clacked grandly and aggressively, and faithfully recorded the peaks and valleys of the glider's flights scratched by the stylus on smoked aluminum foil. The scratches in and of themselves were awe-inspiring.

There on the aluminum foil was the complete history of a given flight by the glider. A long, shallow rising scratch was the reach for altitude as the glider was towed ever up by Dave's C-180. Then a hesitation as the glider released, followed by sharply rising scratches indicating lift in a cloud top. I could imagine the rate of climb by the degree of inclination of a particular scratch. Perhaps one would be followed by a scratch dipping abruptly, indicating a powerful down draft.

Then, just as suddenly, a scratch would mark the influence of an equally abrupt rise by the stylus as the glider caught mighty up currents, peaking at a towering cumulus's top. Such a picture demanded respect for the pilot's expertise.

NCAR had a small complex north of the small farming village of Grover. It consisted of a huge radome housed in a pressurized, fabric globe, with an attached small, wooden building. That was the nerve center of the entire operation. It had an impressive array of lights, switches, microphones, telephones and computers.

There were two other one-story buildings: One was used for offices, the other for a mess hall. It reminded me of a temporary Army post. Personnel were lodged in farm houses and other accommodations scattered in and around Grover. The glider's tow plane pilot, Dave Yokum, myself and two research technicians shared one farm house.

I seldom visited the complex except to eat my meals at the mess hall. It was wholesome food, cooked by three farm women and attractively priced. Actually, eating there highlighted my days, especially the home baked bread and deserts. Then, too, I could observe the strange, to me, population of scientists and technicians who lived in another world. Dave and I were on common grounds in our tiny world of aviation.

The tow plane, a Cessna turbo-charged Model 180, and the glider, were based at a wheat farm's airstrip six miles north of the complex near the Wyoming border. We hangared the glider in a metal Quonset-type building that was also used for wheat storage. The tow plane was hangared in another, shared with wheat farming equipment. A sixteen-foot long travel trailer served as 'operations' and pilot's-mechanic's ready room. Baker Field reminded me of a forward airstrip in a combat zone!

I had known Dave, both owner and pilot of the 180, for several years. He could be best described as a free-lance pilot, at the beck and

220

call of anyone needing flight services. He was an instructor as well, but his true calling was flying, most anything, most anywhere. He was deliberate in both profession and speech, laconic with a subtle sense of humor. I had never seen him angry; he simply ignored any situation that cried out for aggressive oral responses.

Dave eventually resorted to the steady income of a full-time flying job with the Colorado Division of Wildlife. His duties included stocking fingerling trout in the state's high lakes, a task he was well suited for. It involved flying over mountains with peaks as high as 14,000-feet, then descending to lakes cuddled in solid granite up to 2,000-feet below the peaks. Having dropped a lake's allotment of fingerlings it remained only to climb out of these holes to, again, clear the peaks and go on to another location or return to base.

Other tasks entailed flying biologists low over plains and mountain terrain on wild game counts and observations. Obviously, that type of flying wasn't for neophytes, considering the possibilities of being confronted with the rigid and perplexing environment of box canyons, all the while contending with the vagaries of air currents. But Dave flew his assignments without mishap. Towing a glider to release at 18,000 or 20,000-feet was a piece of cake to him.

The roofs and sides of both Quonset huts were liberally splattered with smooth, round dents, some measuring up to four inches in diameter. They were a testimonial to the might of the awe-inspiring plains thunderstorms that haunted the area. Almost daily they marched inexorably out of Wyoming to sweep on to the east and southeast, very often disgorging vast quantities of hail. If thunderstorms needed to be researched, this was the place to do it. It was amazing to me that wheat farmers in the area managed to survive such deadly onslaughts of hail on their fragile crops.

On a typical day of flight operations the telephone would blare

221

incessantly in the ready room, followed by an interval of intense conversation with Dente, the glider pilot. We would prepare the glider for flight and wheel it into position on the airstrip. Then the tow plane would be hooked to the glider with a long, nylon tow rope and then we'd wait for a launch signal from Grover. When it came, the barograph would be wound and glider and tow plane would take-off and I'd report the time to Grover. In about an hour or so the tow plane would return and Dave and I would spend two or three hours doing practically nothing, awaiting the return of the glider.

Grover dictated the target cloud for the day on coordinates from the massive radar there and it fell to Dente to fly into the thunderstorm's heights to obtain data. Generally he released from the Cessna at eighteen thousand feet and plunged into a cloud. Dente rarely talked about his harrowing flights, but the barograph mutely recorded the ups and downs of his experiences in impressive graphics on the foil's smoked surface. Every foil became data over which the cloud physicists would presumably ponder for clues to what made thunderstorms tick.

"One time on an earlier project," Dave told me, "he was spit out the top of a towering cu' at thirty-thousand feet, inverted with his controls iced." That remark increased my already considerable respect for Dente's pilotage abilities and apparent disdain for thunderstorms. It was impressive enough to forgive him for his likewise apparent disdain for society's normal standards of lifestyle and apparel.

He was tall and thin with a body as limp as fish fillet. He resembled Walt Disney's Ichabod Crane in The Legend of Sleepy Hollow cartoon. He even wore wire-rimmed glasses. In fact, with his prominent patrician nose, bony facial features and tawny hair clubbed into a be-ribboned pigtail, he could have won first prize as an Ichabod Crane look-alike. He was scholarly, although his private lifestyle and certainly his wearing apparel wouldn't indicate higher learning. He and his lady lived with four other couples in a commune in Boulder — with one bedroom — when he wasn't out on a research project.

As a matter of record Dente was a degreed nuclear physicist. I didn't ask the obvious question or questions about his living arrangements, or his profession, so I didn't learn how he became a research glider pilot — or how the couples made love in a communal setting!

Dente did not dress normally; that is, pants, shirt and shoes, as the rest of us dressed. He always wore goatskin shorts and well-worn, 'experienced' athlete's shoes — no socks! He also wore an extremely spicy, gamey body odor. When I chanced to step into the little ready room's warm confines I could tell he had been there — when he hadn't been for sometime. Probably the shorts contributed immensely to the aura: They were murky brown and shiny, like a mountain man's deerskin leggings after a long trapping season.

He was certainly durable because he always wore a thin flight suit for his excursions into the clouds. I often wondered how so lanky a body could generate sufficient heat to survive the biting chill of a cloud's upper environment. But it never seemed to affect him.

My duties were relatively light: I inspected the glider after every flight, serviced the oxygen system and barograph and did other minor tasks. Otherwise, I spent hours with Dave discussing the mores of cloud research and hashing over experiences. Occasionally a small group of 'them p.h.d.s', as Dave referred to them, would suddenly appear at the airstrip.

They would bunch up and observe an approaching line of thunderstorms, or a lone one, marveling with each other at its attributes. Invariably, all would have cameras and click away enthusiastically at the object of their group or individual affection, exclaiming in awestruck voices about an outstanding characteristic in a cloud's formation. As if they had some idea of one's optimum appearance.

"Look at them p.h.d.s," Dave would say. "Probably they'll have a group orgasm. You'd think they never saw a thunderstorm before!"

We often conjectured about how much film was exposed and what happened to the data the glider collected — when the vapor collector didn't freeze and cease to operate!

Meanwhile, the two technicians who had remodeled the van chased thunderstorms over forty or more square miles of northeastern Colorado's high plains, ever hopeful of arriving under one that was disgorging hail. They never succeeded in photographing hailstones dropping through the hole in the roof of the van, or measuring dents in the pad under the hole.

Without fail, they arrived too late: The thunderstorm had either passed on or exhausted its ability to make hail. As Dee said, that part of the total research program was out of control.

But if the research at Grover was a startling revelation on how to spend money peering into weather, with little gratification toward modifying it, there was another installation at Miles City, Montana, that was the epitome of the art. It was a tidy empire that researched clouds on a grand scale.

After the project at Grover ended I was retained by a small operation owned by two atmospheric physicists. They had won a very large government contract to study weather and clouds. They were to work in conjunction with the group at Miles City. From the beginning, because of severe personality conflicts, the two seemed determined to rescue defeat from the jaws of success. One of the owners doubled as pilot for the research aircraft. My duties were to maintain an Aero Commander 680F, the first aircraft they used for cloud research. I had my hands full preventing shoddy wiring, planning conversions and otherwise protecting the airplane from the peculiar thought processes of researchers and computer gurus.

To prepare for start-up of the contract it was necessary to mount various data-gathering equipment on and in the airplane. The first major modification consisted of reinforcing the top fuselage structure aft of the cockpit to mount a Knollenberg unit. It was one-foot in diameter and five- feet long. Air particles would be measured and counted between two lenses that emitted a laser beam between them. It weighed about thirty-pounds.

We also mounted a nose boom that extended approximately eight-feet from the fuselage nose cone to take air speed readings and pressures in undisturbed air. There were three probes mounted under the wings to record temperatures, more cloud particles and moisture in clouds. But, in spite of the horrendous opposition to aerodynamic cleanliness, imposed by these elements, the airplane flew well. Two supercharged Lycoming 540 model engines were responsible for providing power; their performance was outstanding throughout the entire program.[47]

While the two owners and their pair of technicians wired the external probes to the data recording equipment in the cabin I would look over their shoulders to make sure they didn't do anything dumb with the installation, and routing of wiring. Meanwhile, I prepared the airplane and its engines for what might be a trying period of operations. That accomplished, I departed with one technician for Miles City in a converted school bus. It was loaded with spares, computers, data recording consoles and other research paraphernalia and, one of my tool boxes.

If I was impressed with the research installation at Grover the one at Miles City was positively over-powering!

Housed in a cluster of one-story buildings and a Quonset hut the complex was situated on the edge of the airport north of Miles City, across the Yellowstone River. There was a huge radome mounted in isolated splendor about one-quarter of a mile west on the vast prairie. Its function was, of course, to sniff out promising — or otherwise — cloud formations.

There were meeting rooms, offices, rooms stuffed with computers and data analyzers, radios and other mysterious electronic devices beyond my comprehension.

Modems connected the computers with a mainframe bank somewhere near Denver and, for all I knew, anywhere else. Leaving nothing to chance, daily satellite reports of weather patterns over the western North American continent were printed out for learned eyes, complete with maps, and there were many of them. 'Them p.h.d.s' were there in force.

The buildings' roofs bristled with communication antenna of unimaginable variety and configuration. There was even a television antenna. Scattered in patterned locations on cattle ranches for miles around out on the high plains were rain measuring stations. The units recorded rainfall — which wasn't much — electronically and transmitted the readings to a low-flying airplane on demand. The information was recorded on tape in the airplane and delivered to the center for analysis; it was a sensible method if one had to collect rainfall data. The high plains of Montana are vast; it would have been a monumental task to collect information by foot, four-wheel drive vehicle, or on horseback.

This high plains research center was well-established, having been there for over fifteen years. It was an empire, within a much more vast empire of the Montana plains that seemed to go on forever.

Officially known as High Plains Experiment, the complex was the largest of three operated by the U.S. Bureau of Reclamation. It had a staff that numbered close to forty-people in the summer, to a low of fifteen during the winter months. There were two other sites: One at Goodland, Kansas, the other at Big Springs, Texas.

If the size of the organization was staggering to me, the goal, as stated in a burst of complicated, scientific language by the director, was positively overpowering to my uncomplicated mental processes.

"The primary goal," he explained, "is the reduction of critical scientific uncertainties concerning natural cloud and precipitation processes and the alternatives in cloud structure and resultant precipitation that occur when warm season convective clouds are seeded in a prescribed manner."

Instead of that long-winded dissertation, he could have said: "We are trying to find a way to make it rain." After catching his breath he went on to say, if any rainfall was induced from cloud systems spread over an area in excess of twenty-thousand square miles during rain-making experiments, it would be 'insignificant.' Well, I thought, one-quarter of a loaf is better than none!'

"We will not be trying to increase any rainfall this summer," he added. At least he had the sense to understand the uselessness in trying to flog a dead horse. I was being afforded an uncommon insight to the machinations of a bureaucracy that had the will to continue life without fear of retribution for its inadequacies and dreams. But the staff there had learned something, too: Most of the summer rainfall produced in and about Miles City came from thunderstorms that originated over the Big Horn and Absaroka mountains, far to the west. Based on that intelligence it seemed to me that natural cloud development was something that no one could really clamp his teeth on. A cloud, any cloud, would not be likely to retain its original physical makeup during an extensive journey that far away from its point of origin.

Elsewhere within the overall empire of the station there were

227

other experiments being conducted. One was the effect of increased rainfall on grain production. Another was a long-range study of species composition and relation to rainfall. There was another: A 'greenhouse' study on how much rainfall was significant to plant production of range grasses. The more I learned the more I felt fortunate, living in another world where I could wear, with dignity, dirt under my fingernails. These people, I thought, would not be capable of accepting simple answers to not so complex questions. Then I found out there were two more experiments.

One was prefaced in the form of a question: When is rainfall during the growing season beneficial? It seemed to me that everyone with a garden patch in the backyard knew the answer to that. There was the other in which a study was attempting to compare native range (grasses) growth versus that under simulated rainfall. I didn't ask how anyone could 'simulate' rainfall. In fact, I stopped asking questions altogether. I still had a fundamental appreciation of reality.

My real world of aircraft maintenance seemed comfortably secure; everything was pretty much straightforward and relatively uncomplicated. At least you knew you had several basic options if a generator quit producing electricity. A broken internal wire; perhaps new brushes were required; the bearings needed to be replaced; a commutator cried out to be attended to. My world was far more elementary and reasonable than one in which cloud physicists held " ...full-scale dress rehearsals of randomized experiments with individual cloud systems." Their words, not mine.

In spite of the constant cloud-probing flights the Aero Commander and its Lycoming engines gave me little trouble. In retrospect it was a relatively easy time for me. Other than doing daily inspections, servicing the aircraft and correcting a few minor discrepancies reported by the pilot, there was little else to do. The research technicians had daily problems with their equipment, but I stayed aloof from their activities, except to make sure they didn't tamper with the airplane's electrical systems. Besides, the technicians weren't of my breed.

Occasionally I would attend pre-flight briefings for pilots. There was an aged Piper Navajo there, too, with both landing gear well-lubricated by oil from its leaking engines. It, too, had a one pilot-owner. Of course, the Ph. D.s attended the meetings en masse. Often, the meetings would be made interesting by the aggressive clash of personalities and opinions between 'them p.h.d.s', the technicians and pilots.

I could never determine how many of 'them p.h.d.s' were in attendance in the   mix of cloud physicists and technicians. At the meetings they reminded me of a flock of penguins. It seemed they all wore clothes that were on the border line between casual and dress. They, without exception, wore beards of various stages of growth — except one. She couldn't grow one being female. She seemed out of place like a rose in a cabbage patch. Did beards give the p.h.d.s a boost in intelligence similar to Sampson who had long hair that gave him physical strength?

Elva lived in California. She was tall, towering above my five-feet ten and one and one-half inches. When we occasionally danced after dinner at a cowboy-oriented restaurant complete with a country-western band, she never complained about the view of the top of my head.

I never complained with my view either, with my eyes even with her breastbones and my chin practically, and comfortably, resting at the apex of her cleft.

We developed a warm relationship during the brief time I was at the airport, hard by the complex. We would, on occasion, drive out on the plains west of the complex and search for chunks of amber. Besides being alone, it was a good time to find amber with the setting sun glowing low over the landscape. The sun provided color spots on the land by glowing through the amber.

Like the gentle evening breeze that flowed over the plains our relationship also gently ceased when I left Miles City. I never heard from her or saw her again. Obviously, she wasn't aware of the ancient rule in aviation that dictated that pilots should be the instigators of such relationships. Not mechanics.

How the weather scientists differences affected the ultimate goal of collecting cloud characteristics data, I'll never know. But, from the tone of the meetings, there was an indication that there was more than a smidgen of egos involved. At times the discussions became so heated it was a wonder to me the various persuasions would talk to each other at all.

I became acquainted with Shelby, the owner of a small maintenance shop on the airport, and spent time comparing notes with him. Now and then a flight of new Taylorcrafts would stop to refuel on ferry flights to Alaska. They were an interesting comparison with the older models, essentially the same but newly constructed with some slight design changes.

Once a Beechcraft King Air suffered a starter-generator problem on its right engine. I earned a generous gratuity by jury-rigging wires so the starter function could spool up the engine for light-off. But I had to send him on his way with the unit totally disabled. The pilot declined to wait for me to find the problem in the generator's side of the unit.

He was grateful to get the engine started and opted to continue his flight home with one generator. Presumably he had a successful flight home!

Suddenly, one day, two seldom seen aircraft landed. One was an ancient B-23 from the University of Washington; the other, a DC-3 owned by the University of Illinois. Both aircraft bristled with probes and antennas, obviously research aircraft.

It seemed that an all-out assault on thunderstorms was planned, but I wondered if the researchers were researching researchers to compare data and keep each other honest. Or, on the other hand, was a truly massive line of thunderstorms approaching and reinforcements were needed?

After two days of hectic flight activities the two aircraft disappeared as suddenly as they arrived. I didn't realize until then that so many institutions of higher learning were engaged in so much cloud research.

I chanced to become acquainted with that Ph.D. I mentioned earlier. I met him one night in Miles City at a bar as old as the city itself. It must have been the first structure built when the U.S. Calvary was there during the Indian Wars. Part of Miles City's history includes a remount station where the calvary bought horses.

During our conversation I learned he was a native of the Hawaiian Islands and told him I was well acquainted with life there. We reminisced at great length over some good bourbon until, gradually, his profession became the center of our talk.

"Don," I said, "I'm truly mystified." We were on a first-name basis by then and he was becoming more open, helped by the excellent bourbon we were sipping.

"This is the second project I've been on," I continued. "I've observed extensive activity in cloud research by any number of people. I've seen facilities much like this one and the equipment, including airplanes, and know there's got to be a lot of money spent to conduct cloud research. There must be tons of data collected over so many years. Really many decades.

"What do they do with the data? Do they really apply it to modifying clouds and weather? What are the end results? What is the real truth?"

Don ordered two drinks and studiously contemplated the amber liquid in his glass, then took a sip. His answer was blunt and brief. "The real truth is," he replied, "what bandwagon you get on. You have to find the one that's carrying money." It was an answer pregnant with options for interpretation.

With the end of summer nearing and, therefore, an end to thunderstorm activity, I was sent home but placed on retainer for maintenance when needed.

The relationship between the two owners of the little company meanwhile continued to deteriorate rapidly. But, before it became totally defunct the following winter, they acquired a Lear Jet 23, to upgrade from the Aero Commander. It would be flown to complete the current contract and, presumably, used in the following year's research. The purchase came as a total surprise to me.

One day, not long after they started operating the Lear Jet I received a telephone call from Miles City. The left engine, I was told, had failed.[48]

"What happened?"

"It ingested the logo plate," the pilot explained.

"What logo plate?" I demanded to know.

"We had one made to identify who the airplane belongs to," he replied and cut off our conversation. "Just find us an engine as soon as possible." He hung up the telephone; obviously he didn't want to talk about it. But I managed to look at a sketch of what could be defined as a badge of egotism. The price would certainly be high for such vanity.

232

The plate he referred to was made of stainless steel, approximately sixty-thousandths of an inch thick with an area of five by seven inches. It had proudly displayed the company's name and purpose and had been attached to the cabin door with adhesive by one of the owners.

It was rather fanciful and horribly expensive when the extensive damage it caused to the engine was considered. The type and quality of the adhesive used to attach the plate was never revealed, nor if the plate had been shaped to the door's curvature for optimum contact. They avoided answering my embarrassing question of why it wasn't hard-fastened to the cabin door.

After making some telephone calls I arranged to have a replacement engine flown to Miles City by an overhaul agency. Their mechanics removed and replaced the failed engine. Within two weeks the telephone rang again. Two tires, it seemed, needed to be replaced.

I rented a Cessna 182 and flew to Miles City, replaced the tires and did an inspection of the Lear Jet. The airplane was in good condition and operating well.

The same couldn't be said for the relationship of the two owners of the little company. The animosity between the two had flourished; from all indications it looked to be a matter of a short space of time before the two would indeed snatch defeat from the jaws of success. I sensed this would be my last episode in maintaining the airplane.

When my separation came, and I was sure it was fairly imminent, I could look back and reflect on the education I received in cloud research — for whatever use I could put it to.

With my work finished I began loading my tools and sundry supplies in the rented airplane I had flown to Miles City, in preparation for returning home. While I was doing that a rancher who had flown his Cessna 182 to Shelby's little shop for some maintenance walked over to me.

If the fact that cattle ranchers, and farmers own and use light aircraft in conjunction with their agriculture operations, it shouldn't be surprising. It is not common practice, neither is it an exception.

Their time is as valuable to them as any profession that depends on the passage of time. And so, living in the vastness of some western states where a trip to town means sometimes multiple hours consumed in a pickup truck versus a fraction flying over the same country, aircraft make sense. They're also efficient in searching out animals for location and general condition, versus hours on horseback or on an all terrain vehicle or in a truck. And aircraft are especially useful during the winter to observe circumstances when ground travel, in any mode, is difficult on a land smothered in snow and replete with snow drifts. Therefore, aircraft that are used as a tool in agriculture and ranching are as valuable as a tractor or a horse.

Aircraft used in farming and ranching in the states can compare to their use in Alaska but, of course, to a lesser degree. Anybody familiar with aircraft operations in Alaska realize the state is dependant on bush flying for multiple purposes: Carrying mail and necessities to far-flung villages; meeting emergencies in various predicaments; search and rescue; carrying passengers; carrying hunters and anglers to remote sites; and the list goes on. The use of helicopters is not as widespread, unlike civil air operations in New Zealand, for example.

In that island nation, distances are much shorter and bush airstrips, as in Alaska, are the exception rather than the rule. That is simply due to geographical features and so, helicopters are common. They, of course, can be set down in the most unreasonable places and generally are. And the operators do what they have to do to accommodate their customers. That means, of course, making use of any clearing that's available.

The rancher and I discussed cattle and politics and talked about flying and the maintenance he needed to have done on his airplane. Inevitably, weather became the leading topic. This led to the research center and its role in the general scheme of things in that portion of Montana's high plains.

In his succinct, measured voice the rancher summed up what he thought to be a local, public perception of the research center. The general consensus, he said, seemed to question its reasons for existence.

"They've been here for fifteen-years," he said, waving his hand in the general direction of the center's buildings. "We've (ranchers) cooperated with them by letting them put their rain collectors on our land and helping them if we could." Exasperation clouded the tone of his voice. His seamed, weathered face bore a look of unresolved anxiety.

As he talked, in my mind I compared two days and two nights at Big Springs, Texas, when the Aero Commander and crew chased thunder storms at night.

They were plentiful, huge and mean where the lightning ripped and dazzled and tore the skies apart. The vast area was a breeding ground for thunderstorms aided by the moist air flow from the Gulf. The crew had no problem finding a thunder storm to probe: Both nights they ringed Big Springs and the airport with dazzling visibility.

The rancher gestured toward the sweltering plains that swept northwest toward the horizon and the distant Canadian border. They were blanketed with shriveled grasses and resembled a colossal sheet of aged parchment. On the horizon, high clouds in clumps of thin, whitish vapor, hung without life and motion. No more than scribbles.

The sky glared hot and blue. Heat waves shimmered over the

landscape, emphasizing the obvious: The absence of moisture. In my month of taking care of the airplane, not once had it rained in the vicinity of the airport. It was a listless, depressing panorama that needed at least two or three days of steady rain to rejuvenate itself. As it was, the days passed slowly in a monotonous procession..

"When," the rancher wondered aloud, more to himself than to me, "are they going to make it rain?"

It was a question I, of all people, couldn't answer. But recalling Don's remark about climbing on bandwagons, I thought with more than a twinge of sarcasm, that maybe the rainmakers could care less.

Job security and building empires know no boundaries!

15

Repetition, Laxity
and Counting Beans...

It's 19:00 hours on a March night and the winds of Wyoming are living up to their fierce reputation.

Cheyenne Ridge, west of the city, does little to impede their bone-chilling onslaught that originates one-hundred miles or more to the west beyond the rolling grasslands east of the Laramie Mountains. The sky is overcast, absorbing Cheyenne's lights in a dirty charcoal sponge. Night is a cold, black cowl. The thin whine of turbine engines on the Wyoming National Guard's C-130 transports across the airport accentuates the bitterness.

A meeting is about to convene in the assembly room of an aircraft mechanics school, a branch of its parent school near Denver, Colorado.

Thirty-five mechanics, including myself, and a handful of FAA agents, mostly from the Denver Flight Standards District Office, sit on chilly, steel folding chairs talking quietly, awaiting the start of an annual meeting of Authorized Inspectors. Seventeen of us are I.A.s. The balance are mechanic-observers who aspire to one day obtain the endorsement to their mechanic licenses.

The meetings are mandatory for I.A.s who wish to retain the endorsement that 'privileges' them to approve repairs, alterations and annual inspections — and expose themselves to potential lawsuits!

I.A. meetings have been going on since the FAA dropped the Designated Aircraft Maintenance Inspector program years ago.[51]

The I.A. designation was created ostensibly, to delegate more responsibility to general aviation maintenance personnel. The endorsement has no place in airline operations nor is it recognized. In actuality, probably some fuzzy-cheeked attorney in the bureaucracy must have opined that DAMIs were, in fact, representatives of the federal government without portfolio. That would not do and the regulations were revised forthwith, eliminating an obviously delicate situation. Undoubtedly the young man was awarded a raise in pay for being so astute.

Younger I.A.s have not been attending these meetings for as long as others like myself and Burnham, a friend with whom I worked on an occasional engine overhaul. He's been in aircraft and engine maintenance and overhaul longer than I have, outdating my career by fifteen-years or more. He cut his engine overhaul teeth on Pratt & Whitney radials. If there's anyone who knows more about them than Burnham I haven't met him. Tall and lanky at six and one-half feet, he abhors mediocrity in maintenance and has a bearish growl to emphasize his distaste. Once I witnessed his use of the growl on a research technician who happened to be working on a project in the hangar. He thought Burnham's tool box was public; and learned instantly it wasn't!

With a career spanning over five and one-half decades, Burnham has been on a first-name basis with some of the early, famous aviation figures. On occasion, in a fit of lucid reminiscence, he has admitted to aiding research, in the early thirties, on the feasibility of transporting illicit liquids by air. Now and then, he told me, he was asked to coax an irascible engine into obedience on an airplane flown by a nervous individual who was anxious to deliver his chancy cargo to an equally anxious buyer.

Ed Beegle was there, too. He had almost as much tenure in aircraft maintenance as Burnham and once owned and operated a highly-respected airframe structures repair facility. Ed was practically fearless in ferrying damaged aircraft to his shop. It wasn't done out of a sense of derring-do, but for a more practical reason: Doing so saved time and paperwork.

If there was no damage to the engine or a broken or bent mount and the engine ran well during a ground check, that was advantageous. An additional positive factor was the extent of damage to the airframe. If, in his judgement, the damage wouldn't affect the airplane's flight characteristics unreasonably, short of casting off bits and pieces, he ferried it.

He looked upon ferry permits and the red tape they presented in obtaining one with disdain and he had a point, if one looked at the practical aspects of a ferrying operation. A signature in a logbook wouldn't make a damaged aircraft any more ferryable than a good visual inspection and the decision to fly it.

There was another member of our unique age and experience group missing and had been for three years. I didn't know him as well as Burnham and Beegle.

Snyder once owned and operated a general repair-inspection-propeller overhaul shop. The propeller overhaul section of his shop was busier than the rest of his services, and many other shops relied upon that; otherwise, propellers would have to be worked on at distant facilities. But the one feature of Snyder's establishment that stood out, to me, had nothing to do with aircraft.

He kept two ancient, asthmatic dogs of questionable ancestry. They were dun-colored with stubby tails, obviously members of the same litter. The odd thing about them was, their heads didn't fit well with their bodies, or vice versa. There was a disproportionate match-up.

Their heads resembled those of bulldogs: Pushed back noses and sagging jowls that dripped constantly. Their bodies, although solidly constructed, lacked the distinctly-bowed forelegs and prominent shoulders of bulldogs. It was a wonder the beasts didn't drive Snyder's customers away. They always catapulted themselves out of the hangar onto the ramp, barking and growling fiercely and stuffing their wet noses against a customer's leg or legs. Then they would follow him into the hangar still bumping and snuffling with blunt noses on his heels and calves of his legs. Oddly enough, they never bit anyone but that didn't excuse their repulsive, abhorrent actions. Yet neither Snyder, or his wife who worked the shop's office, sought to control the dogs.

The two dogs acted like depraved imbeciles to me and I always fervently wished them the worst: Wandering into a spinning propeller came to mind often. Hopefully, they might be consumed by a gleaming disc of cold dedication, engrossed on ridding the ramp of two insults to dogdom.

Snyder was taken with a deadly illness and retreated to the benign landscape of Arizona to live out his allotted time as comfortably as possible.

The mandatory I.A. meetings were but one illustration of the archaic flavor of some Federal Air Regulations.

The first I.A. meeting I attended following the change-over from the DAMI program was, for all practical purposes, the same as the last one I attended. If veteran mechanics/I.A.s were canvassed they would probably verify that statement. The meetings were as interesting and informative as watching paint dry. We attended because we had to — and always hoped the next one would show some improvement.

Normally the meetings began with introductions of the FAA agents present. There was always a period of accusation that I.A.s were remiss in realizing the importance of aircraft and engine record-keeping. Never mind that lax record-keeping has been a historical failing of aircraft owners, as well. Or, the FAA for that matter. A case in point is merely the tip of the iceberg.

On occasion I have found it necessary to call the records section at Oklahoma City for information on an aircraft or mechanic. The results were not entirely satisfactory. In recent years it has been virtually impossible to ascertain the actual number of active mechanics. The last time I tried I was referred to a small company in Boulder, Colorado, that kept such records, in cooperation with the FAA. The official at the company could provide a list but inferred it was possibly inaccurate.

How many active mechanics are there? Does any entity truly know? A reasonable question since he indicated some mechanics long since deceased were discovered in the records. How is it possible that such records have been allowed to deteriorate over time? Or worse, not kept up-to-date. This in the spite of modern record-keeping amenities and the FAA's massive staff!

The I.A.s could always expect charges that repair and alteration forms weren't being completed properly, followed by a review of how to accomplish that feat. Dissertations on how certain FARs affected or would have an impact on I.A. activities was a certain exercise.

Sometimes a brief talk on technical matters would be given by a guest speaker. Most always, if the facility where the meetings took place was generous, coffee and doughnuts were supplied at break time. That was always a welcome pause halfway through the meetings.

While the program of admonitions, rebukes and dire prophecies of our futures if we didn't mend our evil ways was in progress, one of the FAA agents would review our I.A. activities records. All I.A.s are required to keep a running record of the annual inspections and return-to-service approvals they sign-off. The report is mandatory to show proof that minimum activities requirements were met to have his or her I.A. certificate endorsed for the new year.

To my knowledge an I.A.'s report has never been audited against the logbook of any aircraft listed on a report. The present procedure is a sharp contrast to the DAMI years when a report of an inspection, for example, was required to be mailed for recordation in the aircraft's file at Oklahoma City.[52]

Obviously a cross-check would be a routine matter to determine several things: Was the inspection done on a 'ghost' airplane? How many airplanes were certified for service in a given year? If an airplane wasn't inspected when due, why not and was it being flown? A DAMI's activities were easily monitored. The system was a natural for bureaucratic record keeping. But it also was conducive to a better overview of the health of the general aviation sector of aircraft operations.

In all the years I held an I.A. endorsement, no FAA maintenance inspector ever — repeat, ever, — followed up to spot-check my inspection or, for that matter, a major repair I had approved.

Occasionally the opportunity presented itself to shorten our time at the meetings.

During the coffee break we would wander to the table where the agent who reviewed our activities records and endorsed our certificates worked. If he had been diligent, the certificates would be endorsed by him when coffee break arrived. Quite often, several of us would surreptitiously find our certificates and, after finishing our coffee and doughnuts, quietly leave.

On one occasion an I.A., an acquaintance, dramatically shortened his visit to a meeting by simply not attending. He was re-endorsed in absentia by sending his certificate and records with another who returned the endorsed certificate to him the next day. There was no positive identification of certificate holders at any of the meetings I attended. The absentee presumably enjoyed the evening at home while he was being certified for another year.

It would be unfair to declare categorically that all meetings were without substance. On rare occasions formal safety seminars were organized on a regional basis where representatives of industry were invited to take part. These would be interesting and much new support information was made available that helped not only I.A.s but other mechanics as well. But it was the smaller meetings, confined to attendees from small geographical areas that were the epitome of boredom.

There were none more anxious to have done with the meetings or dreaded them more than some FAA inspectors. The extent of their boredom and resentment at wasting personal time was admitted to me more than once by different agents. Yet the meetings persisted as examples of unparalleled exercises in futility. Small wonder that I.A.s, myself included, left the meetings expressing undisguised scorn and disgust. The meetings failed in developing a high level of positive sensibilities among the attendees.

In contrast, the FAA frequently sponsors seminars designed to improve piloting proficiency; maintenance personnel are rarely singled out for the same attention. A gradual change is taking place to include more seminars and additional exposure to the trade because of

243

exhibitors at the meetings. Still, if proposals that I.A.s renew their endorsements every two years become reality, that time span leaves much to be desired in over-viewing an I.A.'s activities. On balance then — although not necessarily true — it would seem that the maintenance aspects of general aviation are well-ordered, pilotage and flight are not.

The law of unintended consequences might have become involved in the FARs when they were written and then caused a vicious cycle of rewrites, additions and revisions. Because of peculiar structuring and language much confusion and misunderstanding has resulted. This is not confined solely within the physical maintenance aspects. Some FARs and FAA documents have the potential of contributing to inadvertent laxity and confusion on both sides of the maintenance coin. As an example, from my notes of the last I.A. meeting I attended, the principal FAA agent presented some official thoughts:

"You mechanics and inspectors must be careful about using aircraft manuals as a basis for making repairs and alterations," he admonished. "Many airframe manuals aren't FAA-approved for making repairs and alterations, but may be used as references in making repairs, unless FAA disapproved." The statement caused considerable amazement among the audience, leaving it in a grey area.

That commentary causes one to ponder one of many mysteries contained in the structure of the FARs and their administration and brings up one of a multitude of questions: Why, if an aircraft design has been approved for a Type Certificate, should not the maintenance and repair manuals for that aircraft be approved, at least selectively? Compare that mindset with the fact that many support documents developed for air carrier aircraft are approved. Who would know better how to design a repair than people who designed the element in the first place?

"Advisory Circulars," the agent continued, "are not FAA approved, but are acceptable for methods of repairs and alterations and other information as a basis for approved data."

That statement reveals one of many paradoxes in the FARs. Advisory Circulars are written and issued by the FAA. In light of that fact it would seem the FAA lacks the courage of its convictions, fearful of commitment. There are a number of air carrier aircraft support documents FAA approved. But generally, especially those effecting repairs, are sanctioned by a factory Designated Engineering Representative. Still, a DER is not an FAA official.

Oddly, the venerated Civil Aeronautics Manual — CAM-18 — remains a valid source for repair examples and, is an approved document. And so, if a repair is made according to an example in CAM-18, it can be approved in-shop. Its validity remains intact to this day.

My copy, acquired at the outset of my career, is in my pilot-son's keeping and is a valuable manuscript. Not only for historical reasons but for practical reference for making approved repairs.

There is nothing heroic about holding an I.A. rating nor does illuminating status accrue to a holder. Many I.A.s are a convenience in the employ of a fixed base operator whose concern is providing punctual maintenance services to customers. Others are part of the maintenance staff of corporate and charter flight departments. In those situations an I.A. is a decided asset, assuring positive, continual coordination in maintenance schemes.

There are many I.As who are employed in work foreign to aviation, but still do aircraft maintenance on a free-lance basis. This means they have no steady affiliation with aircraft maintenance; only sporadic, part time work. Rarely do these 'shade tree' operations meet FAR requirements for adequate manuals, tooling, equipment and base of operations.

I have personal knowledge of an I.A. approving an annual inspection on a retractable landing gear equipped aircraft without performing a gear retraction test. He simply did not have jacks and ignored the test. Generally free-lancers inspect for a miserly fee. But in doing so they cheapen the conscientious efforts and professional images of I.A.s who place a real importance on their rating and the responsibilities it implies.

It's been said that changes are a mark of progress, but I cannot subscribe entirely to that theory.

Remembering the DAMI program and comparing it with the I.A. program leaves much to be desired with the latter. Then, maintenance inspectors normally made their rounds of the various airports in their operating area on a regular basis and visited with the DAMIs. Problems, if any, were discussed. Counsel and guidance were offered and often spot reviews of a DAMI's activities were conducted. It was not a free and loose situation in which any mechanic with the required calendar time as a licensed mechanic could sit for an inspector's examination, never mind his overall record in past maintenance activities.

There's something horribly amiss in a system that does little or nothing to monitor that system for assurance it is meeting the objective (s) it was designed for.

I was asked to inspect a Stearman for renewal of its license after a one hundred hour inspection was performed. It had been completely restored ten-years prior to the inspection; the work was accomplished beautifully. The owner was understandably proud of the aircraft and was constantly in attendance while it was undergoing the one hundred hour inspection, to the point of being a nuisance.

When I glanced at the aircraft prior to starting the actual inspection a major problem was immediately apparent:

There were no inspection rings on the wing panels' fabric,

particularly at strategic stress points. There was no access to inspect the wing panels' interiors at 'N' strut attach points, for one thing. Inspection hole covers were also absent at flying and landing wire fittings-to-wing spars and spar fittings to fuselage attach points.

When I asked that inspection access be provided in the wonderfully finished wing fabric the owner objected and I could understand his reluctance. However, he refused to understand my position; subsequently, I refused to conduct the inspection. The upshot of the standoff was, he asked the mechanics to call another I.A. It happened to be Burnham.

Burnham immediately insisted that inspection holes be cut in the fabric and finally convinced the owner it was necessary. The owner reluctantly agreed with Burnham's reasoning and inspection holes were provided by the mechanics. Burnhams's inspection revealed a cracked wing spar — and other discrepancies. Bear in mind that this aircraft had been relicensed every year for ten-years — subsequent to being recovered — and signed off as airworthy by an I.A., with wing panel interiors uninspected.

In another instance I was asked to inspect a Cessna Model 172; it was to be the second license renewal since new — two-hundred operation hours. The one-hundred hour inspection was normal, with no unusual discrepancies revealed — except one that was extremely serious: The factory had to be held accountable for the imperfection, not operation of the aircraft.

There were several rivets directly above the attach point of the left wing strut to the spar that appeared to have been driven by someone who hadn't achieved even amateur status in sheet metal assembly. They were members of several that connected the wing skins at the wing production break, where the outer panels joined the center section assembly. The rivets were the epitome of how not to rivet.

The rivets were 'golf clubbed', bent as nails would be that joined two boards with the excess of their shanks bent over to clinch them. Some barely had upset heads and there was a generous gap between the wing skins and spar. In short, they were a vivid representation of how not to drive rivets and fit sheet metal.

"I cannot relicense this airplane," I told the owner. He had bought it new.

"Why not...what's wrong?" He was obviously dumbfounded by my statement. I gave him my flashlight and invited him to look at the rivets and the gap between the wing skins and the spar.

"The rivets aren't doing anything more than filling holes in the skin and spar," I pointed out. "Also, since the skins aren't tight against the spar there's a chance that the joint will work excessively under flight loads."

"But it was relicensed last year," the owner protested.

"It shouldn't have been," I said. "There's been no damage to the airplane recorded, so it had to come out of the factory like this."

The upshot of the situation was twofold: The owner took his airplane away and I sent an indignant letter to the FAA with my inspection report. One of the questions I asked was how the airplane could pass factory inspections, given the faulty rivets. I never learned the outcome of the former action, but an agent visited with me two days later, before the airplane was taken away, and looked at the rivets.

"You're right...they aren't according to standard practices," he agreed. And then he said, "But it's the mechanics' and inspectors' responsibilities to correct situations like this."

The discussion threatened to become heated after I asked him what the FAA's role in such matters should be. After all, I pointed out, it issued the Type Certificate and should be closely controlling quality of products made under such authority. I never learned about the interaction, if any, between the FAA and Cessna.

I.A.s have found modifications to airframes, components and engines either not accomplished properly, nor recorded or substantiated by required documents; equipment added or deleted as part of the airplane with, no supporting documentation. Other common discrepancies include structural repairs accomplished, but not in accordance with established criteria or engineering backup; weight and balance changes not computed or updated. Still, these irregularities and the perpetrators are given short shrift by the FAA in spite of being reported.

One Sunday morning I was called to help a pilot who wanted to leave the airport, but was having engine problems. His aircraft had just been relicensed and was presumably fit for flight. After uncowling the engine I found three spark plugs loose in their cylinders and five ignition leads that hadn't been secured to their respective spark plugs. After correcting the discrepancies and running the engine for a ground operational check the pilot took off and went on his way. I was so incensed by the shoddy, haphazard work and subsequent annual inspection sign off — the I.A. had a reputation for being woefully negligent — I called an FAA inspector the following morning. After reading the list of discrepancies I had found I asked: "How could this man be issued an I.A. rating in the first place, but worse yet, keep it, in spite of his reputation for being incompetent and careless?"

"Anyone who meets experience criteria may take the test," he replied officiously. "If he passes the test we have to issue him the rating."

He further stated that an agent would have to be witness to incompetent acts before action could be taken against the I.A. or mechanic. In any event that example isn't an isolated one; from personal knowledge, other I.A.s have had the same experience. Their efforts to somehow sort the wheat from the chaff have been largely fruitless; they can not understand the official apathy.

But the mediocre FAA support aside, why anyone would deliberately play Maintenance Russian Roulette in aviation is beyond
comprehension. The threat of litigation is always present. To hasten
the consummation of that deadly potential with a day, or even days
and weeks, in court by knowingly engaging in less than conscientious,
responsible maintenance activities, is like putting two or three bullets
in the pistol's magazine, instead of one.

In this age of litigation, besides being exposed to possible FAA
enforcement actions, mechanics and I.A.s operate in an environment
wide open to many civil law suits. This is not generally the case for
air carrier maintenance personnel, although there are instances of
record in which mechanics have been disciplined by the FAA for
transgressions not entirely of their making. It's of no concern to the
FAA if a mechanic performed an improper maintenance act under
coercion from a supervisor.

An attorney I knew who specialized in aviation law pointed out
at one meeting that mechanics and I.A.s can, have been, and probably
will continue to be, sued for any number of reasons: Employing
unapproved maintenance methods, poor workmanship, using bogus
parts, using surplus military parts. Also on the list are false, inaccurate or incomplete record entries and even work done years past. This
could be construed as meaning there's no statute of limitation.

"Whatever you mechanics or I.A.s do you're responsible for," he
cautioned. "Irresponsible activities or inadvertent mistakes can result
in lawsuits or prison or both. Be thorough, be careful in what you do.
Be specific and detail maintenance record entries. You have to follow
the rules to survive. The burden is on your shoulders"

"The FAA," he continued, "plays the role of Dr. Jekyll-Mr. Hyde.
It can be your friend or antagonist. One clue to defining what character an FAA agent is playing is when one wants to talk to you about

history — something in the past.

"On the one hand you may become guest of honor in an enforcement case, or on the other, he really is writing a history of aviation and needs your input!"

I took a young man under my wing who wanted to get started in aircraft maintenance; he went on to acquire his A&P and I.A. ratings. His building reputation as having no patience for mediocrity was my reward for time spent with him.

Approximately one month after he completed an annual inspection and relicensed a Cessna 182 the aircraft crashed — no injuries. The owner sued Bill, on the basis of shoddy maintenance, forget the fact the FAA investigation revealed empty fuel tanks. Bill was subsequently exonerated after over a year of litigation and surviving the stress of ultimately proving his innocence. Bill's investigation and research revealed that the aircraft owner was in trouble with the Internal Revenue Service for back taxes and needed money. People will sue for any reason.

In rationalizing the absence of maintenance agents in the field doing spot checks of aircraft, mechanics, repair stations and I.A.s on a regular basis, the phrase 'work loads' often surfaces as a common reason. Presumably the work load relates to the preponderance of paperwork in the FAA's various offices. To the FAA that may be valid when one considers the rapid growth of aviation over the past three or more decades, but not necessarily excusable. Being smothered under the auspices of the U.S. Department of Transportation hasn't helped, nor is it enviable, for an entity charged with monumental responsibilities.

The FAA should be completely divorced from the DOT. Further, I question the wisdom of continually appointing retired military officers to head the FAA's far-reaching empire. This is not to detract from any officer's qualifications in overseeing military aviation affairs.

But, the two fields, commercial and military aviation, are vastly different, not to forget the political aspects of each. Surely there is an individual in aviation's broad, deep expanse with the expertise, acumen and a long term relationship with civil aviation, qualified on those requirements to direct the FAA. Even within the FAA's ranks there must be someone of long service who would have the background and experience to direct the department.

I cannot ignore an incident which serves to illustrate one of many shortcomings in the FAA, but with the realization this isn't a coldly perfect world. The episode elicited a profusion of rather caustic remarks from veteran technical personnel in the airline involved at the time.

During a period when I was employed as an engineering consultant with a regional commuter airline, part of the system of a major Part 121 air carrier, the commuter was audited by a team of fifteen FAA agents. The event was another step in a national effort by the FAA to search out discrepancies in the operations of various airlines. Aircraft and operations documents and record keeping were the primary focus of the audit.

In a conversation with one of the agents, a man in his early thirties, he admitted to not being knowledgeable about airline operations. He had been a mechanic in general aviation and continued as an agent in the field when he joined the FAA. In fact, at the time, he was based at a small general aviation airport in Arizona. Yet he had been drafted for service on the national audit team.

He was plainly at a loss and readily admitted — in confidence — he didn't know what he was looking for. The world of air carriers, he discovered, embodied an entirely different philosophy, crafted for exacting standards as compared to general aviation. Air carriers operated in a vastly different world in all respects. The exercise left us all wondering about the effectiveness of the FAA's effort. Playing at charades was suggested.

I have learned over the years that competition and an aggressive sense of territorial defense exists between various FAA area offices, formerly General Aviation District Offices, now Flight Standards District Offices. This syndrome also carries over into air carrier overview and supervisory offices. Each empire has diverse interpretations, ideas and administration of the FARs. The boundaries cannot be overstepped except by formal agreement.

A case in point occurred when I was in structural engineering at Sky World Airlines, a small air carrier engaged in charter work with nine Boeing 707s and one Boeing 727.

A dispute arose concerning compliance with an Airworthiness Directive (AD). The Principal Maintenance Inspector (PMI) at the air carrier office insisted that an Engineering Order (EO) must be issued to direct compliance and to show approval authority. Meaning approved by a Designated Engineering Representative or the factory DER. I argued that wasn't necessary, based on the fact that if an AD is written and complied with as written, approval is automatic with the proper sign-off.

Issuing an EO was really a moot point and only served to direct that the AD be complied with. Formal approval wasn't necessary and to prove the point I called the FAA agent in Seattle, Washington, who had written and issued the AD and explained the situation to him.

"What the hell is going on down there?" was his immediate and somewhat emotional response. "They (air carrier office) should know that, once an AD is written and issued it becomes the law of the land. The approval to successfully comply with an AD is in its very issuance.!"

The underlying tone of his sensitive reaction was: "How dare they question something I wrote?" But there seemed to be more: The fact that another office could presume to intrude on his territory and, more revolting, question his actions.

On the other side of the coin, when I disclosed the substance of my conversation with the Seattle agent, and his answer, to the head of technical services and the PMI, there was adverse reaction. The PMI took umbrage and expressed his displeasure with the fact I'd call another district office to get a second opinion. The upshot of the whole affair was I was mildly chastised by the head of technical services, my supervisor. It was not politically correct to do so and threaten relationships with the FAA principal inspector. The supervisor did not say as much but the inference was there. The AD was forthwith complied with without unwarranted complications associated with unnecessary paperwork.

Within the FAA there is no such thing as integration in the total system of district offices.

Each is an empire unto itself, even to thinking. There seems not to be consistencies in interpretation of regulations and opinions vary on solving technical problems in the field. From the FAA's perspective, territorial boundaries must remain secure and undefiled. Moreover, the FAA seems to be like an animal that has been caged for a long period of time. When the door is opened, the animal is afraid to emerge. It has been caged so long the creature has forgotten the outside, even though it can see through the opened door. Therefore no decision can be made as to should it, or should it not.

In that respect there is a lack of initiative and decision-making because of being apprehensive about the outcome. This particularly affects promulgating new regulations or revising existing ones.

The process plods through meetings, over desks, through agent after agent. But that isn't the end. There has to be legal matters discussed and the economics that would have cost-effective potential on an operator, not to forget reviewing and deliberating at length over comments from the industry. If, during the regulatory process, a question arises on any point, the mechanism could begin again and more time consumed. That, however, is typical of bureaucracies.

There's a paradox in the scheme of rule-making procedures. On the one hand normal (abnormal, if you will) processes take an inordinate amount of time. On the other, 'emergency' rules — and airworthiness directives — have been written and issued within weeks, or even days. In the former one could question whether the new rule was necessary or was it deemed to be, in order to create a make-work scenario. In the latter, under the auspices of the word 'emergency', could one assume that process to be eligible for the definition of normal, and apply it to the former?

Time is the wind that blows down corridors, opening doors of instant decision-making. But it also can subside to a stagnant breeze.

At the end of my final year of holding an I.A. rating I went to New Zealand and returned one week after the annual, required I.A. meeting. On two other occasions in my career I had been unable to attend the meetings on schedule. The primary FAA agent merely discussed a variety of subjects with me and endorsed my authorization. I know of other like situations in which the I.A. was given the same consideration.

On this occasion an FAA agent, much younger than me in age, and therefore in experience, refused to do so and insisted I sit for the I.A. written and oral examination. I learned he was recently hired by the FAA, but with only a brief time, approximately 10-years, in General Aviation maintenance.

My informant offered the opinion the man found the field too stressful or soured on it, and took the position of an FAA agent, thus assuring himself a comfortable future. Obviously he was determined to enforce the letter of the law as a signal to his superiors that he would, indeed, be worthy of his newly-acquired status.

I refused and shortly afterwards received an official letter from him in which I was threatened with my name being removed from the national I.A. registry. In reply I assured him that if he thought he should, then that's what he should do.

So, after thirty-eight years as an inspector, with no regrets, I chose to remand the rating to retirement!

16

Back to The Drawing Board,
Like Hell....

No one can say the aircraft maintenance spectrum is a coldly perfect world. I've not done research to determine if one exists in other professions. All things considered in life's experiences, it's doubtful if heights of perfection are reached anywhere near one-hundred percent.

The nature of aircraft maintenance often denies a continually, relatively smooth and coordinated atmosphere. Sometimes unrelated activities often interfere and are interwoven in the total scheme of achieving a specific maintenance objective.

Out of less than attractive situations an occasional wet blanket dampens the fires of enthusiasm, which often leads mechanics to ask themselves: "Why am I doing this?" even though they're getting paid to do it.

When I was appointed Director of Maintenance for a new fixed base operation it seemed a golden opportunity on the surface. This wouldn't be helping to dust off a Phoenix that had arisen from ashes. This would be starting with an empty hangar and several excellent mechanics. From the ground there was only one way to go: Up! However, Falcon Aire barely reached the kneeling position.

We started with a bare trickle of local customers needing work on their single engine aircraft. Meanwhile, during the phase-in period, we built several small shops along one wall of the maintenance hangar, and a parts room.

Gradually the influx of customers built to more and more locals with twins and then a subtle buildup of off-airport airplanes needing maintenance. All of that activity was in addition to maintaining the company's trainers and a Bell helicopter. Equipping the shops went ahead on a gradual, comfortable basis.

The very first job in the engine shop was overhauling a Lycoming 0-540 engine for my erstwhile personal client, Leech, the crop duster. We began to make plans for repairing damaged aircraft to take up the slack between inspections and correcting problems on customer aircraft.

On the whole, Falcon Aire's progress was comfortable. Not too fast to be dangerously over-extended, at least as far as the maintenance end of the FBO was concerned. But, up front, in the 'head shed', activities seemed to move at a hectic pace. Too rapidly I thought. It seemed the source of start-up funds was limitless. We were to find out differently.

After a little over a year, problems began to rear their grisly heads in the management hierarchy. The 'team' consisted of a husband and wife and her two brothers, a dangerous combination in management no matter the business.

In a litany of ill-conceived decisions involving one brother who ran the helicopter section, on the strength of his experience flying Army helicopters, let financial affairs degrade from barely manageable to near-total disaster. As far as I knew the new Bell 'chopper never earned its keep. Two firms filed lawsuits on promissory notes of a whopping five-hundred fourteen thousand, four-hundred twenty-seven dollars, plus interest. There was also a one-hundred twenty-seven thousand, five-hundred dollar suit brought by four individuals against Falcon Aire, the helicopter division and the woman who was president and general manager.

But why make little problems when you can create a holocaust?

If she subconsciously adopted that philosophy, she nevertheless adhered to it faithfully in day-to-day affairs. The grand finale came in the form of theft by deception charges and her arrest. According to prosecution records she issued a bad check to a service company that was retained to manage the payroll. She had dug her hole deeper with five-thousand, six-hundred and seventy-five dollars, the amount of payroll checks the service company issued. When the company attempted to collect on her check from the bank, she stopped payment. [53]

So far she had not yet exhausted her considerable talents, based on rumors she had bilked a charitable organization of funds from an air show. It seemed plausible, but was never verified, to my knowledge.

The cash gate receipts were delivered to her office when the attendants deemed it sensible to empty their depositories of cash for safety reasons. It was a large air show and well-attended; receipts were estimated to be over forty-thousand dollars, but when the final settlement was made with the civic organization, it realized approximately one-third of what its estimated total receipts should have been.

Falcon Aire finally succumbed in a smothering haze of lawsuits,

259

sheriff's sales and auctions. The maintenance staff scattered to, hopefully, solid, satisfying positions elsewhere. The men were wonderfully skilled, so I'm sure they were eagerly accepted by viable companies that would appreciate their considerable talents.

In the aftermath of the disaster one incident remains locked forever in my memory. I've often wondered if the demise of Falcon Aire influenced its occurrence. Fate's subterfuge is ruthlessly pitiless at times.

My clerk and secretary, who's duties were shared with the front office, took a position in Honolulu at the fervent behest of her fiance there. She could sense that Falcon Aire's future was frightfully rickety so she departed three weeks before it fell.

Simply put, Lynn was a startlingly attractive young woman. She was tall with a soft, richly evocative smile. But, beyond her physical attributes and outgoing nature, she was intelligent and efficient.

For a person not previously exposed to the peculiar mores and language of aviation maintenance she absorbed terms, phrases and technical vernacular with incredible rapidity. In a matter of three days she grasped the intricacies of typing detailed, accurate invoices that rarely needed to be corrected or otherwise revised.

A month after she left I also abandoned Falcon Aire; my 'whip' was frayed from flogging the dead horse. Shortly afterwards a woman who had worked in the front office called with some dreadful news. Lynn had been murdered in Honolulu, deprived forever of life, liberty and the pursuit of happiness.

She had barely crossed the threshold into womanhood and her life ahead would surely have made the world her oyster. Her husband-to-be and that world are the poorer for her departure from this life. It was a consummate, personal shock to me.

In three short months another lesson in life's continuing education was impressed on me: It was that a woman's natural state is sometimes mysterious. Unexpected, shocking revelations are often the result when inner feelings are exposed. That occurred when Janet, one day, abruptly informed me she needed to 'expand and grow' and summarily exited our marriage, although we had a compatible relationship.

In time I analyzed her decision and attributed it to the whims of her daughter who was living in Denver — which is not to excuse Janet's actions. But the girl could not be without her mother. The loss of her companionship was a severe blow; in a few short years Janet admitted to losing, as well. Whatever!

A sabbatical of several months for me followed in which there were almost endless possibilities: Doing practically nothing; fishing and camping; renewing old acquaintances; assembling memories and notes; rambling in Alaska, British Columbia, Mexico and the Islands. The latter had undergone a dramatic, regrettable transformation. Where once sugar cane fields graced the sweeping up slopes from Honolulu past Pearl Harbor and on to Wahiawa, the land was inundated with houses, hotels and other buildings. The two venerable hotels that had reigned supreme at Waikiki Beach, the Moana and Royal Hawaiian, were virtually overwhelmed with other hotels of horrid architecture. I was grateful I had seen Oahu before the war and almost regretted I had made this trip.

There was also a brief romantic interlude that wasn't wholly consummated by a binding commitment. She was of Irish descent, emotional and cried a lot, but my estate — supply of money — didn't meet her requirements. The liaison faded like a gentle mist before a gracious, placid breeze.

It wasn't that those months weren't unproductive personally; they were constructive, but gradually, the feeling of living in a strange, partial vacuum began to assert itself. In essence, I hadn't begun to learn to cope with total leisure.

From the time of my discharge from the Air Force I had always been busy, never out of work. I hadn't yet recognized that perhaps I was on the cutting edge of a long career. That required another two years or so. But there was an experience similar to the one at Falcon Aire before I began to be impressed with the thought that I had done enough. Something was telling me something.

I joined Skyworld Airlines, a charter company, in engineering. It was an eye-opening experience into the details of an air carrier's ongoing efforts to comply with the requirements of meeting applicable FAR requirements. At the end of my tenure the leading question was not 'Why am I doing this?' It was, 'What was the point in all of that work?'

There was a Boeing 727 that was the odd man out in the beginning of the process of elimination of the company. But previous to being sold there was an exercise in futility, in a sense. However, from the front office's perspective, it was necessary to keep Sky World Airlines solvent. As it turned out, the sale of the 727 was a delaying action; ultimately, the balance of the fleet, nine B-707s suffered a similar fate.

The 727 was a good airplane. It seldom caused trouble as it plied the North American skies carrying vacationers and weekenders to their chosen playgrounds. But it wasn't a whole airplane. It didn't have galleys — even basic galleys.

The area in the cabin at the right service door was strangely vacant. Where galleys should have been, there was a hodge podge of large picnic coolers, containers for cups, coffee, hot and cold water thermos bottles and cardboard trays with snacks and candy. Special receptacles held one-shot bottles of 'tranquilizers' and cocktail mixes. Other passenger comfort supplies were stowed in overhead compartments throughout the cabin.

The storage boxes and coolers were lashed to the cabin floor with cargo straps, an arrangement the FAA Principal Maintenance Inspector (PMI) looked on with a jaundiced eye. He was also getting pushy about it. The situation, he insisted, was dangerously close to violating the

FARs. The airplane was operating under a Part 121 certificate.

The 727 had galleys, but the PMI was extremely distressed about them. They had been modified several times before the airplane began flying in Part 121 operations. He questioned the modifications: Where was the engineering data supporting the alterations? How were they approved? Moreover, he brought their basic physical condition into question.

In all fairness, the PMI had valid reasons for his concerns. When I first saw the 727's galleys their primary structure, frames, sidewalls and partitions confounded acceptable standards for sheet metal installation and repair. In any event, the galleys were removed by virtue of a Supplemental Type Certificate to appease the FAA.

Thereafter, our flight attendants were forced into the embarrassment of serving their passengers from a collection of containers on the cabin floor.

Before I took the position of structures engineer with the company, the airplanes operated in a private travel club mode.

Reorganization of the company resulted in operating them under Part 121 rules with a separate name to expand their usefulness. I learned from the maintenance department that the travel club president presided with an iron hand over technical and flight operations with a one-man, one-voice, one-vote policy — his!

"If we objected to an idea of his as being unsafe or possibly in violation of regulations," a veteran mechanic told me, "he would tell us to do it or leave." He interpreted his mechanics' predicaments as employment security through intimidation.

When the status of common carrier was acquired, immediate pressure from the FAA to bring the airplanes into compliance with the regulations governing common carriers was inherited. This meant establishing a records section and bringing airframe and engine component pedigrees up to date. A quality control and quality assurance department was formed. There was revising maintenance manuals to be done, certifying interiors for fire-blocking and a multitude of other concerns. A technical services section was also formed which included a small engineering group.

The transition was costly, which probably contributed immensely to the deadly influence of the law of unintended consequences.[54] Although the Boeings were busy generating income flying travel groups and other charters throughout the Western Hemisphere and, indeed overseas, still more money was required to stay airborne.

A loan of approximately fifteen-million dollars was arranged with an east coast bank which, as it turned out, set the stage for the eventual culmination of a promising company. In a matter of months the bank that, understandably, held title to Sky World's assets, especially the Boeings, began procedures to satisfy the loan. It was not the kind of news anyone wanted to hear, when it leaked down from the head office.

Immediately after the engineering section was established, one of the first directives to reach it was: 'Get galleys into the 727!' It was explicit: 'Delays would not be acceptable'.

New galleys were, economically, out of the question. They would cost a tidy one-million dollars, according to the original manufacturer. Nor, would the manufacturer help us attempt to find used ones fit for service. Not-so-subtlety, the company said it wasn't about to help us with information when it could sell new galleys, and it was the only source. That left us with only one option: Rebuild our galleys to certifiable condition.

They had been shipped to Flight Structures, an engineering firm near Seattle. I took what background data I could gather, went to Flight Structures and saw the galleys for the first time. Everything the mechanics had told me was true. In plain terms they were a mess, structurally and operationally. Subsequently, Flight Structures was engaged to re-engineer and rebuild the galleys and deliver them certified for service. The program would cost sixty-thousand dollars — freight additional.

There followed several months of searching for parts removed when the galleys were 'reworked'; ferreting out information about their original materials and design; establishing their status as original equipment when the 727 was built. There was a myriad of dimensions to assemble: Galley mounts on cabin floor structure; positions of water supplies, drains and electrical provisions. After an exhaustive search of our spares, we managed to find the original data plates, an absolute necessity to certification.

The research, telephone calls, letters and Fax messages seemed endless. The PMI had to be soothed with progress reports, as well. In addition there was the daily work of developing repairs, managing cabin interiors, fire-blocking and a myriad of other duties to perform. It was a hectic time, to put it mildly. Meanwhile, the long-suffering flight attendants continued to serve their passengers from the demeaning stoop and squat position.

There was one episode that stands out in my memories and notes. It exemplified diverse frustrations that were encountered during The Time of The Galleys.

The galleys were equipped with food service carts — as most are — which were stowed in compartments for takeoffs and landings and during severe turbulence. Since Flight Structures' drawings specified white oak side spacers to prevent cart sway in the compartments, the mechanics dutifully made them from white oak obtained at a local lumber yard.

The FAA agent handling manufacturing — rework of the galleys was defined as manufactured — raised a perplexing question. I had known him for several years and found him fairly reasonable and helpful , although he could be extremely irritating at times. Now he seemed to have attained the ultimate in being unreasonable when he demanded certification that the wood indeed was oak. Maybe it was because he was due to retire in three weeks and was also getting a little long in the tooth.

"I need some documentation saying this is white oak," he declared. "How do I know this is white oak? It could be any kind of wood."

His demand stunned me; even the most amateur do-it-your-selfer could identify the wood as white oak. Nevertheless, I returned to his office the next day with the sales invoice.

"This doesn't tell me anything except it was sold as white oak," he snorted. "They (the lumber yard) might sell you anything for oak." Was it possible the old boy held a personal grudge? His comment did sound suspiciously like he had an unfortunate experience with the lumber supplier. It specialized in catering to home owners who liked to do their own work.

At that point my head temperature had crept high into the yellow arc. His obstinacy was bordering on childishness. Even the FAA engineer who had been monitoring the galley program was becoming exasperated.

"You tell me. Do you want something from God?" I asked with undisguised sarcasm. "After all, He did grow the tree these strips came from."

The matter was finally resolved, to the agent's satisfaction, when I produced a document from the American Forestry Association defining the characteristics of white oak. The information wasn't much more than a journeyman cabinet maker could have given. The difference was, it was on an official letterhead and, therefore, an acceptable, viable document to him. Still, the information didn't address the background of the particular white oak we bought from the lumber yard. But I didn't volunteer that observation. Not surprisingly, the agent never personally examined the white oak spacers to satisfy his concern.

The galleys arrived a few days before the 727 was scheduled for an intermediate inspection and stood resplendent awaiting installation. Meanwhile, a steady stream of flight attendants flowed in and out of the hangar, admiring the galleys while exulting in the promise of serving their passengers properly. Our mechanics installed them and the FAA finally gave them its blessing. The 727 was once again a whole airplane.

No sooner had the galleys been installed, and before the 727 was due out of its inspection, the airplane was sold to a Central American airline. News of the transaction stunned all of us.

There was absolutely no hint that negotiations with the Central Americans were in progress. Suddenly, two days before the 727 departed, representatives of the airline appeared and began gathering the airplane's documents and records. They simply gathered them without an orderly system and stuffed them into boxes.

That accomplished, the boxes were loaded aboard the airplane and the 727 disappeared. With startling rapidity the 707s began to be sold, almost, it seemed, on a regular though spaced schedule.

I cannot deny that there were provocative, interesting times at Sky World, but when my supervisor was dismissed and the director of maintenance assumed his duties, preceded by the resignation of the head of quality assurance, the proverbial hand writing on the wall began to be more clear.

Then, the head of quality control was dismissed, his chair occupied by a person with little or no experience in the field. It became obvious that these moves were no more than the last, desperate gasps of a person drowning.

No one needs to hit me with a barn door to impress me that a 'delightful affair' is doomed to extinction. I opted to use my accumulated paid vacation, and went to New Zealand for two weeks where I did some research on aviation and fished. One month after returning I resigned.

Shortly thereafter, Sky World Airlines became history.

Reflecting on Sky World Airlines I cannot help but agonize over the awful waste of its potential and the efforts of the people below the inner sanctums of the head shed to make it work.

There was a rumor that the lending bank deliberately initiated its demise on the strength of the marketable value of the airplanes. That, of course, was never proved or disproved. But, given the dedication of Sky World's working staff, and with a little time and help over the rough spots with more astute management, it would have become a more viable operation than it was — and I would have remained, as would the others.

There is a lesson to be leaned considering the amount of Sky World's loan if the lending bank were perceptive and given to ethical customer relations.

The bank should have encouraged — no, insisted — on doubling the amount of the requested loan. Doing so would have assured enough money to provide for adequate funds to accomplish final repairs and modifications to clear the slate with the FAA. The balance could then be applied to improved operations for more revenue, to begin paying off the mortgage. .

When the airplane was sold, my attitude changed from unbridled enthusiasm that something had been accomplished to about as much personal satisfaction as making love to a hungry woman on a cold floor. Had things turned out differently, and we would have kept the airplane, I would have felt a wealth of personal satisfaction.

But the affair had a more dramatic, profound effect on some of the flight attendants, bordering on outright trauma. A few actually cried unabashedly when the 727 was sold.

The flight attendants never served their passengers from the galleys as God and the Boeing Commercial Airplane Company intended.

17

Linchpins in
The System....

In the beginning there was the designer/builder/pilot. Then the order evolved into designer/builder/pilot/mechanic. Finally, after aviation's embryo began to mature, natural progression changed once more. Designers/builders became to busy to do anything else; pilots became too busy to maintain their aircraft and the full-fledged mechanic materialized. Thus the sequence ultimately became designer/builder/ pilot /mechanic.

That pecking order was established in the lineage of aviation professionals as we know it today. That's how I interpreted the thoughts of the mechanic beside me.

"Where did you ever come up with that theory?" I asked Robbins. We were sitting on the hard ramp, our backs against the main hangar wall, eating our lunches.

The hectic activities of evening arrivals and departures had diminished, leaving the airport relatively quiet. But now and then an airplane would arrive, or one would depart, punctuating the slowly settling silence with their engine noises. By midnight, Washington National Airport, for all practical purposes, would be almost asleep until dawn, when it would slowly awaken.

Off to our left, about five-hundred yards away, the terminal lights glowed softly in the night. It seemed to be preparing for slumber. An Eastern Airlines Martin 404 was nosed up to the last gate on the south end of the curved gate complex like a horse tied to a hitch rail.

"It stands to reason, doesn't it?" Robbins didn't sound thoroughly convinced of his personal philosophy. Or he wanted confirmation.

"Some guy wanted to fly, so he designed an airplane. Then he had to build it. After that, he had to learn to fly and then, he had to maintain it. So there you have the designer/pilot/ mechanic." He was really warming to his theory now. I rudely interrupted his soliloquy.

"Look...that Eastern Martin is actually standing there on all three of its landing gears," I remarked with a tinge of sarcasm. Eastern was noted for having landing gear problems, strangely at Washington National. One notable incident was when a Martin landed, taxied to the terminal to off-load its passengers and stopped. The nose gear promptly collapsed. The airplane rested in that incongruous tail high position well into the next day before it was rescued. Any longer and some wit could have suggested it become a monument or reworked for a kids playground.

Robbins ignored my comment as though it was never offered. "That's how it all started, like when the Wright brothers first flew. They designed and built the Flyer and then flew it. Naturally, when they broke it they had to rebuild it. Besides, they started out as bicycle mechanics. Now doesn't that make sense?"

Without waiting for my response Robbins descended farther into his analysis of how the wheat and chaff were divided as aviation progressed. He took another bite from his baloney sandwich, as though he needed fuel to encourage further dissertation.

"When things really got rolling the designers got too busy to build and fly, so the pilots/mechanics did it," Robbins continued. "Then the pilots got too busy to maintain their airplanes and mechanics began to do that exclusively. So that's how the line of progression ended up as designer, pilot and mechanic."

He leaned back and thoughtfully finished his sandwich, suddenly quiet, as though his analysis had exhausted him. Robbins was scary at times. He was a marvelous mechanic, but was prone to these unexpected outbursts.

Privately I had to admit his reasoning made some sense, but wouldn't tell him, for fear it would start another windy dissertation. Besides, we had to get back to work. Thirty-minutes for lunch didn't last long.

The Wright brothers did indeed earn an honored niche in the chronicles of aviation. They were, in fact, bicycle builders and mechanics who knew absolutely nothing about flying or the theory of flight. Through persistent research into what was known about flight then — which was very little — they managed to build the Flyer.

During their efforts to prove it would fly they should have been killed or severely maimed. Instead, they were highly instrumental in opening the doors to a wonderfully imaginative age even de Vinci could not have foreseen.

I learned throughout the years that Robbins' theory of progression wasn't entirely set in concrete. Many maintenance men have changed hats to become pilots, engineers and managers. Pilots have exchanged cockpits for drawing boards and executive desks. Designer/pilots have mutated into becoming owners of aircraft manufacturing establishments. Walter Beech and Clyde Cessna are two well-known examples. There are others.

Of the three professions, that of the aircraft mechanic is unique. It embodies a long list of fields in which he or she is required to be solidly versed. No other profession demands those attributes.

The fields in the directory of theory and practical application of that theory in aircraft maintenance is long. It lists electrical and hydraulic systems, engine and accessory overhaul and maintenance; propeller overhaul and maintenance; structural repairs and a host of other disciplines. It is necessary to interpret and understand federal air regulations — if at all possible — affecting aircraft maintenance and the mechanic.

Also calculating weight and balance, understanding the theory of flight, and now the ever-increasing prominence of the use of electronic and computer-generated elements controlling engine and airframe systems that were once manually controlled, confronts many maintenance people. Some requirements have been victims of progress, such as dope and fabric and woodworking.

Sniffing dope fumes wasn't considered a fad. Getting light-headed was simply a function of dope and fabric work, and one was paid to do that. But progress has a price: Unfortunately, many mechanics' skills are degrading into a remove and replace syndrome because of black boxes.

There have been, and still are, mechanics who have an admirable measure of inherent engineering sense. That quality has been manifested in improvements to existing designs, fashioning structural repairs or designing new components and even aircraft.

Unfortunately, there have been many who showed real promise in engineering who chose not to, or could not, for any number of reasons, pursue the profession, aviation being the loser.

Etched sharply in my memory is one example of using mechanical imagination. It was a impermanent modification an acquaintance adopted purely out of self-perceived desperation to accelerate making a permanent repair. At the time I couldn't help but admire his presence of mind, but hesitate to recommend his solution to a minor inconvenience involving a few days of aircraft down time.

As anyone who is acquainted with the line of early, fabric covered Piper aircraft knows, the general design of some engine exhaust systems were similar: The exhaust stacks, from both sides of the engine, terminate in a muffler mounted behind the engine on the firewall. An overboard tail pipe exits from the bottom of the muffler through the bottom engine cowl.

I was inspecting a Beech E-18 when I noticed, through the open hangar doors, a Piper J-3 land and taxi toward the hangar. Nothing unusual except its engine sounded strangely different. Curious, I walked to the airplane as its pilot climbed out. To my surprise it was Bannister, a young A&E based at a small airport about seventy-five miles away.

"Why does this engine sound different?" I asked, after we exchanged greetings.

"I rearranged the exhaust stacks," he said. His sheepish grin told me what

273

he did wasn't according to Hoyle or anyone else for that matter. "Take a look. What I did works pretty good!"

I did and became somewhat flabbergasted. He had reversed the stacks: Right to left and vice versa! The muffler had been removed. Before the modification the ends of the stacks should have been inserted into each end of the muffler; now they protruded from the side cowling about six-inches. I had never given any thought that was possible, but there it was.

"Why did you do that?" I asked.

"The muffler was completely eroded and going to pieces," he explained. "I knew John (the repair shop owner) had a new one and, rather than wait for him to ship it to me, I thought I'd just fly over here, get it and install it here. I didn't want to take the chance of flames shooting out of the muffler."

Fortunately the ends of the exhaust stacks extended well into the propeller's slipstream away from the section of sheet metal that wrapped around the fuselage aft of the firewall. Otherwise, flames emerging from the pipes could have burnt the finish on the wraparound. In the extreme, the finish could have caught fire easily if the pipes had been closer. The paint was actually pigmented nitrate dope.

The Supplemental Type Certificate (STC) list is a lengthy catalog of interesting examples of conversions and design changes to airframes, engines, accessories and other components. They are illuminating tributes to the potential engineering capabilities of mechanics and, other maintenance personnel. Many are also factory-generated.

STCs have resulted because someone recognized that either a design cried out for purely upgrading an element, or there was a compelling need to increase mechanical or flight efficiency. Others have been developed for specialized operations, but still, FAR requirements must be met.

If a reader has a good idea and wishes to develop it and an STC for the concept, he should not be mislead into believing the process is a simple one. It is not! When I developed one and finally completed it, I was again reminded of that book I already mentioned: Pilgrim's Progress.

The plot had religious overtones wherein the leading character set out on a journey to accomplish the goal of purity of mind and ideals, in addition to everlasting salvation. During that tedious, seemingly endless journey he was constantly confronted with enticements and obstacles designed to sway his purpose. He prevailed, although it was a long arduous excursion. In my situation the obstacles were there, but not the religion. One can easily lose what little, if any, one has, when dealing with the FAA to develop an STC!

Little appreciation of the intricacies involved in developing an STC can be had by simply reading the published, bland description of one. In my experience I learned it wasn't so much the planning, design, installation and general mechanics involved, but the monumental amount of paperwork. There seemed, I thought at the time, to be no end in sight trying to satisfy the FAA.

The STC in point was a joint effort by myself and Pittsburgh Plate Glass Company. It was a conversion to replace production windshields in Lockheed 18s with electrically-heated units made by PPG. In retrospect PPG had the easy part: Manufacturing the two windshield panels.

The physical conversion was relatively simple. There was only the matter of removing the original windshield panels and replacing them with the new heated units, following factory-suggested installation procedures.

Installation of wiring circuits, power relays, switches and overheat warning modules was no more complicated than rewiring any major electrical system. It was the almost overwhelming effort compiling documentation to satisfy the FAA's insatiable appetite for more information — some demands were pointless, in my view, at the time — that tried my patience and soul.

Once the FAA demanded information about how the new electrically heated windshields were made. That, of course, was propriety information and summarily

275

refused by PPG. During the course of the project it struck me as strange no FAA engineer appeared to monitor the conversion as it progressed over seven months. In fact, the windshields were operational — and were operated — two weeks prior to the inspection for final approval.

At the conclusion of the exercise I had a file approximately three-inches thick, excluding blue prints, and an official document proclaiming an STC had been issued.

I learned later that the approving inspector erred because he intruded into the affairs of an FAA office out of his bailiwick. He was from a district office, not from FAA engineering. In any case, nothing resulted from the internal conflict, as far as the conversion was concerned. But I learned through the grapevine that a heated conversation and discussion had ensued between the two offices.

World War II can be credited — if any war can be given credit for anything — with at least two major contributions to the growth of aviation after the conflict: Out of necessity new aircraft designs evolved, as well as the education of mechanics. Many would maintain post war civilian aircraft. The controversy seemed to have awakened minds and inherent mechanical aptitudes that would be of immense help in aviation later.

Without question, the war was an outlet for personal desires to enter aviation that could not be satisfied for any number of reasons as a civilian.

After a brief indoctrination in Air Corps service schools the new mechanics were plunged into the throes of an explosive expansion of combat squadrons scattered over the face of the earth. It was in those far-flung outposts that they started to blossom and acquire maturity.

With little more to rely on than their limited service schooling, personal ingenuity and inherent mechanical sense and skills they managed to maintain their aircraft with remarkable efficiency. Many relied on theft and deception: It was not unusual for members of one squadron's maintenance staff to steal a part from another squadron, in order to keep their aircraft combat ready.

The deception was in the form of lying if any suspicions grew into downright accusations. Pride was a mighty incentive in meeting flying schedules, and competition was fierce. Therefore, lying was acceptable and, customary.

For the maintenance men who elected to continue into civilian aviation after the war what they learned in military aviation was a solid base on which to build.

Atypical of those maintenance men urged on by their latent potential was Max Bietcher, a personal acquaintance.

Early in his life Bietcher was deeply interested in things mechanical and enrolled in Pratt Institute of Technology, taking classes in hydraulic engineering. "Halfway through (his studies) I found out that hydraulic engineers were operating elevators at Macy's Department Store for fifteen-dollars a week," he recalled, "so I quit and went into aviation instead."

His first job was at Vultee, later becoming Consolidated Vultee, building primary trainers, B-24s and LB-30s. Because of an illness in his family he moved his little group back to the New York area from California, where he hired in with Eastern Aircraft — not to be confused with Eastern Airlines — at Linden, New Jersey. The company was building FM-1s and FM-2s for General Motors.

Disenchanted because of production methods '...they thought they were building cars...' and faced with the real prospect of enlisting, Bietcher joined the U.S. Overseas Air Service Command. He worked his way up to become in charge of the flight line at Newark, a stopover for aircraft passing through on their flights overseas. These included P-61s, P-51s, B-24s, B-17s and '...practically everything the Air Force had.'

It wasn't a one-way street and it was busy. As in any war, equipment falls into enemy hands and there was no exception in that war.

Westbound ships occasionally off-loaded Italian Arados and German Me-209s and ME-262s. They were then shipped to Newark and reassembled. But while the aircraft were intact, they arrived with little if any documentation. Without benefit of maintenance manuals, assembly instructions and blueprints, the aircraft were assembled and flown to Wright Field.

Under the keen scrutiny of Air Force engineers the aircraft's design features were closely studied. They wanted to know what the Germans and Italians were designing into their new jet fighters, the 262 and Arado. Maybe there were some properties or methods of manufacturing that could be used in the new YP-80 Lockheed was developing. But other German aircraft were given the same studied attention.

By the war's end Max had acquired his A&E License (now A&P) and like many others cast into the civilian world, looked for a medium in which to use his expertise and skills. He found an outlet when he joined a group with like desires. They had diverse experience and persuasions, but together they formed an all-cargo airline, appropriately named Sky Freight Airlines. Max's engineering sense would be an advantage, as well as his maintenance skills.

"We bought six C-47s (service designation of DC-3s) with less than one-thousand hours, on the surplus market," Max told me. "I realized we'd need engines and I had an idea the Pratt & Whitney 1830-43 was what I was looking for. It was the same engine we installed on B-24s at Vultee."

Max bought forty 1830s, again on the surplus market, and trucked them to Newark, home base of the new airline. There was a problem, however: They wouldn't fit a DC-3 engine mount. With the benefit of his nimble mind, Beitcher made a pattern and from that, had an aluminum casting made that would adapt the 1830s to the DC-3 engine mount. In a time when simplification was paramount, the design was approved on an ACA Form 337. Later, adapters were sold to other DC-3 operators so they, too, could take advantage of the surplus of 1830 engines available.

"That was the beginning of using the P&W R-1830-43 engine in DC-3s,"

278

Max told me years later. His pride was evident — and justified. After the conversation I wondered: 'Did Max install those R-1830s on some of the B-24s based on Oahu during the war?' It was apparent his motivation was instrumental in the mix of engines that powered DC-3s. At Capital Airlines we had DC-3s equipped with Wright R-1820s while National Airlines, whose DC-3s we serviced, were powered with R-1830s.

While there are still opportunities for aviation mechanics to exercise their inherent or acquired abilities to enhance aircraft operation with new ideas and innovations, it may be that those latitudes have narrowed somewhat. This perception was brought out in a conversation with my son, Earl Jr., a fine, natural pilot in his own right.

"In your time," he remarked, "there was much to do, things to accomplish, and there were goals to look forward to. Aviation was growing and needed help." As an afterthought he wondered aloud.

"Maybe that's what's wrong today: Young people don't have much to look forward to, or accomplish something as you and others in the early days did." He might have added that thought could apply to a wide variety of young people not necessarily involved in aviation.

There was considerable validity in his assessment, but still, engineering without portfolio continues where necessity demands changes to improve aircraft operation and air services. This is especially true in areas such as Alaska or the upper reaches of Canada's provinces.

There aviation is the common denominator, binding outlying towns and villages together. An observer would be hard pressed to find a bush aircraft without modifications to its original configuration.

"An engineer is nothing more than a mechanic with his brains beaten out." I've heard that old saw from time to time, its attribution lost in the mists of time. It's a bit far-fetched and patently unkind, in general, but instances have arisen that

279

have vividly illustrated the non-application of imagination, common sense and foresight, or an absence of experience in an engineer's design efforts.

Probably the quote originated when some individual, in a fit of rage and frustration, encountered a situation which he thought, could have been better conceived during the design stage.

I'll agree that many aircraft structures and assemblies may lack something in design and installation but that's hindsight. Anyone can criticize another's work easier than creating an original. This is not a coldly perfect world, by any means. If there is an anomaly, though, that cries out for correction, or improvement or change to better serve a purpose, sooner or later revisions are accomplished, whether from factory or individual field action. There are some that take longer than others, to address and design.

There have been modifications and even original works, designed and engineered by mechanics that come very near deserving of the mark of genius. In a few instances the mechanic had a smattering of engineering theory in his background; in most, a reliance on good, solid judgment and practicality. The latter attributes are generally garnered during years of realistic maintenance experience. Add common sense, which cannot be taught, as a major contributing factor.

Another acquaintance I've known for years is an individual who began his maintenance career in the United States Army Air Force when radial engines prevailed as the primary power source. After he was discharged, he opened a small shop overhauling not only radial engines but flat Continentals and Lycomings, too.

He even overhauled a Ranger engine: An in-line, air-cooled inverted type out of production for many years. Anyone who has had experience with Ranger engines will understand why I mention overhauling one as a distinctive accomplishment.

His outstanding contribution to one segment of aviation came not from overhauls, perse, but converting good, dependable Lycoming engines, mostly four-cylinder types, to produce more horsepower for aerobatic aircraft. The idea germinated because competing pilots wanted more power, not a newer, larger engine. In that case the man filled a niche rather than, by definition, improving a design.

The engines dependably accomplish what their conversions were designed for and are powering aerobatic aircraft even in international competition. However, Lycoming refuses to admit they exist.

A product, such as an airplane, often is not all things to all uses. To meet specific operations the configuration must be designed in, and then produced as a specialized use aircraft. Otherwise changes and re-design can be made, in the field, after the fact, to accommodate an aircraft's individual owner's perceived, specialized purpose or a fleet operator's desires. There are also innumerable small companies producing spares for older aircraft and engines and new parts and components for newer ones.

In spite of my son's seemingly bleak analysis, mechanics are still in a position to not only recognize opportunities for improvements; many have the ability to effect those modifications and changes. This is not to say, however, that everyone should suddenly decide they are full-fledged engineers. Perish the thought : "Yesterday I couldn't spell 'engineer', today I are one." The point is, there are still horizons to march toward, although some may not appear to be as broad or distant or challenging, as they once were.

The argument can be that during the 1930's it was private flying that led the public's gradual acceptance of aircraft as a viable method of travel, not the opposite. This by no means meant private aviation declined. It's rise was interrupted by World War II, and continued by leaps and bounds in its aftermath.

This phenomenon became General Aviation, an appellation that includes practically every aspect of aviation, excluding transport and armed forces aviation. And so, more and more mechanics were required, especially for maintaining transport aircraft, which is to say, commercial aviation. This is especially to the point since power was provided by internal combustion engines — piston engines, to be specific. They required, and still do, considerable attention; to a lesser degree, so did the airframes.

With the advent of turbine engines the pendulum began to swing in favor of a lessening of the concentration. If for no other reason than the fact that turbine engines have very few moving parts — lowering vibration-induced problems to practically none. There's one outstanding feature about turbine engines: If a vibration problem arises you can be sure that your options are very limited. In fact, there is only one: Remove the engine from service until a determination of the cause of the vibration is made.

I know of only one engine make, the Franklin — now made in Poland but regaining a foothold in this country — that is so free of vibration inherent in horizontally-opposed engines it makes one wonder why Lycoming and Continental have not adopted the feature.

It is the design of the flywheel. The flywheel is hollow and filled with a silicone-type product, then sealed with a metal plate. It is an extremely effective innovation and removes incipient vibrations from the crankshaft and other elements of the power section induced mostly by piston rods and pistons. A Franklin engine is a real joy to fly behind.

Airframes kept pace with turbine engine design with improved engineering and materials. Now, systems are more and more self-sustaining with elaborate, highly technical electronic measures. Structurally, they have become so enhanced the need for repairs, in comparison with piston-engine equipped transports, has declined markedly. Still, the need for maintenance personnel remains consistent, if not strengthened, simply because there are more large aircraft; also competition with commuter and feeder aircraft personnel requirements.

General Aviation has remained a steady field for mechanics, but, unfortunately, wages have not risen markedly in comparison to airline wages. Also, the FAA seems to consider General Aviation as a step-child, deserving only of sops. Although the FAA cannot influence higher pay for General Aviation, nevertheless, there's nothing that says it cannot encourage and promote progress; that it is supposed to do anyway. Signs surface that it will improve — albeit slowly. One aspect that will help mechanics is the inevitable introduction of small turbine-powered aircraft, in the four to six-place class. So, if a mechanic takes training in that field he or she will fare better in compensation with FBO's.

In corporate flying, a segment of General Aviation, small turbine-equipped aircraft — and not so small — have become the rule, rather than the exception.

This segment of General Aviation is the lush pasture of maintenance. What relatively few mechanics are needed, in comparison with other divisions of aviation, generally remain until retirement. Overall, whatever the future holds for aviation mechanics, the more dedicated and responsible will prevail. It will be a matter of natural selection as to who has the potential for upward mobility, to coin an upscale term, — as in nature's options for improving species.

I have never known, or heard of, a mechanic one could consider as 'great'. That has never been a consideration or opinion of those mechanics deserving of being prominent and exalted, within the maintenance spectrum. Like the lyrics to a song, they have always worked in the shadows of the 'greats' during the Golden Years of Aviation from before World War II to even this day. The Roscoe Turner's; the Wiley Post's;Eddie Rickenbackers. the aces of World War II and now, the astronauts.

In recent years there is much ado about the absence of public perception and understanding of the role of aviation mechanics industry-wide. Mechanics as a whole, and over the years, haven't helped their image. Many, especially in general aviation, have ignored their physical appearance, demeanor, attitude and the mindset that they are just as important as a pilot.

Appearence, however, is gradually changing, particularly in some FBOs and corporate aviation; airlines have always dressed their mechanics to present a uniform, appealing image. Egos need to be polished and impressed but with diplomacy.

When asked what their occupation is many answer: "Oh...I'm just a mechanic." Not, "I'm an aviation mechanic and a dammed good one. I put those airplanes in the air. Pilots keep them there!" Self-advertising, in the proper vein, is a distinguishes a mechanic from being perceived as a person who could lose himself in a crowd of two or someone who has the will to not be seen as out of place by virtue of his profession. In recent years there has been much ado about the absence of public perception and understanding of the role of aviation mechanics industry-wide. One major reason is that industry has made no concentrated move to initiate a public relations effort to educate the flying public.

Seldom, if ever, will there be a story in a daily newspaper about aviation mechanics other than when one or more is associated with an aircraft accident. Never a human interest story about a career in the field. On the other hand, it's difficult to convince a newspaper editor such stories should be printed since they wouldn't generate sales, lacking sensationalism.

And so, the Wright Brothers went on to deserved public acclaim, but Charles Taylor who built the Wright Flyer's engine did not. It's doubtful if there will ever be a Maintenance Hall of Fame with deserving installations of well-known maintenance men and women. In the final analysis doesn't it all come down to maintenance?

Still, the ones that stood out are legendary, known only to, and respected by their contemporaries — and the few greats who are still alive and remember them.

18

Knotting The
Strings of Time....

The months and years of my aircraft and engine maintenance career accumulated like so many growth rings in a tree. The memories are like jewels of varied intensity. Some glitter with undiminished light, others not quite as intense. Thus are marked the good and not so good experiences and relationships. But the enjoyable surpassed the flawed, by far, while enhancing the cultivation of forty-six rings.

The very first step into civilian aviation was when I labored with Carson around the clock on a war surplus Piper J-3. They were used as artillery fire spotters, but this one hadn't penetrated the smoke of battle. The completion of the work we did on it, a subsequent inspection and approval for flight by the CAA was of foremost importance to the birth of Pacific Skyways. A crop spraying contract would get the company off the ground and we had to meet a deadline. After that, we could look forward to a regular paycheck. That would substantiate our willingness to invest personal time and living expenses in a dream.

The years that followed Pacific Skyways' demise were the first footholds on the steep steps to the heights of personal achievement After that episode ended in frightening reality, I began to draw regular paychecks, that steadily increased in value.

Working up through light, fabric- covered aircraft to more and more complicated heavy single engine 'planes helped immensely. Early on, there was a variety of war surplus aircraft, transitioned for use in civil aviation, which I feasted on. There followed, the venerable commercial radial engine transports followed by turbine engine equipment, both pure jets and turbo props.

The transition into the dawning world of whining compressors and screaming turbine wheels marked a new era. I became a part of it on the Viscounts, Beech 99s, King Airs, Lear Jets, Boeing 707s and 727s. It was a bountiful period.

The men and women with whom I associated over the years, foremen and supervisors, mechanics, pilots, stewardesses — now 'flight attendants' — radiomen, parts men and helpers, and that woman who owned the doomed fixed base operation, are all segments of the kaleidoscope.

Government agents figured in the scheme, too. Representatives of the CAA were followed by those of the FAA. With most, I had a palatable relationship; a few, clashes of professional opinion of varying degrees of intensity.

I discovered, in that exposure to officialdom, that those characters are as human as the rest of us — and many were technically inadequate. There were personal emotions, jealousy, machoism and monumental egos. Several suffered from traits that sometimes overruled common sense and objective administration.

I cannot help but think of how the onus of responsibility in policing federal rules governing aircraft technical support has gradually shifted to civil field maintenance personnel, especially in General Aviation. I'm not convinced that control can be achieved entirely from an office, to the exclusion of a physical, official presence in the field.

Without even quasi-official status it's often difficult for maintenance personnel in the field to convince an owner his aircraft condition violates certain FARs. Or prompt a shop owner, supervisor, or foreman that a mechanic or inspector should not be placed in the difficult position of ambling his sense of right against what is wrong. Administration of regulations in the air carrier spectrum is much more effective since an FAA agent's presence is regularly in place.

Those characters in my personal play arrived, paused for varying periods and continued on their way, as I did mine. From time to time, a few have reappeared by rare chance; most have not been seen again. But that remarkable medium of communication, the aviation grapevine, now and then has revealed their presence and activities — and their passing — with uncanny, timeless accuracy.

Hammond and Fox, who profiled my beginnings, have undoubtedly vanished into the Long Silence. Both chastised me severely when I transgressed, but were wonderfully generous with praise when I hewed to the line of their excellent instruction and advice.

They regaled me with stories of the very early days when radial engine crankshafts were fixed and the cylinders and propeller, as one unit, rotated. Those were the rotary engines. Probably an adventurous engineer thought that perhaps it would be better if the horse was placed before the cart. And so they decided that the crankshaft would rotate and the cylinders be fixed, so true radial engines were born out of the short lifespan of rotary engines.

Of all the maintenance men I've known, those two had knowledge of and rapport with engines, that was nothing short of eerie. It was Hammond who started me on my career by wisely immersing me headlong into stark basics: Long dreary months of hand-cleaning carbon, cement-hard varnishes and residues from gears, shafts, valves and pistons. Unwanted elements that had been baked on after the parts were subjected to exquisite torture in the finest of all oil refineries, an operating piston engine.

During that internship Hammond and Fox insisted that their credo, "You don't let anything go until it's right," be followed to the letter. In later years some young mechanics, shop owners, private aircraft owners and foremen had difficulty accepting my insistence that the precept be applied. Especially when I held an inspector's rating. There were times when it was trying to convince them, but I never got into trouble by adhering to Hammond's and Fox's instructions. And the unforgiving nature of flight always reminded me they were right.[55]

Colter departed life early on, victim of that mysterious scourge that grows with often inexorable deadli-
ness in a body. It sometimes takes years to achieve its
ultimate goal, sometimes not so long. His was a very
brief encounter and the dreadful affliction triumphed
over him at thirty-two years of age. He had an excellent technical mind, a quick wit and a never-ending
awareness of his responsibilities to his role in
maintenance. When he succumbed to cancer he had a
jump-start on a rewarding career. I have no doubt
whatsoever he would have been an undeniably valuable asset to aviation, not only as a mechanic but in the
higher echelons of supervision or, quite possibly, management.

One dark night in Australia at a forward airstrip,
Boor was smitten by the No. 2 propeller of a B-17; his
death, of course, was instantaneous. He was a high
school classmate. In a brightly-lit hangar at Washington National Airport Nelson died in appalling, searing
agony. He had been cleaning a fuel tank cavity in a
DC-4 wing when the bucket of methyl ethyl ketone
spilled on him. His extension light shorted during his
hasty exit from the wing, causing a calamitous spark!
Miraculously, he lived for three hours and then departed life, leaving his leather belt and shoes — and his
memory.

Tools and tool boxes are as personal to a mechanic as a purse is
to a woman. I never bought a roll-away from the commercial market.

When my original Air Corps issue, wooden roll-away became too small for my needs and tools, I built another, larger and also of wood. I still have both. Also the tray from a small, metal hand tool box I began my career with.

It was a hip-roof design and the split lid opened outward, with the tray nestled inside. The box had four small casters and a length of aircraft control cable fitted on one end for towing. This was a common tool box among mechanics I worked with years ago. They served us well until expansion into roll-aways was affordable.

A mechanic offered to buy the Air Corps roll-away from me, saying it had historical value. His offer left me in a grey area: Was I also historical and what was my value?

Many of the hand tools I began my career with I still have. Others have fallen by the wayside through attrition, wear and borrowing. A mechanic at John Rogers Airport at Honolulu borrowed a wooden-handled screwdriver. He returned it with the handle split. He used it as chisel. Thereafter I limited borrowing to very rare instances. Except for socket sets I never made it a practice to buy open end or box wrenches in sets, as a matter of course. I preferred to be selective.

Some tool designs have evolved from trim patterns into unnecessarily heavy shanks and heads better suited for Caterpillar tractor work than aircraft and aircraft engine applications. My tools included Plomb (Proto), Williams, Bonney, Blue Point and Cornwell. Those names were mainstays in hand tools at the inception of my career. Those I still have recall vivid memories at the touch.

I still have two tap and die sets nestled in solid American oak cases. One was made by Blue Point. A Snap-On tool salesman tried desperately to trade for it, but I refused. In my collection there is a pair of surplus Cleco pliers. They cost me twenty-five cents in 1952. They were stamped from heavy sheet steel, are light and easy to use and remain durable to this day. About that time a right and left cutting pair of Wiss shears was purchased with moonlighting money. I still have them, and their sharpness hasn't diminished dramatically. There are other sheet metal tools dating to that era and still operating well. The air-operated drill and rivet gun were surplus as were the bucking bars, clecos and rivet sets.

Although my new wooden roll-away drew much admiration from mechanics it paled in comparison to one Norman built; it was a magnificent creation. Fully five feet high by approximately six feet long, Norman's roll-away was constructed with a heavy angle iron frame and mounted on five hundred-pound capacity casters.

Its commodious interior contained shelves and drawers and racks of such quantity and capacity as to make the conventional roll-aways mockeries and miserably inadequate. It even had a small compartment that housed Norman's technical library.

One end of the behemoth had a thick, wooden work surface that folded down when not in use; in the operating position it was well-braced. At the opposite end the ingenious Norman devised a small table and chair which could be swung out from a stowed position. Being the studious type, he would swing the unit out, lock it in position and sit in haughty comfort eating his lunch while he read. We always thought 'Norman's Marvel' easily could qualify as a monument to aviation maintenance.

Carson, who had been a wonderful personal friend and neighbor when he was with United Airlines and I with Trans Ocean, at Honolulu, died in California while enroute from Germany to his beloved Hawaiian Islands and retirement. Death often denies with icy insolence. Carson was the epitome of generosity and cooperation when we needed to borrow a set of Loran units or other equipment from United's stores. He and United were the direct antithesis of Pan American's cold, disdainful attitude. He was affable and outgoing — and 'All American'.

He made an attempt to go into the cattle business, a short-lived effort. When he was returning his first cow home from having it bred, on a wobbly, flat bed trailer with rickety side rails, Carson was overtaken by (then) Japan's Prince Akihito's entourage. The official convoy was being escorted by Honolulu police on a tour of Oahu. It was the first visit by a high-ranking Japanese official after the war.

"You'd better pull over, Clyde," his neighbor and passenger advised. "I don't imagine they want to expose the prince to a cow's ass staring him in the face."

"To hell with them," Carson retorted indignantly, "I'm an American and this is America. They can go around us!"

The matter was resolved when a burly native Hawaiian policeman drove his motorcycle alongside Carson's truck and trailer and ordered him, in no uncertain terms, to pull over. The prince's group drove sedately by while Carson seethed with rage on the side of the highway.

Carson's ashes were given over to the Pacific Ocean off the coast of Oahu in an ages-old Hawaiian rite of passage. Norine keeps the faith in California. I've often wondered if his last words were, 'Keep your knees tight.

Don't let anybody get into you,' to whoever was there when he died. It was an admonition he generally uttered when parting company with his friends and close acquaintances.

Gardiner and Collins were close associates during the Hawaiian Air Depot days and knew Carson as well as I did. It was the former who told me of Carson's passing.

Like Carson, Gardiner spent a considerable portion of his career with the FAA, as did Collins, but Gardiner achieved higher status. Several years have passed since he took early retirement.

"I had enough," he said. "I came to my senses and bailed out." The implication was one of utter disgust at the direction the FAA was taking in conducting the administration of aviation affairs in Gardiner's bailiwick. .

Sobeck was one of the finest sheet metal repairmen I've ever been associated with. But to work with him in the tight confines of a Constellation's tail cone could put one at risk of becoming intoxicated by default, much like 'they' say, inhaling second-hand cigarette smoke will give one cancer. He consumed beer before and after work with an almost religious devotion. But his penchant for the brew never affected his expertise in structural repairs. I never commented or asked how many bottles he had, but he was never out of control. Our foremen also never questioned him.

Sulley was accident-prone. He never failed in providing us with interesting occurrences during his work assignments. The night he attempted to start the

*No. 1 engine on a DC-3 the entire left wing and fuse-
lage side became lit up when the engine back-fired and
caused a carburetor fire. Luckily, there was enough
battery power to keep the engine turning until the
excess fuel was disposed of. Sully simply had not yet
achieved dominance over the oft-times sensitive nature
of Holley carburetors. It was a spectacular event!*

*Two weeks later he pierced the side of a DC-4 with
the forks of a fork-lift while unloading seats from the
airplane's cabin. Then Sulley was disposed of; foremen
weren't known for liberal attitudes then. There are
many other mechanics and incidents that surface
occasionally from my memories and then retreat to its
depths. I never worked with a female mechanic, or
knew one in all of that time. They simply had not
appeared.*

Except for a few pilots in corporate aviation, the commuters and
those who flew the Boeings at Sky World Airlines there are none I remember. Nor did I associate with or know any of the various ones who
were prominent in the public's eye. I didn't realize Ernie Gann flew
for Trans Ocean until I read his book, *Fate is The Hunter.* Undoubtedly we looked at each other from time to time; he from a DC-4's
cockpit, me from the ground, during the Korean Air Lift.

It was simply a matter of circumstance that the pilots who flew
the DC-3s, DC-4s, Constellations and DC-6s were nameless faces
peering down from cockpit side windows. They completed their flights
and disappeared, only to reappear a day or so later on another flight;
from this repetition a few faces were remembered, but not the names.
There was little personal contact with ground crews, as compared to

other, smaller operations where the same pilots were present on a daily basis.

Among my thoughts about the era of aviation I grew up in are the dramatic changes that have since occurred, particularly with respect to environmental and electrical systems and, of course, engines. The first high technology we were introduced to was engine analyzers on the Constellations. Black boxes have become the rule, rather than the exception. Tools have mutated as well.

Now it's an age of specialization, with much removing and replacing, primarily in air carrier maintenance, to a lesser degree in general aviation. And high-profile testing equipment has emerged to support the advance of technology in aircraft systems. In different times mechanics were machinists, welders, sheet metal technicians, electricians, engine overhaulers, clerks in everyday practice. These varied activities were part and parcel of their normal working lives.

"You fellows," a maintenance manager with United Airlines once told me, "were the repairmen and fixers. Today they (maintenance) are changers."

Time and personal responsibilities didn't permit me to pursue the credibility of Bill Sessions' report that Jacque Costeau's PBY needed a co-pilot/mechanic. The airplane was scheduled for an extended mission throughout the South Pacific, he said. Sessions said he recommended me to Cousteau and called me from Miles City where the airplane had stopped on a research and filming mission in Montana. I didn't get the message, until three-days after the PBY departed Miles City. But I've often wondered: What if...?

Richardson was a fellow mechanic on Oahu when
I was on Kauai. He had re-covered his J-3 and called
to say he would fly it to Kauai from Honolulu, to brag

about it. He didn't arrive. A colossal navigational error of approximately 90-degrees resulted in a ditching at sea when he ran out of fuel. He was on a heading to Johnson Island, five-hundred miles away to the south-west instead of Kauai, a mere eighty-mile flight, to the northwest. A Navy sea-going tugboat, inbound to Pearl Harbor, plucked him and his girlfriend from the Pacific Ocean, but couldn't save the J-3. The pair was extremely fortunate that Fate arranged matters so that the tugboat and the J-3 intercepted at the location of the ditching.

There was a wrench that fell from a wing inner brace and confused the flux gate of a Lodestar's compass. After a brief period of diagnosing the problem, I found the wrench lying immediately under the compass unit. It had the initials R.V.B. engraved on the shank. Obviously, my friend, Tex Blanscet, at Qualitron Aero in Burbank, had left it there after re-wiring the compass system.

"I have a wrench that belongs to you," I told him via long distance telephone. "You left it in the right wing of the airplane. It really threw the compass into a tizzy."

"It's not mine," he declared.

"Your initials are on it...R.V.B."

"They're not my initials."

"You won't get it back," I warned him.

"Since it's not mine I don't expect it back," he retorted. His refusal to acknowledge the wrench was honored — I have it still. It's a valuable memento of him.

A close acquaintance with an innate interest in aviation once remarked he envied me living through and being a part of the time when aviation was evolving into its present state. But during those times of bone-chilling days and nights, sweltering heat, cut hands, cracked fingers and often irascible piston engines while not having the advantage of sophisticated equipment, tooling and supplies available now, we probably didn't think of being part of a particular era.

If a role needs to be defined we were supporting a continuous experiment that began with the Wright Flyer's brief flight over the sand dunes of Kitty Hawk, continuing through the liftoff of Columbia. With that momentous event, another phase in the Great Experiment began.

That continuing exploration has not been without price.

In any endeavor in man's endless quest to satisfy an inexhaustible appetite for more knowledge or progress, there will be tragedies. They are inevitable; nothing is easy when a new idea or concept is put in motion. This truth applies to maintenance men and women, as well as air crews. There's always a risk when one integrates one's part in the total system.

Men and women have perished in explorations, wars, laboratory experiments, testing new devices, pursuing dreams. The people directly involved know this is so, but press on in their work to transpose new ideas into practicality. In aviation maintenance, military and civil, there were some mechanics who fell, but not as many as in aircrews. The ones who prevailed remember the hard work, frustration, heartache, derision, injury, danger and tragedies — and sometimes names are recalled. If names are understandably forgotten, the images remain.

The holocaust that consumed the Graf Zeppelin, and the Macon, Akron and Shennadoah disasters were only incidents during our experiment in aviation — as were the many airplanes that fell. Now, in this next phase of evolution into creative daring, Challenger's passage into history should not have come as a surprise. It was a singular reminder we must pay the piper if we're to take a concept into a new dimension.

If the world lasts long enough, two hundred years or so into the future, space vehicle maintenance men and women and astronauts will doubtless reflect on the 20th Century exercise to exact an alliance with airspace.

Probably they will wag their heads in reverence and astonishment at the procession of, to them, crude aircraft and the present space shuttles resting in the archives. They will wonder aloud: 'How did they do it?' Much like the spectator at a display of World War II combat aircraft who was overheard talking to his companion:

"You mean to tell me we fought a war with those airplanes!" he exclaimed to his friend. Would he have considered an array of very early commercial air transport types with the DC-2 as the crown jewel, with like astonishment? Those were the aircraft that truly opened air travel to an adventuress public.

As Taylorcraft's J-2 , later evolving into the Piper J-3 put thousands in the air, so DC-4s and DC-3 s convinced the public that air travel was far more appealing than trains and other mass surface travel. The two designs proved their worth in the crucible of war as being capable of transporting freight and humans long distances with unremitting dependability. After the war they carried-over into public, commercial air travel without pause..

Of the new breeds Lockheed Constellations remains conspicuous in my recollections. They were the embodiment of design grace in flight and reasonable when demanding attention in maintaining them.They, and the Boeing Stratocruisers, could be deemed as the types that introduced luxurious air travel at appealing speeds.

In time, they gave way to the awesome Boeing 707, a gigantic step forward in domestic air travel and global air voyages, at astonishing speed. Insofar as General Aviation types are concerned — with no apologies — the Ercoupe does not enjoy favor in my remembrances. But it's two-control design was an honest attempt to promote ease of flight for private pilots — and it did have some appeal to many.

Every professional aircraft mechanic will experience incidents throughout his or her career that will remain prominent in their memory banks. In spite of two insignificant incidents I can say with understandable pride I was never responsible for a life-threatening incident; nor for being faulted for an aircraft's well-being. The years are irrevocable but memories are not so even those two stumbles remain with all the strides.

If there is one piece of advice to offer maintenance technicians — using the present, vocational term — it is this: Reject compromise. Maintain professional perspectives to authentically guarantee distinctive, quality results. You will lose nothing, but gain much.

The examples and thoughts set down in this work are just a few of many for me. The bits and pieces contributed to the whole. There are many more that occasionally surface, quietly, without warning, as though revealed by a curtain that has been gently raised.

In all of my career I can count on one hand the number of bastards I met. Aviation seems to preclude their presence. There is a persistent demand that inter-dependence between personnel is evoked in a common cause of maintaining and flying aircraft, no matter in what segment of the spectrum. The few adverse ones I encountered either moved out of aviation or were convinced they should change their attitudes.

I regret not being involved in space shuttle maintenance. That would have been the crowning achievement at the end of my career's avenue.. But I was glad to have entered the turbine-powered age and played a major role in the totality of the aviation I weathered.

There's always a beginning and an end in everything. In reality, my career began when Lou Hogler took a chance and hired a neophyte with a license to learn at Capital Airlines. My time at Fairchild Aircraft can be discounted to a degree in spite of it being a learning process. Manufacturing was not for me. At Capital Airlines I began using what I had learned since the P-26 starter incident.

It's difficult to define precisely the point at which a subtle feeling began to infuse me that enough was enough. After Falcon Aire and SkyWorld Airlines.

I've always felt that a sense of personal accomplishment transcends the fact that one gets paid for his or her efforts. Later, working as a consultant for two commuter airlines was satisfying to a degree, still I was not a thread woven in the fabric of the company.

Ninety-percent of the time with the last commuter I was with was consumed auditing file cards that tracked times and changes on aircraft components. I was, in fact, doing what the FAA should have been doing!

In the ultimate analysis there was no decisive, final date or time established to withdraw. It was, in effect, an incremental, graceful phase-out. In the beginning it never entered my mind to seek fame and fortune. Fame, to a mechanic, bears a distracting connotation if he or she has mis-directed his or her misfortune, thus instantly becoming well-known.

Otherwise, fame, in the commonly-used definition, is a nebulous word — and fleeting. I have no heros in aviation. Only admiration for those who accomplished much for the furtherance of flight. My heros are the thousands laying in military cemeteries scattered over the globe. They have met the true definition of the word.

Fame is not wide-spread in the aviation maintenance community, where it exists at all. Fame is fleeting at best. Charles Taylor, the mechanic/machinist who built the engine for the Wright Flyer, is barely known.

This is mystifying given the importance of an engine to that historical first flight.But there *is* an excellence in maintenance award in his memory. It surfaces for a brief time at a ceremony, once each year, and then its exposure and his memory expire.

All that aside, if young men and women that are entering aviation maintenance as a career choice can persuade themselves to prevail, there are exciting opportunities in their future. Small general aviation aircraft are in a period of transition and beginning to fly with small, turbine engine power. There is need to maintain transport types that will be powered with more sophisticated propulsion. Turbine power as we now know it has reached its limit.

As far as me or any of my contempories leaving a legacy in aviation, it exists only as an unknown quantity, in general. However, a legacy is there in the older aircraft we nurtured until modern aircraft, now flying, could appear. Thus, anyone who eats cornbread is bound to leave a few crumbs on the table.

"You've done enough in aviation," friends have remarked.

Maybe so, but how much is enough?

END

As in a Tale so is Life: Not How Long it is,
But How Good it is ,

Seneca

Notes

[1]   Nearing the final stages of this work I received a brochure advertising High Times, a career aircraft mechanic's biography. It is the first documentation dealing with an aircraft mechanic's profession I am aware of.

[2]   My brother David served with 358 (H) Squadron, 303 Group (H), Eighth Air Force as top turret gunner/engineer. His B-17 was shot down during a raid on Schweinfurt, Germany. He was fatally wounded.

[3]   Mexico Farms. Reportedly the second oldest, continually operated airport in Maryland. It opened in November, 1923. A part was leased to the Army Air Service. Among the greats who stopped there were Wiley Post, Eddie Rickenbaker and Howard Hughes. College Park is the oldest.

[4]   The Pitcairn PA-4 was restored by a Harold Armstrong, of Rawlins, Maryland. It's original owner was 'Torque' Landis. Reportedly the last example of the type, it is based (at this writing) at the Cumberland Maryland, Municipal Airport. It earned the Experimental Aircraft Association's 1991 Grand Champion Antique and Clasic award.

[5]   Spartan Executive, for one. It was designed and built by Spartan Aircraft. The basic design was a sleek, all-metal, low-wing, 4-5 place type. Two engines were offered: The 225 h.p. Jacobs and the P&W Wasp Jr of 320-400 h.p. With the former, the Executive cruised at 165 m.p.h, with the latter 205 m.p.h.

[6]   The Macon's wreckage was found in June, 1990, off Point Sur, California, by the Navy's deep-diving craft Sea Cliff. It went down February 12, 1935. The Akron went down in the Atlantic on the night of April 3-4, 1933. There was a third, the Shennadoah, that crashed in Ohio, September 2, 1925. The Macon disaster sounded the death knell for the Navy's excursion into the use of dirigibles. The Macon and Akron carried four Curtis F9C Sparrowhawks for protection against attack. The tiny fighters were launched and retrieved with a trapeze-type arrangement on the dirigible and a hook on the aircraft. The concept was never proven since there were no attacks.

[7]   Boeing's P-26 heralded the departure from fabric-covered bi-plane type fighters to all metal, low-wing types. The Army Air Corps took delivery of the aircraft in early 1934; they remained operational until WWII. P-26s saw limited combat against the Japanese in the Philippines at the start of the war.

[8]   A mechanic at Bellows Field made an unauthorized flight of over an hour in one. He was an accomplished pilot in civilian life, but that didn't preclude charges of mis-appropriating government property. He was court-martialed and sentenced

Notes

to two years in the Army stockade at Schofield Barracks. The flight was uneventful. He simply wanted to fly!

[9] Electric motors were in use to spin starter planetary gears on other aircraft, but as far as I knew, P-26s weren't retrofitted. Several months after my introduction to inertia starters I watched a P-26 crewman make seven cranks before the engine started — after the eighth. I didn't volunteer to relieve him.

[10] Years later I was astonished to see one at Greybull, Wyoming. It was used as a slurry bomber by Hawkins & Powers.

[11] 'States' and 'Mainland' were colloquial references to the Continental United States. The two words were (and are) commonly used in the Hawaiian Islands.

[12] The Maj. Gen. Oscar Westover, official Air Corps designation P-11. Seventy-five feet long it was originally built to chase bootleggers in the Caribbean and was capable of a top speed of thirty-five knots. It was armed with a fifty caliber (heavy) machine gun.

[13] I was told the Tornados powered the ponderous Keystone bomber, a formidable bi-plane type with open cockpits and nose gunner's position. I saw the fuselage skeleton of one relegated to eventual decay in a swamp near Bellows Field.

[14] Hardness testing of metals should be familiar to maintenance technicians. The Rockwell method makes a smaller indentation and may be used on lighter materials. It is simpler and more rapid than other hardness testing methods because hardness numbers can be read directly. Therefore, they need not be calculated.

[15] Link rods were 'H' shaped in cross-section, but did not have provisions for bearings and bearing caps on one end as do piston rods. Instead, one end accepted a piston pin, the other a link pin. The link pin connected the link rod to the perimeter of the master rod. The arrangement is peculiar to radial engines.

[16] By definition, from the Hawaiian language, 'haole' means stranger. While that could apply to anyone not a native Hawaiian, it commonly refers to people from the Mainland U.S., and is not complimentary, as a rule.

Notes

[17] After studying one in the Hawaiian Air Depot hangar at Hickam Field, shot down during the attack of the 7th, it appeared, in many respects, to be a copy of the Curtiss P-36. There is argument the Zero had an unadulterated lineage.

[18] It was standard procedure to park the B-17's in neat rows on the bomber squadrons' hangar ramps when not flying or, scheduled for maintenance. The Japanese pilots couldn't miss!

[19] There's no question in my mind that if the Japanese had landed a crack, heavy division during the attack they would have secured the island and anchored a valuable base in the Pacific — and prolonged the war immeasurably.

[20] B-24s operated from an airstrip that is in use today on the North Shore of Oahu, at Mokuleia. It is used primarily for glider flying. While my crew and I were changing the No. 2 engine on a B-24 there, a five-hundred pound bomb was accidentally released by a member of the aircraft's crew working inside the fuselage. Fortunately it didn't fall far enough to arm. I still hear the thud as it hit the ground! B-24s also werestationed at Kahuku Pt.

[21] Buzzing and mock strafing became so rife the Air Corps put up a few P-38s to act as aerial cops.

[22] Formerly John Rodgers Airport. When it was expanded after WWII it was renamed Honolulu Airport. Further expansion and improvements resulted in today's Honolulu International Airport.

[23] The designation was changed by the FAA to Aircraft and Powerplant. The noun, powerplant, is misleading, since it could also include a powerhouse and powerplant; both produce electricity commercially. But semantics are an artform in the FAA.

[24] The prices were irresistible. The J-3s were $100 each; the L-5 was $200; the UC-78 a paltry $500 with a spare engine. All the aircraft were operational.

[25] The tidal wave of April 1, 1946.

Notes

[26] The P & W 4360 design was the high water mark of practical radial engine design, but it wasn't the largest engine ever made; Lycoming's XR-7755 was. Liquid-cooled, it had 36 cylinders with 6.375 bores, 8.5 to 1 compression ratio and 6.75 inch stroke. It was fuel-injected, had two high-tension magnetos and four distributors. Development of the turbine engine with its high power to weight ratio doomed the XR-7755. It never went into production.

[27] The commercial derivative of the military C-97 with B-29 wings and empennage. Service ceiling was 32,000-feet, range 4,300-miles. Cruise speed at 25,000-feet was 340 m.p.h. using 1,900 h.p. power settings.

[28] Pratt & Whitney engines played a prominent, if not major, role in aviation's development. The first Wasp engine, a radial weighing 650-pounds and developing 425 h.p. was assembled, December 24, 1925. It was test-run five days later. By 1930, P&W engines were on ninety percent of commercial aircraft. Practically all Navy aircraft and a majority of Army Air Corps 'planes were equipped with P&W engines during that period.

[29] Pan American docked the Clippers at Pearl City on Oahu. The Clippers would taxi to Pearl Harbor's outer buoys marking the entrance channel. They would turn around and make their take-off runs into the harbor and prevailing winds. The sight was nothing short of spectacular as they came by the Hickam Field dock, four engines roaring mightily to break the water's adhesion to the hulls, spray flying from under their bows and sponsons. Finally — it seemed almost miraculously — they would lift-off ever so gradually and with water showering from the hulls in ever-decreasing volume, turn grandly away from the rise of land, over Honolulu, to take up their courses.

[30] Rhesus monkeys. Said to be untainted by Herpes B virus and other infections from the world outside their jungle haunts, according to Dr. Joseph Heid, Charles River Laboratories.

[31] Considering how sensitive the Hawaiian government was (and is) to the arrival of items on the list of banned agriculture and animal species, not one official was there to be sure no monkeys escaped. There would have been an uproar if one had!

Notes

[32]   I returned to Burns Field in 1988, a brief, poignant retreat into time. The small brick building that housed the CAA's flight service station was an empty hulk; Pacific Skyways' little wooden office building and hangar had succumbed to the ravages of time and had completely vanished. It was a haunting still familiar place. It seemed to be listening and waiting. I didn't stay very long.

[33]   'Squawk' is commonly used when referring to a reported mechanical discrepancy. By definition, it is a harsh, loud cry or a noisy protest. One night I was told to go to the terminal to check a pilot's squawk on a Constellation ready to depart on a scheduled flight. He told me he couldn't see his left aileron trim tab when he rolled the control wheel left. His embarrassment was obvious when I explained how a servo trim tab operates. But then, I couldn't fly an instrument approach.

[34] Although the FAA chooses to include corporate aviation in the general aviation category I feel they should be separated. Corporate aviation is distinctively different in concept, operation and maintenance,
when one considers the use of highly-sophisticated pure jet, prop-jet and piston engined aircraft.

[35]   Often we loaded passengers on airplanes that had been parked in an open hangar to cool their aluminum skins. After they were pushed out and the engines started, the planes would taxi away for an immediate take-off. There were no sophisticated de-icing facilities then.

[36]   We had DC-3s, too. Their steam heating systems were remarkedly efficient and would warm the cabins quickly — if one knew how to operate them. 'Moose' Miller had the uncanny ability to put them into operation faster than anyone I knew. He often gave the flight crews pointers on how to operate them.

[37]   There's a marked difference between the environment of a combustion chamber in flight conditions as compared to a ground run. Manifold pressure and mixture settings change, for example. During a ground run, if the mixture is changed, quite often a rough engine will result during a magneto check. If an engine is running properly in flight, don't try to find out why.

Notes

[38] Often we returned to base late at night, to find we were scheduled for an early departure the next day. Rather than driving home to sleep, after servicing the aircraft and correcting any discrepancies, I slept in the hangar. Two hours of rest by eliminating driving time made a difference.

[39] News on the aviation grapevine said Fairchild sold a few twin-engined, low-wing aircraft to Japan. As I remember from photos of the Japanese Betty bomber and seeing the Fairchild there was a startling resemblance. Quite possibly, the Bettys were copies; the Japanese excelled in copying.

[40] The C-82 was followed by the C-87 and the C-119. They were variously referred to as 'Packet', 'Crowd Killer', 'Flying Boxcar' and 'Dollar Nineteen', depending on the mood of their aircrews and application.

[41] There is a shocking contradiction in the river's appearance between its source in the Colorado Rockies and the Mexican Border. It struggles through El Paso as a despondent trickle in a gritty wash. At its headwaters, it is vibrant, cold, clear and exuberant — and an excellent trout stream.

[42] On a regular basis Hoagler, our supervisor, would insist we meet at a sea food restaurant and enjoy a purely social evening together. He was wise in assuring that his men had a good personal relationship with each other, which was manifested in a good working relationship. He was a wise pelican indeed — and all business during working hours.

[43] Whittle was granted a patent about July, 1931. The first production engine, the WX1, was a single-shaft, single-stage unit. It had a centrifugal-flow compressor and single-stage turbine. The engine was rated at 1,290-pounds thrust. Whittle patented the first turbo-fan design in 1936.

[44] Arguably Henri-Marie Coanda (Kwan-dah) flew the first jet-powered airplane on December 10, 1910, but the event faded into oblivion. History is vague about the incident.

[45] Production spanned 16-years, and 444 were built. Reportedly, there were 85 in service worldwide, as of 1990.

Notes

[46] It's my contention that used oil, if re-refined properly, is as good as, or better than, when it originally emerged from a refinery. A piston engine is a remarkably efficient refinery. Oil companies, of course, would disagree.

[47] A few Howard DGAs (Dammed Good Airplane) were used by the Navy as instrument flight trainers. This aircraft was purchased from war surplus. It was capable of high-altitude flight because of a geared induction blower.

[48] In spite of an enormous Knollenberg laser, particle counting tube, a Cambridge dewpoint recording unit, an eight-foot long nose boom and an array of heavy data recording cabinets in the cabin, it managed to achieve 21,000-feet — barely.

[49] In order to retain the structural integrity of the pressurized fuselage a new cabin door, lower half, was installed. It was re-designed to accept compact atmospheric probes mounted externally. The step-door, the original lower half, was removed and a modified door installed. Entry was gained by stepping over the lower half.

[50] The General Electric CJ-610. A derivative of the J-85, the engine is credited with being instrumental in introducing corporate aviation to the jet age. Bill Lear and his Lear Jet share equal recognition. Lear was GE's first customer for the C-610.

[51] Designated Aircraft Maintenance Inspectors (DAMI) were appointed by CAA Maintenance Inspectors. We were required to carry photographic identification, a requisite that should be continued, amongst others. Appointment was based on overall experience and longevity in the maintenance field.

[52] Mechanics were required to send 'report cards' listing their maintenance activities. The requirement was effective in confirming currency in maintenance and eliminating now-and-then activities.

[53] Not long after the inevitable, and the remains of Falcon Aire were salvaged by its creditors, an acquaintance told me she had made off with her

Notes

chief flight instructor, abandoning her children, husband and hearth. If true —
there was no reason for my source to lie — it was the icing on the cake of her
chaotic management of the FBO.

[54] Two B-707 engines were removed from service; the history of their turbine
wheels could not be established amongst available records. Replacing them
imposed an additional, severe setback to the company's overall economy.

[55] In one incident I began to inspect a Taylorcraft BC-12D, but stopped after
writing 27 very serious discrepancies. I suggested the owner have a thorough
100-hour inspection done. He opted, instead, to have a CAA agent inspect it and
flew the aircraft to an adjacent airport to meet the inspector. After the
inspection the agent refused to issue a ferry permit to return the aircraft to its
home field, a 10-minute flight. The owner flew it anyway and was fined $50 for
the violation. He later accused me of being 'un-cooperative'.

[56] If there's one piece of advice to offer technicians starting an aviation
maintenance career it is this: Reject compromise! Maintain professional
perspectives to authentically guarantee distinctive, quality results. You will lose
nothing, and, ultimately, gain an exceptional proportion of respect and, self-
esteem. It is far better to maintain a commitment to responsibility and integrity
and keep a clear conscience than to succumb to coercion and risk a pathetic
career in conformity.

✈

This collection of notes was compiled from personal notes, memory, conversations with others and public
information documents. They are accurate to the best of my ability to make them so. Some readers may contest
information but should remember that the passage of time and repetition of information sometimes influences the
accuracy of history.

The Airplanes

These are the airplanes I was involved with in various degrees of overhaul, modification, general maintenance and engineering. The gliders are not powered types.

I have not listed that Boeing P-26 of my Air Corps recruit days. I worked with its infamous starter, not the aircraft!

Aeronca: 7AC Champ, Chief, Sedan
Aero Commander: 520B, 680F
Bellanca: 8KCAB, 17-31ATC, 1739A
Boeing: PT-17(Stearman), B-17(various models) 707-200/300, 727-100
Beechcraft: 18(C-45), T-34, D-17S, 58P, C-23, N35, V35, E55
CE-288, E33A, V-35B, J-35, 65, B-90, D-95A, B-99
Cessna: UC-78 (Bamboo Bomber), 195A, 170A, L-19, 120, 140, 150,
152, 172, R172K, 172M, 172N, 172P, 177B, 182, 182D,
R182, 182G, 182Q, 185E, 185F, 188, TU-206F, 207, 210D,
210L, 210M, 210N, P-377, 401A, 411, 421
Consolidated-Vultee: B-24, BT-13
Convair: 580
Curtiss: P-40B, P-40E
Douglas: DC-3 (C-47), Super DC-3, DC-4 (C-54), DC-6
Fairchild: 24, C-82
Forney: Ercoupe
Globe: GC1B Swift
Grumman: F6, GI
Howard: D

The Airplanes

GA-16
Interstate: Cadet (Army L-6)
LearJet: 23, 24
Lockheed: 18-56 (Lodestar), L-049, L-749 (Constellations)
Luscombe: 8E
Mooney: Mitsubishi MU-2, M20E, M20J, M20P
Navion: B Model
North American: B-25, P-51D, AT-6, T-28
Piper: J3C, J4, PA-12, PA-14, PA-17, PA-18, PA-20, PA-22,
PA25-260, PA28-140, PA28-161, PA28-180, PA32-300
Stinson: L-5, 108, 108-1, 108-2259
Supermarine: Mark IX (Spitfire)
Taylorcraft: BC12D

And Gliders

Leister-Kauffman: Flattop
Schleicher: KA-6, ASW19
Sweitzer: 1-23H15, 1-26, 1-32, 2-32
Vickers-Slingsby: T-65A

There wasn't time for more!

Epilogue

Well, I thought, at least I'm not cutting grass. On the other hand, though, if I were I'd be outside in the wine-like Hawaiian air and balmy sunshine. But here I was, stuck in Operations!

A little over two months had dragged by while I chafed under an onerous routine, typing orders, operational directives and filing or retrieving paperwork at the files. The business in Operations there on the flight line at Hickam Field was neither hectic nor entirely passive. It simply went on at a bucolic pace. There was a certain advantage, however: I could look out the windows from time to time and watch flight activities.

It was the beginning of a learning experience, I'd find, that never ceased throughout my new life. Not just in a professional, workaday sense, but in the sub-conscious as well. That realization seldom comes early in a young person's life. Rather, its spawning is subtle and grows apace with the passage of time until, in later years, one begins to become aware of its presence.

I hadn't applied to be a clerk in Operations. I was assigned to the position when a request for one had been sent down to the 23rd Matériel Squadron of the 17th Air Base Group. The First Sergeant ordered me to comply with the request simply because my records indicated I could operate a typewriter. But it was doing something constructive and definite instead of the daily uncertainty of what would be in store for me.

I learned, while looking out the Operations file room window one day, that there were engine starters other than an inertia starter. Had I not been there, I may not have known there were 'shotgun'

313

starters. When a pilot strode to a P-36 parked on the ramp I watched closely. He climbed into the cockpit of the trim fighter, strapped on his parachute and busied himself with preparing for engine start.

Suddenly, there was a loud BANG! Instantly I thought the airplane was going to blow up, but it didn't. Instead, the propeller began turning and the engine started. I also learned I wasn't cut from the same cloth as a born clerk. I didn't like confinement or paperwork as a steady diet. Nevertheless I learned to cope with both. It was a learning experience that helped immensely, in my later maintenance years. Sporadic paperwork was easily addressed, since it didn't confine me to a desk permanently.

When I applied for a transfer to the air-sea rescue boat unit I was unknowingly starting on the path to what I truly wanted to do: Become physically involved with airplanes. The path would be like one made by a wandering calf. It would have its bends and curves, but ultimately straighten.

I took naturally to the duty and enjoyed it, except for the aftermath of unfortunate flying accidents. There was pathos and rare humor. We plucked injured and whole pilots from the ocean and pieces of some.

There was a time when the early model P–40's were having coolant problems. Once, a pilot bailed out of his stricken aircraft hitting the right horizontal stabilizer. One of his legs suffered a compound fracture. It was not an unusual injury since the P–40's fuselages were short. Another time a Navy pilot 'buzzed' our boat in the Grumman TBM he was flying. His propeller dug into a wave, causing the engine to begin vibrating horribly. His only recourse was to ditch.

We had a close-up, unobstructed view of the scene. Within five minutes he stood chagrined, soaking wet and unhurt on the boat's deck, watching the TBM briefly bob up and down on the waves and then sink. "I don't know what I'm going to tell them at Pearl Harbor," he said. "I suppose it will be, there was an engine failure." An acceptable half-truth.

Those years in air-sea rescue, before and after Hammond's tutorship and the Hawaiian Air Depot interlude, weren't without personal compensation, as far as exposure to aircraft was concerned. There was some insight into flying operations, although somewhat distant. I did meet Hammond, which was critical and wholly rewarding.

When I was detached with a boat to 20th Air Force Headquarters in the Western Pacific there were airplanes everywhere. Especially the hundreds of B-29s that were pounding Japan from Guam and Tinian. After hostilities ceased I felt a sense of personal loss with the number of aircraft of all types no longer needed and remanded to the gloomy depths of the Pacific Ocean — with other battle equipment of every description.

With the launching of my career I learned that getting wiser doesn't necessarily keep pace with getting older — or vice versa. A person has to be open to change and options, if he or she hopes to succeed to any degree. Mechanics who never change, whether from inability or refusal to do so, much like some farmers, may suffer in the backwash. I met many that remained bucolic and unaffected by the admonition: 'If you're not the lead dog, the scenery never changes.' Their work, however, was acceptable.

There were a few who, while not being careless, in the strict sense of the word, tended to become somewhat lax, personally and professionally. They had fallen victims to that syndrome that often affects many: Familiarity breeding contempt, compounded by self-induced mental boredom. Perhaps they were never made aware of the truth in the old axiom: "You must drive rivets as though each rivet is a project unto itself", as applying to every event in their lives.

Epilogue

Thus the bolts around the circumference of a turbine housing or a compressor section are not to be considered en masse. Each and every one must be torqued individually and with care, as a distinct operation, before moving on to the next. And so it is with living a life.

If assignments mean accomplishing the same task on several aircraft of the same model in succession, it's only human nature that possibly a 'rut' will form, into which an individual easily could fall, and quality suffers. Factory work on an assembly line is a fertile ground for such pitfalls. I still believe, though, a short period of work in a factory environment is an asset in any mechanic's learning process.

It's been one of my observations throughout my career that maintenance people have gone about their business in a grey area. That is, as far as a personal kinship with others was concerned. There were no social inter-activities on a noticeable scale.

The invisible line between pilots, stewardesses, dispatchers, operations and management was seldom crossed. Only the pilots, out of necessity, encroached in the maintenance sphere to discuss or explain some in-flight discrepancy or other related anomaly. As far as I know and experienced, there were few personal, close relationships established between mechanics and other professionals within the aviation community — as in intimate friendships.

I firmly believe one of the reasons, if not the leading one, for this irregularity in association lies in the title 'mechanic', assigned to maintenance personnel from the beginning of aviation. Mechanic does not have a distinctive flavor, as befits a person who maintains a vehicle as distinctive as an airplane. Especially since a mechanic has an awesome share of responsibility for its safety, as much in his hands, as in a pilot's.

The appellation 'Mechanic' is generic, all encompassing, without character. It leaves the public with the impression of a person with grimy gnarly hands, an inadequate education and semi-skilled work performance.

Compare this perspective with the British designation of Ground Engineer. That denotes a person with higher than average intelligence and mechanical expertise, and immediately demands respect. But, on the other hand, 'Engineer', is commonly attributed to an entirely different discipline: Designing, constructing, managing. Aviation Maintenance Technician enhances status and is profoundly more distinguished than mechanic, considering the explosion in aviation technology, in lieu of Ground Engineer.

I recall a newspaper story in which '...eight aviation pioneers were inducted...' into a state aviation hall of fame.

One was a woman who donated her long hair for use as crosshairs in the Norden bomb sight. Another woman was cited for having four thousand, three hundred flying hours in the Civil Air Patrol — and being editor of an aviation magazine. A man was recognized for being a leading aircraft salvager and parts supplier. But he wasn't a maintenance technician. There was also the curator of an aviation museum. The balance were pilots with varying though, on the surface, not exceedingly impressive accomplishments. Were the Hall of Fame officials desperate to add to its membership list or was the induction criteria generous to a fault to accomplish the same purpose?

It was not surprising that no maintenance people were listed. The large wonder to me is: Why not?

During the ending years of my career I detected a certain atmosphere of malaise, subtlety permeating aviation maintenance, although maintenance in itself, had not degraded. It seemed that the personal relationship between the aircraft and mechanic was demea ning into a cold, distant, purely mechanical venture. That was not to my liking!

An aircraft is remarkedly unique in all respects, being not of the earth and highways. It is not a product of heartless machines, as with earthbound vehicles. There is, or should be, an intimacy between it and the human element since the first driven rivet to and beyond its first flight. There were airplanes that seemed to derive a perverse pleasure from constant ails, and some that operated hour after hour, doggedly, dependably without complaint.

One stands out in my personal chronicles that had an unusual, productive life. Its career began as a patrol bomber in the South Pacific arena of combat and then into commercial service in New Zealand. After serving for several years carrying passengers and suffering an occasional mishap, it was converted for corporate service where it recorded years of trustworthy hours. Finally, it was remanded to retirement, to make way for one that blended into the turbine-powered age.

Were they possessed of souls? At times it seemed they were but that's indulging in science-fiction fantasies. The more un-romantic assessment would be: Some were built when the constructors were at the top of their personal skills' peaks. Others, when the constructors were not so zealous in applying their skills to the task.

As in the Book of Ecclesiastes, everything has its season; and so concluded mine with airplanes and their engines, and the multitude of facets embodied in aviation. The courtship was frustrating at times, but finally consummated. It was not wholly perfect throughout the union, but the small distractions did not sully the whole. I can look back on that period with immense satisfaction.

Aviation was good to me and I was good to aviation. Our relationship was wonderfully compatible.

It was a good time!

E.R.W.

ISBN 155212776-1